D1179962

Film and Revolution

JAMES ROY MACBEAN, a noted film critic, is
author of articles appearing in *Film Quarterly,
Sight and Sound,* and other journals.

MacBEAN, James Roy. Film and revolution. Indiana, 1975. 339p il 75-1936. 15.00, ISBN 0-253-32189-1; 4.95 pa. ISBN 0-253-20191-8. C.I.P.

CHOICE   *MAY '76*

Performing Arts

Film

MacBean is a Marxist for whom the major significance of films lies in their position as conveyors of ideology within the class struggle. The approach sheds much light on Godard's self-consciously revolutionary films. Though MacBean claims that this analysis can be applied to any film, all that he discusses have been carefully selected for their social and political themes. MacBean is most scornful of the unacknowledged "bourgeois capitalist" assumptions behind André Bazin's ontological realism and the more recent semiological approach of Christian Metz. He proudly acknowledges his own ideology, one that would necessarily sell short many fine films. To argue that any film will reflect in some way the class ideology of its makers is one thing; to suggest that seeking out that ideology will always reveal what is most essential about the movie is another. Nevertheless, the book is quite readable and is a very significant work of Marxist criticism. It is worthwhile if only for the excellent discussions of Godard and the very topical critique of semiology. Thirty pages of stills.

film and revolution

James Roy MacBean

INDIANA UNIVERSITY PRESS

Bloomington and London

Published in Canada by Fitzhenry & Whiteside Limited,
Don Mills, Ontario
Manufactured in the United States of America

Library of Congress Cataloging in Publication Data

MacBean, James Roy.
  Film and revolution.

  Includes index.
  1. Moving-pictures—Political aspects—Addresses,
essays, lectures. I. Title.
PN1995.9.P6M33   791.43'0909'3   75–1936
ISBN 0–253–32189–1
ISBN 0–253–20191–8 pbk.   1 2 3 4 5 79 78 77 76 75

Contents

v

Part Two: *Film and Revolution on Many Fronts*

Part Three: *Post-Bazin Aesthetics: The Theory and Practice of Marxist Film Criticism*

Acknowledgments

I would like to express my appreciation and thanks to the
following people, who in many different ways have helped me
to bring this book forth: to Ernest Callenbach, editor of *Film
Quarterly,* for his advice throughout the entire project and, above
all, for his friendly and comradely support of my work; to Berna-
dette MacBean, for her insights and advice, for her warm gener-
osity in the sharing of responsibilities, and for her emotional
support; to Susan Fernandez, for working so hard and so well on
the final editing that I simply can't envisage doing without her on
my next book; to Hubert Dreyfus, for his critical observations and
encouragement; to Bertrand Augst, for his stimulating enthusiasm;
to the editors of *Cinéthique,* Gérard Leblanc and Jean-Paul Far-
gier, for their many friendly and comradely discussions in Paris;
to Henri Langlois, of the Cinémathèque Française, for having provided me and so many others with such a marvelous cinematic
education; to Tom Luddy, of the Pacific Film Archive in Berkeley, for his intelligent programming of films; to Herbert Marcuse,
whose interest in the cinema may be small but whose interest in
the struggles of men and women for liberation is grand; to Dusan
Makavejev, whose intensity of personal feeling and of social commitment is an inspiration; to Valerie MacLean, whose own intensity of personal feeling is an inspiration; to Masoud Mostowfi,
for his friendly support and solidarity; to Jules and Helen Seitz,
for their warm logistical support; to Robert and Leslie Carabas
and to William and Marie-Joseph Horwich, for their warm en-

couragement and frequent hospitality; to Gino Lofredo and Carlos Broullón of Tricontinental Film Center in Berkeley, for their friendly and comradely support of my work; and to Jean-Luc Godard and Jean-Pierre Gorin, without whose films, as the saying goes, this book would not have been possible; and, finally, to The Mabelle McLeod Lewis Foundation, of Palo Alto, California, whose generous grant helped me in the writing of this book.

The following chapters, which first appeared in *Film Quarterly*, have been reprinted with the permission of the University of California Press and the Regents of the University of California.

"Politics and Poetry in *Two or Three Things I Know About Her* and *La Chinoise*," Summer 1968.

"Politics, Poetry, and the Language of Signs in *Made in USA*," Spring 1969.

"*Weekend*, or The Self-Critical Cinema of Cruelty," Winter 1968–69.

" 'See You at Mao': Godard's Revolutionary *British Sounds*," Winter 1970–71.

"Godard/Gorin/The Dziga Vertov Group: Film and Dialectics in *Pravda, Struggle in Italy*, and *Vladimir and Rosa*," Fall 1972.

"*La Hora de los Hornos:* 'Let Them See Nothing but Flames!' " Fall 1970.

"The *Ice*-man Cometh No More: He Gave His Balls to the Revolution," Summer 1971.

"Rossellini's Materialistic *Mise-en-Scène* of *La Prise de Pouvoir par Louis XIV*," Winter 1971–72.

"Sex and Politics: Wilhelm Reich, World Revolution, and Makavejev's *WR: The Mysteries of the Organism*," Spring 1972.

"The Working Class Goes Directly to Heaven, Without Passing Go: Or, The Name of the Game Is Still Monopoly," Spring 1973.

"Godard and Rocha at the Crossroads of *Wind from the East*" originally appeared in *Sight and Sound*. Permission to reprint this material was given by the British Film Institute.

Illustrations have been obtained through the courtesy of the respective distributors of each film and through the generous assistance of Tom Luddy of the Pacific Film Archive, Ernest Callenbach, editor of *Film Quarterly*, and Mel Novikoff of San Francisco's Surf Theatres.

Introduction

Film theory is very much in a state of flux at present. And so is film criticism, or at least the only film criticism worth taking seriously—that which attempts to base the practice of film criticism on sound theoretical foundations.

Among film scholars there seems to be general agreement now on only one thing: we have entered a "post-Bazin" era of film theory and criticism. There was not even this much general agreement as recently as the winter of 1970, when I launched a controversial reevaluation of Bazin's aesthetics in a guest-lecture at UCLA. But although I have been in the forefront of those pointing out that Bazin's aesthetics of "ontological realism" lacked valid theoretical foundations and were rife with hidden ideological bias, nonetheless, there is one important way I would like to pay homage to André Bazin. And I find it particularly timely to point out now, when most attempts at film theory are so turgidly abstract and abstruse, that Bazin had a wonderful ability to do theory and criticism simultaneously. He utilized his marvelous sensitivity and intelligence to elucidate individual films and the workings of cinema throughout film history; and he developed the theoretical position of his aesthetics in the practice of the critical analysis of particular films.

Not that I am arguing that *all* film theory should be developed within the format of a criticial analysis of individual films. But I am pointing to a gap between theory and criticism that has been growing wider for some years now. And the situation has reached the point where theoretical critiques and counter-critiques of various forms of structuralism and semiology are carried out in a vacuum, with hardly a reference—much less any critical application of the "theory"—to particular films. Too often in the hands of pedants whose academic penchant for writing commentaries upon commentaries upon commentaries rivals the obscurantist excesses of medieval scholasticism, today's attempts at film theory are retreating further and further from the critical discussion of films. Not only does this impoverish our discourse about film, it also raises serious doubts about the relevance of film theory in general.

My own approach has been quite different. Deploring that ever-widening gap between theory and criticism, I have sought to develop theory in the critical analysis of certain key films that have forced us to pose the theoretical issues in new ways. These films have not only challenged our expectations of what a film should be; they have also challenged our notions about how the cinema—and art in general—functions in the advanced industrial societies of Western Europe and America.

Numerically, of course, such challenging and politically provocative films represent a tiny drop of water in the huge torrent of worldwide commercial film production. However, because of the peculiar "tastemaking" function of that marginal and politically shifting class of petit bourgeois intellectuals, it occasionally happens that in an industry like the commercial cinema, where the vast majority of products (films) are so appallingly mediocre, a film that seriously challenges the status quo may be given the sort of critical attention that establishes it as a kind of cultural benchmark. As such, its influence is potentially quite important.

However, the bourgeois press and the petit bourgeois intellectual journals usually deal with potentially subversive films in the same way they deal with all the other films. Thus, reviewed in terms of whether or not this particular consumer product offers enough spectacle to make it worth the price of admission, or critically examined in terms of its place in the pantheon of film masterpieces, even an explicitly militant film is to some extent co-opted by the *commodity* structure of the intellectual art market. But it is only *relatively* co-opted; and we must be careful to emphasize that by no means all of the subversive power of a politically militant film gets defused; quite the contrary, the struggle at the level of conflicting ideologies can be extremely effective, for the hegemony of bourgeois ideology may be pervasive but is by no means *absolute*. Nor is bourgeois ideology itself some eternal, impregnable entity that is invulnerable to attack.

Thus, it is of the utmost importance to deal with politically challenging films in another ideological context, which, unlike the commodity context of bourgeois capitalist ideology, will enable us to illuminate and emphasize the political as well as the artistic challenges manifested in these films. This is the direction, then, and the urgent task to which my own critical and theoretical work has been devoted.

In this undertaking, the films of Godard—and of Godard and Gorin—have obviously proved particularly fruitful. But not only can the Marxist theoretical analysis developed in this book be applied fruitfully to Godard's films and to the other films I discuss, but also it can be applied successfully to *all* films. My own choice has been to concentrate on films that not only challenge and demystify capitalist ideology but also offer, either explicitly or implicitly, a socialist ideology. And I made this choice because I believe it is of the highest priority to seize the *offensive* whenever we have the opportunity.

In the cinema, unfortunately, there are few films that enable us to take the offensive against capitalism and the ruling bourgeoisie; and it would be a drastic error to let such opportunities pass us by. But it is also useful—although in my mind it is a *secondary* task—to apply the Marxist analysis to some of the multitude of films that serve to reinforce the dominant bourgeois capitalist ideology. Two fine examples of this other application of Marxist film criticism are the *Cahiers du Cinéma*'s collective text on John Ford's *Young Mr. Lincoln*[1] and Charles Eckert's insightful analysis of the 1937 Warner Brothers production *A Marked Woman.*[2] (For more extended consideration of the issues explored by these texts, see Chapter 17.)

In any case, I think it is fair to say that the films of Godard—and of Godard and Gorin—have been seminal influences on all of us who have been developing a Marxist critical methodology to apply to the cinema. And many of our insights into the relations between cinema and ideology could not have been achieved if Godard and Gorin had not pioneered the way by performing their own analysis of these relations in images and sounds.

For myself, I readily acknowledge how closely involved my own work is with Godard's. Some of the same radical developments are clearly evident in my writings as in his films. And this of course is no accident. Not only am I working in the same conjuncture of art and politics as Godard, but, more directly, I developed a great deal of my own theoretical position in the process of examining the issues raised by the films of Godard.

The reader can trace this development quite easily in the section of *Film and Revolution* dealing with the Godard films. Thus, in the chapters on *La Chinoise* and *Two or Three Things I Know About Her, Made in USA,* and *Weekend* (chapters 1–3), theory is dealt with implicitly rather than explicitly, at least to a large extent. And in the succeeding chapters the Marxist theory of ideology, which underlies all that I have written, only gradually comes to the forefront in an explicit and pointedly political way.

Between the "Critique" section of the chapter on *Le Gai Savior* and the "Auto-Critique du Critique" section of that same chapter, there is clearly some sort of break. In some ways one can even speak of an "epistemological break" here. (Certainly, it is not one I take any personal credit for: it derives of course from my reading of Althusser at that time,[3] and, indirectly, from Godard and Gorin's reading of Althusser, which clearly influenced their film-making.) In any case, what is involved theoretically are the epistemological foundations of our understanding of knowledge. And what involves us, in film, in these issues are the episte-mological foundations of the cinema's way of getting at, or producing, knowledge.

The philosophical issues are complex. But let us say simply that Althusser credits Marx with founding in *Das Kapital* a new, more scientifically valid conception of knowledge in which the emphasis is on the *practice* of the *production* of knowledge. This materialist theory of knowledge rejects the empiricists' subject/object split and its bias toward *contemplation,* which conveniently removes knowledge to a detached, passive, and purely men-tal (idealist) realm. Thus, in simple terms, turning even Hegel around and standing Hegel's idealist dialectic back on its feet on solid ground instead of on its head, Marx asserts that knowl-edge is not "found" by a thinking subject's contemplation of objects but is rather *produced* in the *practice* of material inter-action between men, women, and things.

As Julia Kristeva expressed it in the pages of the influential French journal of Marxist film theory, *Cinéthique:*

> Practice thus becomes . . . the locus of the contradiction (iden-tity and/or difference) between the subject and the object, between sense and *matter.* Practice is thus the hinge on which turns the relationship between the subject (and thus of its "signifying systems") and its exterior, or, if you will, its *nega-tive.* There is no object which is not already given in a practice (of the subject, a signifying practice); but neither is there a subject which is not refounded, modified, by practice, within the object as its negative.[4]

For film-makers like Godard and Gorin, the concern with epistemology has entailed some major shifts in our understanding of the relations between film and "reality." And this in turn has entailed some major shifts in the relations between a film and its audience. Rejecting as illusion (and as an ideologically biased illusion) André Bazin's notion that film somehow "reveals" the essential, transcendental "truth" of reality, Godard and Gorin openly acknowledge the *practice* and *work* of the film-makers not just in producing a film but also in producing *significations* about reality. Moreover, "reality," itself, comes to be understood as having no meaning apart from the significations we *produce* in our *social practice* with men, women, and things. Making a film—and likewise viewing a film—are thus ways of producing significations: they are *signifying practices*. And "truth" itself is no longer understood as immanent in things and beings, as if lying there waiting to be "revealed" (like God's grace); it is ultimately nothing more and nothing less than the significations and material transformations we *produce* in *social practice*.

It is only appropriate, of course, that where the cinema is concerned, an epistemological break should occur when one really begins to understand *Le Gai Savoir*. For in that film Godard himself (he was still working alone at that time) attempted to explore the epistemological issues raised by Althusser, to express in cinematic terms that *coupure* (break) which was more than a break with the system (although it was definitely that too); and to lay out the ABC's of a new, epistemologically valid cinematic approach to the production of knowledge.

A difficult task, to be sure, and even in *Le Gai Savoir* the underlying theory is far more cryptically implicit than explicit. And that is also the case obviously for Godard's next film, *One Plus One*. And this still not very explicit character of theory (in films which contain very little that one would recognize as spectacle) is precisely what makes these transitional films of Godard's own break such maddeningly difficult films to grasp.

Let us not assume, however, that theoretical explicitness is as much of a virtue in art itself as it is in art criticism. After all, even Brecht guarded against overexplicitness in his art. And when I asked Gorin and Godard recently about the increased theoretical explicitness of their films, Jean-Pierre laughingly replied that "the most explicit film of them all, *Struggle in Italy*, was undoubtedly our worst." And Jean-Luc's comment was "Why be explicit? That's just playing God."

In any case, let's avoid making another fetish of "theoretical explicitness." Even in film criticism let's not overreact to the absence of theoretical foundations in what passes for film criticism but is mere journalistic reviewing, for if we overreact we are in danger of making such a fetish of theoretical explicitness that we may never get around to examining critically even the few films that would help us to pose the theoretical issues in a more useful, productive way.

For example, where Godard's work "before the break" is concerned, I find much that is useful—even if theoretically implicit rather than explicit—in all his films, but particularly *Two or Three Things, Made in USA, La Chinoise,* and *Weekend.* Epistemological breaks aside, I have not ceased to appreciate *La Chinoise*'s lucidly self-critical exploration of the artist's role in society. For it has seemed to me that this must be the central issue for the artist who seeks to carry out his or her* political commitment not just on the side, in press conferences or fundraising speeches, but right there, as Walter Benjamin put it (in "The Artist as Producer"), where he *works,* where he really *produces* something. Godard, it was clear even at the time of *La Chinoise* (and let's not forget that this film came *before* the French "May Events" of 1968), accepted the responsibilities and limitations, or, better yet, the *contradictions,* of his position as an artist who sought to involve himself in the political struggle . . . *in his work as an artist.*

Moreover, as the French May Events and our own "events" in the U.S.A. bore out, what was particularly electrifying was the fact that students, artists, and intellectuals were at last beginning to recognize and rebel against the way in which they too, like the blue-collar workers, are invariably exploited, alienated, and co-opted, even in their limited avenues of protest, by a bourgeois capitalist system whose ideology permeates all social relations and which threatens—as Godard's *Made in USA* and *Weekend* offered grim reminders—to reduce all of us to "one-dimensional men," passive consumers of *la société du spectacle.*

For me, writing film criticism has meant fighting that ruling-

* I have tried in this book to avoid using the male pronouns he, his, and him in the generic sense. Hereafter, if these forms slip in because of habit, I do not mean them to exclude women.

class ideology where it operates in the cinema, and that has meant carrying on class struggle in what I wrote. As Walter Benjamin put it (again, in "The Artist as Producer"), "The place of the intellectual in class struggle cannot be situated, or better chosen, in any other terms than according to his positon in the process of production."

To put it plainly, the much-heard phrase "bring class struggle into your own life" does not mean that everyone should immediately become a factory worker; but it does mean that everyone should stop to analyze the class struggle, sometimes blatant, more often hidden, that operates in our everyday relations to men, women, and things. And, of course, once that analysis is made, we are confronted with the imperative of choice. The first question is simply whether we take sides with the exploiters and oppressors or whether we join the struggle for revolutionary liberation. The second question, more difficult, is what is to be done?

The present book took shape from my own commitment to the struggle for revolutionary liberation and from my growing conviction that the struggle must be carried out on all fronts, even in film criticism. As I developed my own understanding of Godard's films—and as I encountered other films like *La Hora de los Hornos, Ice, WR: The Mysteries of the Organism,* and *The Working Class Goes to Heaven,* which also probed the potential and the need for revolutionary liberation—the more I realized that there were more useful and more urgent tasks than adding to the bookshelves yet another "auteur" study, and that the real subject of my writing was not Godard alone (and by this time Godard was no longer alone), but *film and revolution.*

However, in examining the relations between film and the struggle for revolutionary liberation, I have purposely resisted, for the most part, the temptation to stake out boundaries and to define characteristics of some new genre of film that might go under the rubric "the revolutionary film." Categorizing films this way does not seem particularly meaningful to me. And the task of exploring relations between a given film and its ideological situation seems to me a far more fruitful and urgent task than simply carving out a new compartment of film history.

Thus, the films examined in this book range from explicitly militant films like Solanas's *La Hora de los Hornos* and Godard's *British Sounds* (two films that would almost certainly figure on anyone's list of "revolutionary films") to certain other films like Rossellini's *La Prise de Pouvoir par Louis XIV* and Marcel Ophuls' *Le Chagrin et la Pitié*, which, although they seem to me to explore certain relations between film and revolution, would nonetheless hardly be categorized as revolutionary films.

On the other hand, I would contend that the richness of insight with which Rossellini develops a materialist analysis of history in *La Prise de Pouvoir par Louis XIV* and the insistent emergence within *Le Chagrin et la Pitié* of a class analysis of French political attitudes make these particular films more productive in heightening revolutionary consciousness than such films as *The Battle of Algiers, Burn!,* or *State of Siege*. These latter films are useful in stirring up emotional support and sympathy for the revolutionary cause, as well as in stirring up a healthy sense of revolutionary outrage at the paramilitary machinations the ruling class uses to maintain its power and privileges. But *The Battle of Algiers, Burn!,* and *State of Siege* (to name only the best of such films) do not go very much beyond the emotional level; and we have seen from Leni Riefenstahl's *Triumph of the Will* just how frighteningly easy it is to use the emotional power of the cinema to arouse masses of people to support even the most unjust and ignominious causes.

If revolution is to be truly liberating, it must be much more than just the emotional revenge of the oppressed. And if a film-maker's commitment to revolutionary liberation is more than just an emotional identification with the oppressed, then his cinematic practice must address itself to the viewer in a way that calls forth *all* his human faculties, rational and emotional, instead of relying on the emotional manipulation of the viewer's tendency to *identify* with the characters on the screen.

For me, then, examining the relations between film and

revolution has meant, among other things, *not* artificially separating content and form, and then privileging content by simply
noting that a given film takes sides either for the ruling capitalist
bourgeoisie or for the proletarian and Third World forces of
liberation. Instead, whether writing on individual films or (as in
the third section of *Film and Revolution*) examining the theoretical foundations of film criticism, I have found it necessary
to concentrate on the *whole range of relations between film and
ideology* that are manifested as much in the relations between
images and sounds on celluloid as in the film-maker's (or the
theorist's) selection and treatment (or omission) of political
themes.

part one

Godard/Gorin: Rethinking the
Function of Art in Society

1

Politics and Poetry in Two or Three Things I Know About Her *and* La Chinoise

"Words, words, words." Hamlet's reply to Polonius when questioned about his reading might well be the response one would make when questioned about these two films by Jean-Luc Godard, for never has the cinema been so wordy as in *Deux ou trois choses que je sais d'elle (Two or Three Things I Know About Her)* and *La Chinoise (The Chinese Girl)*. But with Godard, as with Hamlet, there's a method in the madness. And, in any case, rarely have words been held up to such painful scrutiny, to such a desperate search for *sense,* as in these two maddeningly provocative films.

Deux ou trois choses, however, is particularly maddening in that, first, the narration (by Godard himself, in a running commentary on the film and its making) is spoken in an often barely audible whisper. Second, all of the commentary and much of the dialogue are spoken off-camera or away from the camera, thus eliminating any real assistance from lipreading. And, third, both the commentary and the dialogue are systematically covered, and often smothered, by the noise of construction machinery, low-flying jets, pinball machines, electric appliances, huge tractor-trailer trucks, passing automobiles, etc. Consequently, the "viewer-listener" of *Deux ou trois choses* has to strain at every moment to pick up even two or three words, and to attempt to assimilate the words and reconstruct the *sense* of what has just been said, while all the time trying not to fall behind the torrent of words that continues to pour forth. However, the strain of coping with such an overwhelming tidal wave of words and noise is really what *Deux ou trois choses que je sais d'elle* is all about. And one of the "two or three things" Godard knows about Paris (nominally, the "elle" of the title) is precisely the fact that within such an urban environment an individual is unable to find a moment's peace and quiet. Moreover, by letting the viewer-listener *experience* this alienation—through noise, among other things—which separates us from our own thoughts and from others, Godard succeeds in putting across a message in the way best calculated to leave its imprint on the audience, for it is the viewer-listener who realizes during the course of this film (in case he or she hasn't realized it before) just how intolerable is this constant roar of noise in which we live in the modern city.

It is worth pointing out, by the way, that Godard's manipulation of the sound track in *Deux ou trois choses* is by no means a radical new departure for him: while it is true that he has always (or at least from *Une Femme est une Femme* on) relied heavily on direct recording of natural sound, he has also experimented a great deal with various ways of arranging, or composing, the raw material into what we might call "sound-blocks" of alternating levels of intensity. *Une Femme est une Femme,* for example, juxtaposes sound-blocks of a tremendous variety of sound possibilities—dialogue recorded in studio, dialogue recorded over natural sound, fragments of music, entire songs, dialogue over music, silence, etc.—and in *Bande à part,* in particular, the sound track is no longer the harmonious counterpart of the visual image but is rather the audio counter*point* to the visual image.

This contrapuntal form of composition is developed most fully, however, in *Deux or trois choses,* where Godard's insistent forcing of the spectator out of his normal passivity is carried out in a relentless flood of seemingly unrelated images and sounds—

of *signs*, both audio and visual—which, in the words of the main character, "ultimately lead us to doubt language itself and which submerge us with significations while drowning that which is real instead of helping us to disengage the real from the imaginary." In short, Godard both tells us and shows us, in *Deux ou trois choses*, that we in Western civilizaton are adrift on a sea of significations, victims of our own signs, the only escape being to sink or swim: to drown in *non-sense* or to struggle for *sense*.

One of the main problems, then, in the struggle for sense, is the problem of endurance. At the beginning of the film, presumably, everyone (or at least everyone who knows some French) will be willing to *try* to hear the words and assimilate what is said, but over a period of more than an hour and a half, with only occasional and very brief "rest stops" (snatches of Beethoven's last string quartet and, once or twice, a few precious moments of sweet silence), it seems unfortunate but inevitable that sooner or later a certain portion of the audience is going to sink (or, as happens, simply walk out), exhausted and exasperated by the constant struggle to separate words from noise, sense from non-sense.

One might be tempted simply to ignore the often unintelligible dialogue and commentary, and to look for sense exclusively in the visual image; but perhaps it is not until and unless the spectator begins to understand how noise in the context of this film makes sense—how noise in this film does not impede sense but rather is a vehicle of sense—that the film as a whole can begin to emerge from the bewildering complexity that is at first glance deceptively similar to non-sense. The act of confronting the bewildering complexity of modern urban society and of learning two or three things about it is, after all, the not so easy task Godard himself has undertaken: is it then asking too much of us, as we confront the complexity of this film, that we, in turn, attempt to learn two or three things about cinema?

This double action of analyzing society and how it works, and at the same time analyzing art and how *it* works, is precisely the double action of *Deux ou trois choses,* a film in which Godard *qua* sociologist scrutinizes the "social pathology" of the modern city at the same time that Godard *qua* film-maker scrutinizes the cinematic means of transposing the social analysis into art. Moreover, in the whispered commentaries in *Deux or trois choses,* we overhear Godard questioning himself (as he does in *Far From Vietnam*), as both sociologist and film-maker, as to whether these are the right images, the right words, and whether his perspective is from too close or from too far. In short, *all* is put in question in *Deux ou trois choses:* the impersonal cruelty of Gaullist neocapitalism; the prostitution, in one form or another, of the modern city-dweller; the American imperialist aggression in Vietnam; the fragmentary assimilation of culture in a society flooded with paperback books; the thousand and one amenities of modern life (radios, beauty salons, super-sudsy detergents, the latest style in dresses, and the modern bathroom plumbing still unavailable to 70% of the French people): *all* is put in question, including, and perhaps especially, the notion of cinema.

Godard, it is clear, wants a revolution in both art and society; and he hopes to make his contribution to the revolution of society by accomplishing in film the revolution of art. It is this double action, in art and in society, that Godard advocates when he speaks of the need to "struggle on two fronts"[5]—an idea he seems to develop more fully in his fourteenth film, *La Chinoise.*

Godard has very often acknowledged that in his view art is a very serious matter with a most important role to play in the social revolution he sees taking place today in Western civilization. Moreover, Godard's art (like Gide's *Les Faux Monnayeurs* or the play-within-a-play that Hamlet stages for the king) is very calculatingly constructed of a most disquieting mixture of the fictional and the real; and one of the dominant refrains that haunt *La Chinoise* is the Hamlet-like assertion that "art is not the reflection of reality, but the reality of the reflection." There is, indeed, something very Hamlet-like in Godard's hyper-lucid introspection, in his intense desire to understand a situation and at the same time to act upon it and influence it; in his genuine desire to commit himself to the social and political life around

Two or Three Things I Know About Her: isolated . . . adrift on a sea of significations

Two or Three Things I Know About Her: the prostitution of everyday life

Two or Three Things I Know About Her: the cash connection . . . making ends meet

La Chinoise: In the beginning was the Word.

La Chinoise: a little exercise in revolutionary reading

La Chinoise: the cinema as a gun

him and in his aesthetic inclination to maintain an ironic distance from that life, to play with words, to pun, to mimic, to jest. But where Hamlet found social commitment and aesthetic distance incompatible and the wavering between them inimical to an active life, Godard seeks to resolve the dilemma, not by eliminating one or the other of its horns but by jealously guarding them both in the creation of a work of art, like *La Chinoise*, that is at the same time sincerely and sympathetically committed to social revolution and yet ebulliently ironic in its insistence on delineating the sometimes infantile and dangerous excesses of the very heroes and political stands with which he, Godard, and we, the audience, may sympathize and perhaps identify. *La Chinoise*, like all of Godard's films, contains within itself its own self-critique: it is social thought and the critique of social thought, art and the critique of art. For an audience accustomed to having their politics and their art be one thing only—serious or funny, pro or con, tragedy or comedy—*La Chinoise* must indeed be very perplexing; but it would be a grave mistake to reduce this film, as some viewers seem to do, to one category or another—hilarious spoof or dead-serious militance, insouciance or hard-line propaganda, aesthetic dilettantism or didactic non-art. Godard, one should have learned by now, cannot be explained away so easily; and his well-known taste for contradictions might better be understood as the ability to achieve a dynamic balance amid seeming oppositions.

Godard is in many ways a Hamlet who has found his calling: he is Hamlet as playwright, Hamlet as artist. It is art which enables Godard to achieve and maintain that dynamic balance; and, conversely, it is his intense desire to achieve such a harmony amid seeming discord which brings him inevitably to art. As Godard himself puts it in *Deux ou trois choses*, the goal of achieving a new world in which both men and things will know a harmonious rapport—a goal both political and poetic—explains, in any case, the rage for expression of Godard the writer-painter, of Godard the artist. Hamlet, too, knew that art and politics could serve each other, that art could be the mousetrap for the conscious of society; but it is significant that Hamlet staged only one play and from then on attempted to deal with life "directly," without the mediation of art, whereas Godard stages play after play after play, and deals with life by dealing with art.

In *La Chinoise* this interplay between art and life, between reality and the reflection of reality—and, most important, the inevitable interdependence and overlapping of the two—are expressed dramatically in the memorable sequence early in the film when the young actor Guillaume (played by Jean-Pierre Léaud) begins by reciting in very traditional style several lines from a text he is rehearsing, then stops short, grins, and, in answer to a question unheard by the audience (again, it is more or less whispered by Godard himself), acknowledges that "Yes, I am an actor" and then launches into an impromptu monologue on the dilemma of an actor committed to social revolution. At the close of this scene, however, Guillaume protests vigorously that one must avoid the temptation not to take his words seriously just because he is an actor performing in front of a camera, and he insists that he is sincere. At this moment we are suddenly shown a cameraman (Raoul Coutard) who has been filming Guillaume's speech and who is, in turn, now filmed himself in the act of filming the actor Jean-Pierre Léaud for the film we are presently watching. However, Godard's use of this complex procedure evokes little, if any, of the Pirandellian confusion of illusion and reality, but emphasizes rather the very Brechtian paradox that the film-within-a-film, like the film itself, must be seen not only as a work of art but, like all art, also as an activity engaged in by real people who may be sincerely committed to the ideas they are acting out in artistic form. As Godard explained when answering questions from the audience in Berkeley, Guillaume is an actor committed to the revolution who hopes to make his contribution to the revolution by *acting* in a revolutionary way in revolutionary films and theater. In this sense, Guillaume's revolutionary activity with the Marxist-Leninist cell is not so much a *secondary* activity as it is a *corollary* activity of the committed art he practices as an actor. In short, Guillaume is a revolutionary actor acting for the revolution; and this, too, seems to be what Godard is getting at when he advocates the "struggle on two fronts."

Godard recently indicated in a *Cahiers* interview that he was interested in the film-maker's opportunity to create in his own modest way "two or three Vietnams in the heart of the immense empire of Hollywood-Cinecittà-Mosfilm-Pinewood, etc., and economically as well as aesthetically—that is to say, in struggling on two fronts—create national and free cinemas that are brothers, comrades and friends." From this statement and from others like it, we can see that Jean-Pierre Léaud's role in *La Chinoise* as a revolutionary actor acting for the revolution is, in a very real sense, the role which Godard believes is the most authentic role he himself can play as a committed artist.

This problem of the artist's particular kind of commitment arises again in *La Chinoise* as we witness the very intense dialogue in a train compartment between Véronique and Francis Jeanson, the deeply committed colleague of Jean-Paul Sartre at *Les Temps Modernes* and the man who was in the forefront of political agitation in opposition to French colonial rule in Algeria at the time of the Algerian uprising. Jeanson, in *La Chinoise,* willingly puts himself in what is for him the rather paradoxical position of seeking to oppose or at least restrain the revolutionary activities advocated by the young would-be terrorist played by Anne Wiazemsky. Jeanson senses very acutely and very visibly the uncomfortable paradox of his position vis-à-vis the younger generation of radicals, but he argues sincerely and penetratingly —and with a wonderful feeling of warmth and genuine personal concern for his youthful student—as he attempts to make her realize the need, first and foremost, of creating a solid base of mass popular support for social change. Without this popular support, he points out, his own revolutionary activity in the Algerian crisis would have been futile, if not impossible; and it is precisely this need to create popular support for social change which involves Jeanson at the moment in a project designed to bring revolutionary theater to the people in the provinces.

Once again, the notion of the revolutionary actor acting for the revolution seems to be the artist's way of carrying on the "struggle on two fronts"; but even here, in presenting what is essentially his own view and what he believes to be the only authentic role for the artist in contemporary France, Godard's extreme honesty, sincerity, and lucidity force him to acknowledge, as we see in the scene with Francis Jeanson, that the artist's position will inevitably appear an equivocal one, for the militant activists will never consider the artist's contribution bold enough or even of any real significance in the revolutionary struggle; and the artist's particular way of committing himself will always contain at least a hint of self-interest, inasmuch as the artist continues to pursue his artistic career while at the same time claiming to align his art with the revolutionary cause. In both of these respects, then, it is understandable that in spite of Jeanson's obvious sincerity and the excellence of his arguments, we find it difficult to listen without slight annoyance, slight embarrassment, or both, when he speaks of the way his little theater troupe will enable him to engage in social action and at the same time enable him to get away from Paris, where he no longer finds himself able to concentrate on the books he is writing. "In going to the provinces," he explains with enthusiasm, "I'll be able to carry out this social action and, moreover, carry on my writing at the same time."

It is hardly surprising, however, that Jeanson's arguments, however right they may be, do not dissuade Véronique from advocating, and then committing, acts of terrorism. The artist can speak of the "struggle on two fronts" precisely because for him there are the two fronts of art and society, but for the ordinary individual (like Véronique, Yvonne, or Henri, the young man expelled for "revisionism") there is only the single front of a world that is not right, of a world with something rotten at its core, of a world that must, in one way or another, be taken apart so that it can be reassembled in a better way. While the artist can create on paper, on canvas, or on film a new and "perfect" world (and perhaps encourage others to attempt to create a new world in real life), it seems that the dirty work of going out and attempting to create this new world in real life falls inevitably to the ordinary individual who deals directly with life without the mediation of art; and it is the ordinary individual who, no matter how much he may be encouraged by the example of "committed art," must bear the burden of the fact that a bullet fired in reality takes a man's life, whereas a bullet fired in a film is art.

Hamlet himself, one will recall, found great sport in creating a work of art (his play-within-a-play) in which the king was murdered; but the same Hamlet found it nearly impossible in spite of the best of reasons to kill the king in real life. Given this predicament, the ordinary individual can react in many ways, the two extremes being either to sit back, do nothing, and, like Hamlet, complain that "the time is out of joint. O cursèd spite that ever I was born to set it right" or, like Véronique in *La Chinoise*, to accept the consequences of setting it right and go out and shoot somebody. In Berkeley Godard admitted that while he himself would never take up a gun, he now felt that he had to support those (like the North Vietnamese, or Régis Debray, or Che Guevara, or the Black Panthers) who, in the name of positive social reform, were willing to pick up a gun and if need be, use it. Godard also expressed admiration for a society like China, which he sees with the advent of the Red Guard youth movement as virtually turned over to the young people between fifteen and twenty-five years of age. As Godard puts it, "there are lots of things in this world that would be better off if they were turned over to the young people who have the courage to start again from zero."

This notion of starting again from zero (which was Juliette's conclusion at the end of *Deux ou trois choses*) recurs repeatedly in *La Chinoise*: Véronique wants to close the French universities so that the entire notion of education can be rethought from zero; she would bomb the Louvre and the Comédie Française so that painting and drama can likewise be rethought from zero; and Guillaume pushes his own investigation of the nature of theater to a notion of "The Theater of the Year Zero"—which is visualized cinematically by a shot of two individuals (an older woman in a sort of bathing suit and a young girl nude) knocking on either side of a large panel of transparent plexiglass through which they can see each other but which separates them—an image, perhaps, of the first primitive nonverbal efforts to communicate between one human being and another. Moreover, this notion of starting again from zero is implicit in the fact that in both subject and form *La Chinoise* is a film of revolution, a film that traces the progress of movement around the circumference of a circle until one completes the circle and returns to the point of departure. There is a strict logical sequence (as an inter-title states in announcing the film's final shot) which demands that the film end with the same shot with which it began—the shot of the balcony of the activists' apartment.

In beginning and ending at the same point, the film itself can be said to undergo a complete revolution; but to say that the film ends at the point of departure is not to say that the action within the film accomplishes nothing. On the contrary, it is the action within the circle which permits the return to the point of departure and the opportunity to start again from zero. Although they contain the same shot of the balcony, the opening and closing shots of the film reveal very different actions and attitudes within the development of the film narrative. In the opening shot, we see the balcony with its bright red shutters opened, and we hear, and then see, a young man (Henri) reading aloud. Then, as the film unfolds, Henri is seen to be the character who develops the least, the one who adheres most rigidly to the French Communist Party line, the one whose attitude remains static (and it is significant that Henri is the one character—aside from Kirilov, who is also extremely rigid—who is always filmed in static shots without cuts).

In the closing shot of the film we see the same balcony, at that very moment being reoccupied, so to speak, by the bourgeoisie—represented by the girl whose parents have let Véronique use the apartment during the summer vacation. The girl scolds Véronique for having made such a mess in the apartment and tells her it must be cleaned up before the return of her parents. Finally Véronique is left alone on the balcony with the parting advice to "think over carefully all that she has done." As Véronique leaves the balcony and closes the red shutters, we hear her unspoken thoughts explaining that she has already thought over her actions, that the end of the summer means the return to the university and the continuation of the struggle for her and for her comrades, and that she has now realized that the summer's activity with the Marxist-Leninist cell, which she originally thought represented a major breakthrough in revolutionary action, represents in reality only "the first tiny step in what would be a very long march"—words taken by Godard from a speech by Chou En-lai. Thus, the sequence of events that began on the balcony with Henri mechanically reading comes to an end on the same balcony with Véronique thinking out for herself the realization that what she has done is merely a beginning in an ongoing struggle ten thousand times longer. As Godard indicates in the final inter-title, the "end" of the sequence of events that comprises the film is only "the end of a beginning."

Godard himself gives the impression that the end of each new film is only "the end of a beginning"; and it is clear that as Godard develops as a film-maker, more and more he is putting into question both the entire notion of Western civilization and the entire notion of cinema. He has often remarked that when he made *A bout de souffle* (his first feature), he had lots of ideas about films, but that now, after making more than a dozen of his own, he no longer has any ideas about films. This confession, however, should not be taken as an indication of despair; rather it is for Godard a genuine liberation. He is clearly a man who has the courage, as well as the will, to start again from zero and to do it every time he makes a film. Even Hamlet, after all, despite his hesitations, managed at last, even if only inadvertently, to wipe the slate clean and enable Denmark to start again from zero. "Readiness is all," he proclaimed. Godard, at the end of *La Chinoise*, seems ready.

2

Politics, Poetry, and the Language of Signs in Made in USA

The films of Jean-Luc Godard, and particularly the films from *Une Femme Mariée* to the present, are pushing at the boundaries which have stood—more perhaps through habit than intrinsic necessity—between one art form and another. *Deux ou trois choses que je sais d'elle*, for example, defies all categorization, and can only be described, in Godard's own terms, as "a sociological essay in the form of a novel, written, however, not with words, but with notes of music."[6] *La Chinoise*, at the same time that it probes the nature of revolution, probes as well the nature of theater—especially the "dialectical theater" envisioned by the later Brecht. *Made in USA* (which Godard finished just a few days before *Deux ou trois choses*) takes a few jabs at the political intrigue film and thrusts its real assault at the tenuous boundary between film and the painter's canvas.

Moreover, just as painters today are themselves challenging the notion of the canvas and are reaching out into the world of everyday objects as media for their paints, so too does Godard reach out both to paint and to film the walls, the billboards, the posters, the gasoline pumps, and the comic-books which surround us today; to create of them, in his films, a series of semi-abstract collages which stand—more perhaps than any other contemporary art form—as the icons of our age. In *Made in USA* the style is a combination of the comic-strip iconography of pop art and the violent splashes of color of the "action painters." The compositions are out of Pollock, Poliakoff, Hofmann, Francis, Gorky—and there is even a flayed skull leering out at us obscenely, like one of DeKooning's terrifying "Women." But Godard has, in his own way, gone beyond the action painters to discover still another medium with which to paint—blood. *Made in USA,* as Anna Karina comments on the film's sound track, is the marriage of Walt Disney and Humphrey Bogart, in short, "a Walt Disney with blood." And blood there is, flowing, spurting, splattering over the whole works; but it is a photogenic blood that looks— and is used—suspiciously like paint. A man is murdered in bed and the blood-spattered sheet is cropped and photographed to resemble a composition by Jackson Pollock.

Along with Antonioni's *Deserto Rosso* (*Red Desert*), Agnès Varda's *Le Bonheur,* and Bo Widerberg's *Elvira Madigan, Made in USA* belongs to the burgeoning genre of what might be termed "painter's cinema" due to the way in which so much of the film narrative is "told" in color, composition, and light. Godard, who recognized in *Deserto Rosso* the sort of film he himself had long wanted to make, has spoken of the impression he had, while watching that film, that the colors were not in front of the camera but *in* the camera, that the camera did not merely photo- graph *Deserto Rosso* but *created* it—a stylistic effect which God- ard himself sought to achieve in *Made in USA.* "What I wanted," Godard revealed, in talking about both *Made in USA* and his short film *Anticipation,* "was to get *inside* the image . . . just the way certain paintings give one the feeling of being within them, *inside* them, or give the impression that they can never be un- derstood as long as the viewer remains outside."[7] But Godard is well aware that the ordinary film-viewer's habit of concentrating on the anecdotal structure of the "plot" often presents a formid- able obstacle to his getting inside the film and understanding the more subtle language of color, composition, and light. To help the viewer overcome this obstacle is always a difficult task, and the opening words of *Made in USA*—"le bonheur, par exemple"—

may be Godard's way of attempting to alert the viewer at the very outset, by referring to Varda's experiments with colors in *Le Bonheur,* that the film he is watching belongs to a genre of films that do not tell a story so much as they show it. Godard has even declared that the film which *Made in USA* resembles most is *Les Parapluies de Cherbourg* (by Varda's husband, Jacques Demy)—a film in which all of the dialogue is sung instead of spoken. In *Made in USA* Godard explains, "the people don't sing, but the film itself sings."

Nevertheless, *Made in USA* reveals a hard-edged contemporary sensibility which has far more affinity with Antonioni's cool abstractions than with the Romantic lushness of *Le Bonheur, Elvira Madigan,* or *Les Parapluies de Cherbourg.* Godard's sensibility, it should be pointed out, however, does not lack its own particular brand of Romanticism—a more tempered lushness— which reveals itself, for example, in *Le Mépris* and *Pierrot le fou,* in Godard's lucidly despairing but nonetheless poignant nostalgia for Mediterranean harmony; and which reveals itself in all his films in his attitude toward love, in the poignancy of his characters' perpetual search for love, in his own special way of letting the camera dwell caressingly on the gestures, the expressions, the *moues* of his actresses.

In *Made in USA* it is Anna Karina once again whose every gesture, every blink of the eyes, every swish of the hair is offered up to our visual caress. She is on screen nearly every instant of the film, usually in close-up, usually standing in front of a brightly colored wall—as if in a series of painted still compositions which might be entitled "Anna Karina on Blue," "Anna Karina on Red," "on Yellow," "on White," etc. Her face is now a little fuller perhaps, and at times the make-up gives her a slightly washed-out look: the gestures and expressions are the same we have seen so often in the earlier films that in *Made in USA* we sometimes have the impression we are watching an old pro's parody of the "real" Anna Karina we know and love. But when she fluffs out her hair in that feminine gesture so well-loved by

Godard, we capitulate, and, like Bruno Forestier (Michel Subor) in *Le Petit Soldat*, we lose the bet and have to admit that we have fallen in love with her . . . all over again and in spite of the lack of depth (this time) in her role and in the film as a whole.

However, the notion "lack of depth" seems to have been quite consciously integrated by Godard into both the subject and the form of *Made in USA*. Visually, the film has a markedly flat quality; and one has the claustrophobic feeling that nearly all of the film takes place in the closed space of what the French call a *plan américain;* with the camera framing just above the knees on a person standing directly in front of the wall. There is even one remarkable sequence in which Paula (Anna Karina), seeking possible clues to the disappearance and presumed murder of a man she loved, keeps a rendezvous with various underworld types in the prop and publicity storage-room of a movie theater. She walks to and fro amidst a maze of life-sized cardboard cowboys, commandos, and sex-queens—a two-dimensional pop world of violence and sexual fantasies which serves as a mirror both to the American movie industry's exploitation of the aggressive tendencies and sexual frustrations of American society, and to the superficial and basically false social and political situation of a Western Europe which, in rebuilding itself in the postwar years, has come increasingly under the influence of American ways.

France's Ben-Barka affair, to which *Made in USA* often alludes, was a gangland-style kidnapping and murder, which, if it hadn't happened right before their eyes in the heart of the Latin Quarter in broad daylight, 1965, would have seemed to most Parisians something out of an Al Capone movie of the twenties, or, for that matter, still another manifestation of America's present wave of violence and political assassinations. In any case, the title is neither gratuitous nor whimsical: Godard, like most Frenchmen (and this is the one issue on which Godard and De Gaulle would agree), feels very strongly about the insidious effect of the Americanization of Europe; and, in *Made in USA*, Godard has attempted to depict in his own cryptic way Europe's floundering efforts to extricate herself from the stultifying morass of American "cultural" exports—guns, gangs, gadgets, and Coca-Cola—as packaged by MGM.

But Godard is by no means a crude xenophobe sputtering with indignation and rage at the sight of everything American. On the contrary, Godard's attitude toward America betrays that certain admixture of attraction and repulsion, of fascination and fear—the love/hate relationship that America seems to inspire so readily in its intercourse with the rest of the world. There are aspects of America which Godard clearly admires and seems even to love. Action painting (or, if you prefer, abstract expressionism), to which Godard pays homage in *Made in USA*, found its beginning and its most fecund development in America; and in addition to American film style of the thirties and forties, even American comic-strips are admired by Godard (as well as by Resnais and many other French film-makers) for their lively, concise syntax, their quick-cutting shorthand which puts across its message with a minimum of signs and a maximum of emotive energy.

Made in USA is, itself, very much in the comic-strip style, even using "balloons" (the single expletive "BING!" the instant Anna Karina is slugged on the head by an underworld tough popping out from an alley doorway) and dialogue carried on from one frame to another (back and forth, with a cut each time the conversation switches from one speaker to another—the two speakers never appearing together in the same frame). There is, however, more than one comic-strip style; and given the telegraphic economy of the individual comic-strip *sign*, one can, simply according to the proliferation of individual signs, create of each frame either a "simple" or a "complex" unit of expression. This distinction (basically a stylistic one applicable to most art forms) can easily be perceived by a glance through the comic section of any newspaper: some comic-strips, like "Peanuts" or the Jules Pfeiffer cartoons, are extremely spare and convey their visual message with very few lines and little or no background; while others, like "Dick Tracy" or "Batman" or "Steve Canyon," are extremely dense and convey their visual message with an overwhelming mass of detail, each individual part in its own cryptic way conveying a certain signification. The *sense*, for example, of a frame from "Dick Tracy" is as much the electromagnetic ray-gun lying on the table in the corner as it is the punch being thrown at the hero's prominent jaw by his latest adversary.

Godard has, of course, utilized both simple and complex styles, but he has leaned increasingly, in his latest films, toward the latter; and, in particular, has experimented with the dynamic tensions which can be set up by a density of signs with conflicting and even contradictory significations. Thus, in *Deux ou trois choses*, both the viewer and the chief protagonist (Juliette—Marina Vlady) are inundated with signs clamoring for their attention, bidding them to do this, to do that, *not* to do this, *not* to do that, until the struggle to separate *sense* from *non-sense* reduces both Juliette and the viewer to a "zero-point" from which, hopefully, they will be able to start afresh. In *Made in USA*, too, the style is often complex in such a way that individual signs work against rather than with each other.

Before discussing the various types of sign-conflicts which occur in *Made in USA*, however, we should look closely for a moment at the very exemplary demonstration of sign-conflicts which Godard included within the dramatic structure of *La Chinoise*. This simple lesson shows the way two signs can come at us at once with contradictory significations, baffling us momentarily (or longer) until we refine our sensitivity to the more discrete units of meaning within a single sign and are thus able to decode the *sense* of a given sign or sign-cluster. In fact it demonstrates precisely the sort of critical operation we have been called upon to perform in *Made in USA* and *Deux ou trois choses*. I am referring to Véronique's demonstration to Guillaume of what it means to "struggle on two fronts at the same time." She tells Guillaume, by means of the spoken word, that she no longer loves him, while at the same time, by means of a Romantic piano sonata which she plays on the phonograph, she tells him just the opposite. Guillaume, like the audience, does not know at first what to make of this procedure and stares at Véronique bewild-

Made in USA: ''A Walt Disney with blood''

Made in USA: a narrow and constricting world

Made in USA: Anna Karina up against the wall

Made in USA: ''The barman is in the pocket of the pencil's jacket.''

ered, then becomes frustrated at the confusion in his decoding process and shouts angrily, "What's going on?" until finally he catches on, relaxes, smiles, and admits that she had him scared for a moment.

Normally, of course, there are not just two but many signs presented simultaneously in a particular shot or even in a particular frame; and it is worth noting that Guillaume, confused by the two conflicting auditory signs, immediately searches for a third sign—a visual one—by staring intently at Véronique's face. She, however, maintains as neutral a sign as possible by remaining impassive—and Godard himself safeguards that neutrality by avoiding a front close-up, keeping the camera to the side and at middle distance.

When two signs conflict, of course, there is no need for one sign to cancel out completely another sign. Given any two signs presented (aurally or visually) at the same moment, sign A could cancel out sign B, or B cancel out A; or A could predominate over but not cancel out B, or B predominate over but not cancel out A; or A and B could be contradictory and yet each of them half-true (for example, as in the case of a love/hate relationship); and, theoretically at least, they could be present in equal parts, that is, in a 50/50 ratio; or, finally, A and B could be mutual reinforcements or redundant statements, either both 100 percent true or both 100 percent false.

Among the various signs, it happens that words (although they are present in great abundance in Godard's films) are often systematically undercut or overruled by visual or other auditory signs such as music (as in "demonstration" by Véronique) or noise. The latter is utilized by Godard as a particularly effective source of tension, especially when what we might call random noise (that is, a sound usually not considered to occur for the explicit purpose of conveying sense: the sound of a car's motor or the drone of a low-flying plane) occurs simultaneously with a sound (such as the spoken word) which *is* normally considered to occur for the explicit purpose of conveying sense. When these two sounds occur simultaneously, our normal reaction is to consider the random noise as pure "interference" and therefore to dismiss it as much as possible in order to concentrate better on the supposedly more meaningful words. In *Deux ou trois choses*, however, Godard systematically turns the tables on us by letting noise convey as much sense as the words we strain so hard to hear —and often noise, in that film, conveys more sense than the words. In *Made in USA*, however, there are only three basic situations in which noise per se predominates over or cancels out the spoken words. Each time it is pronounced, the name of the man whose disappearance and presumed murder Paula is investigating is completely drowned out by a ringing telephone, low-flying jet, or honking auto-horn, so that even at the end of the film he is known to us—unless we are excellent lipreaders—simply as Richard. The noise, by systematically smothering the name, pretty clearly signifies to us the relative unimportance of the name; and the history of the past few years has provided all too many names we could fill in: Kennedy, King, Ben-Barka, Oswald, Evers, and even (perhaps most appropriate) the name X (as in Malcolm).

A second instance of noise interfering with words is a nicely ironic example wherein the noise is, itself, made up exclusively of words, but words spoken simultaneously by two different people (Paula and Widmark—Laszlo Szabo) who, standing side by side and facing the camera, deliver simultaneously two rapid-fire monologues which melt quite helplessly together to form an incomprehensible jumble. Finally, the third, most important, and certainly most irritating conflict between noise and words occurs on the two occasions when Paula listens to a tape-recorded speech which Richard (our Mr. X) had prepared for a meeting of the PCF (the French Communist Party). The tape is played, however, at such a high volume and on such a small tape-recorder that the sound is horribly distorted, producing a deafening, haranguing rasp (it is Godard's own voice, by the way, which is distorted), permitting us to comprehend little of what is said. What few fragments we do manage to comprehend (such as the statement that the Communists in France must offer a concrete alternative to the "nuclear adventure and patriotic publicity of the Gaullist police-state") indicate to us that the speech, although rambling, might (in Godard's own allusive and elusive way) be quite interesting and even instructive; but, as it stands, it is instructive only as another example of the way the rhetoric of the Left (as well as that of the Right) so often deteriorates into an incomprehensible harangue. And this is not the first time that Godard has dramatized the inability of the French Left to communicate its political programs articulately.

But if words can be so easily overruled by other auditory signs such as music and noise, what happens to words when they come in conflict with visual signs? It is precisely this problem which provides what is undoubtedly the most extraordinary sequence in *Made in USA*—the incredible "conversation" at the bar in a small café. (This sequence, by the way, is all the more extraordinary by virtue of its being filmed over a duration of what seems like ten minutes without a single cut—capturing, through subtle camera movements and the slow, preoccupied pacing of Paula, as well as through the rhythm of the words, a ballet-like ebb and flow that is absolutely hypnotic.) The conversation takes place between Paula, the barman, and a young laborer who has come in for a few quick glasses of *vin ordinaire*. It begins with a seemingly nonsensical mélange of words and numbers. When Paula states that she is twenty-one, the laborer remarks that he is only two years older than she is (so far so good), to which Paula replies, however, that she is surprised to learn that he is nineteen (?)! The barman butts in to object that 22 and 35 (?) do not make 19, to which Paula agrees, except, she adds, that, during war, 70 plus 14 made 40. Mathematically, of course, this is all *non-sense;* but the last equation, at least, makes *sense* if one catches the reference to war and to the "snowball" effect of war upon war upon war in the last hundred years. (1870 was the year of the Franco-Prussian War, the first of France's humiliating defeats at the hands of the Germans; 1914 was the year in which Germany invaded France in World War I; and 1940 saw Germany once again occupying French soil.) Moreover, these wars—at least the last two—have brought increasing intervention of the United States in Europe's affairs, and the wars are thus key chapters in the Americanization of European life, which comprises the subject of the film.

Following this playful but straightfaced game of numbers, the conversation switches to an equally straightfaced but far less playful game of words, which, it is demonstrated, can be put together in perfectly correct syntactical relation and yet make sheer *non-sense*—and even a most poetic but most disquieting form of *contre-sens.* "The barman is in the pocket of the pencil's jacket." "The counter is kicking mademoiselle." "The doors are throwing themselves through the windows." "The windows are looking out of my eyes."

These statements are delivered matter-of-factly by the young laborer between sips of his wine. But while he uses words to turn the world upside-down and inside-out, Raoul Coutard's magnificent color photography shows us a world so *visibly*—and, for the actors who move about in it, so *palpably*—right-side-up and right-side-out, so irrefutably solid in its thingness, that ultimately we realize (as did Juliette in *Deux ou trois choses*) that instead of helping us to disengage the real from the imaginary, language submerges us with significations which threaten to drown that which is real, and only lead us to doubt whether language itself is of any help in our intercourse with the world.

There is, as everyone knows, an old saying that "one picture is worth a thousand words"; and Godard, in *La Chinoise,* coined a cinematographer's version of that old adage and had it painted on the wall of the activists' apartment. "One must confront vague ideas with clear images" reads the maxim of moralist Godard, who, in his exploration of the world of *signs* and in spite of his own love for words, finds the visual sign—the clear photographic image—a far more faithful indicator of the reality of a given situation than the fickle and all too malleable word.

But the question arises as to why in his films, Godard occupies himself with exercises in signs, with comic-strip syntax, with pop art, with the sharp, bright graphic style of *Elle* and *Marie-Claire.* Some have attributed it to caprice, others to perversity, while still others have somewhat enviously accused Godard of cashing in on the cult of modernity. The answer, I would maintain, is that Godard does, in fact, interest himself in the cult of modernity, *not* in order to cash in on it, but rather because it is where today's action is, because it is where today's "mutations" (to use one of Godard's favorite words) are taking place, and because Godard, as a committed artist, seeks both to understand the social-political-biological-emotional situation as it exists today in Western Europe, and, at the same time, to act upon it, to influence it, to change it by goading, pricking, and cajoling people into a greater awareness of—and, concomitantly, a greater use of—their *responsibility*.

The nonsensical conversation at the bar in *Made in USA* provokes Paula to assert (echoing Nana's famous acknowledgment of her individual responsibility in *Vivre sa Vie*) that even though existence may be relative, "one can place in the very center of that relative existence a point of absolute reference: *morale*" (which, in the French sense of the term, comes closer to the English word "ethics" than to the narrower "morality"). One is, she affirms, responsible for what one does. Moreover, the very fact that there is nothing outside of existence to justify it shifts the entire problem of existence (as the French existentialists have pointed out) from the realm of metaphysics into the realm of ethics. That "point of absolute reference at the center of one's relative existence" is nothing other than the *nothingness* which each person is, and which forces him to *choose,* to create himself anew at each new moment. One is not only responsible for what one does, one *is* what one does. Or, as Godard himself once phrased it, "the very definition of the human condition should be in the *mise-en-scène* itself."

Godard's style of *mise-en-scène* in his films is, above all, a Brechtian attempt (both in theatrical means and philosophical end) to coax the viewer-listener into a closer examination of his own individual, existential *mise-en-scène*. On the subject of theatrical means, however, it should be pointed out that Godard uses not only certain theatrical techniques associated with Brechtian Epic Theater, but also certain techniques associated with Artaud's Theater of Cruelty. For example, the bombardment of the viewer-listener's senses throughout *Deux ou trois choses,* the unbearable rasp of the tape-recorder in *Made in USA,* and the latter film's numerous "jets of blood" all reveal a strong affinity with—and may quite consciously be derived from—Artaud. Nevertheless, it is quite clear that what Godard seeks in the theatrical experience (and that includes film) is *not,* as Artaud would have it, the trancelike participation of a religious communicant in some eternal oneness, but rather the lucid participation of a critical and self-critical individual in the day-to-day dialectic of existence, à la Brecht. In short, what Godard seeks, like Brecht and like the existentialists, is lucidity, responsibility, and *engagement.*

But Godard is very much aware of how easy it is for an individual living in modern urban society to abdicate both his lucidity and his responsibility by passively submitting to and unconsciously assimilating the mass media's perpetual bombardment of signs and significations, which, as much by bewildering and benumbing the individual as by direct exhortation, succeeds all too often in planting notions and arousing needs in which conscious volition plays little or no role. "To live in society today," Godard once stated, "is like living in one enormous comic-strip"; and in films such as *Bande à part* and *Pierrot le fou* Godard has clearly demonstrated the way even those who attempt to live outside of society bring their comic-book notions with them.

It is, in fact, precisely because the human being is so malleable, so adaptable, because he can assume and appropriate patterns of behavior so readily, often without even knowing he is doing so, that Godard is so much concerned with the problems of lucidity and responsibility. The individual confronted by what McLuhan calls the "electronic implosion" of *signs* pouring at him from every corner of his environment, finds himself in a vulnerable position if he does not quickly develop an ability to handle signs in a sophisticated way, to read them correctly, to decode them and process the information in a rapid and precise manner. Without this ability the individual is a prey to what Herbert Marcuse describes under the rubric "The New Forces of Control" in *One-*

Dimensional Man—a book, by the way, which may very well have been a source of inspiration to Godard in his depiction of the flat, depthless world of *Made in USA*. As a matter of fact, Godard's films are full of characters who have succumbed to what Godard (in *Deux ou trois choses*) calls "The Gestapo of the Structures" and who have become, in a very literal sense, one-dimensional men. (I am thinking particularly of Charlotte in *Une Femme Mariée*, Madeleine and "Mlle. 19 Ans" in *Masculin-Féminin*, Ulysse and Michel-ange in *Les Carabiniers*, and, of course, the citizens of Alphaville.) Then, too, there are in Godard's films the individuals (like Michel Poiccard in *Breathless*, Odile and Franz in *Bande à part*, and Ferdinand in *Pierrot le fou*) who dream of a Romantic escape from contemporary problems and who are always setting out, if only in their imaginations, for exotic places. But Romantic escape in Godard's films always ends in death—if not physical, then spiritual death. It is not considered by Godard to be an authentic solution.

On the other hand, Godard's most positive characters (Nana in *Vivre sa Vie*; Lemmy Caution in *Alphaville*; Paul—until he "steps back too far" and falls to his death—in *Masculin-Féminin*; Paula in *Made in USA*; and the group of activists in *La Chinoise*) all steadfastly refuse to run away from reality, refuse to abdicate their responsibility, and involve themselves in the day-to-day struggle for mastery of the vague, impersonal forces that in modern society weigh heavily upon them. The electronic age is here whether we like it or not, and it is here and now that the "mutations" are taking place. Godard's exercises in signs in *Made in USA*, *Deux ou trois choses*, and *La Chinoise* constitute his way of helping, coaxing, almost forcing the viewer-listener to refine his processes of perception, to develop his ability to handle signs, and thereby to protect himself psychically from those who would willfully manipulate the unsophisticated. Only through mastery of the complex system of signs and significations, Godard seems to be warning us, can we hope to extricate ourselves from the hypnotic web they spin around us.

In *Made in USA* that spider's web of manipulation, intrigue,

coercion, and violence has had its day. Near the middle of the
film we are told, by means of a quiet, brooding song by Marianne
Faithfull, that we have reached "the evening of the day." The
song is like a lament. The same mistakes are being made all over
again. "We sit and watch the children play, doing things we
used to do, doing things they think are new." And we just sit and
watch . . . and cry bitter tears. The new Europe is repeating the
mistakes of America, and America is repeating the mistakes of
the old Europe. It is all a vicious circle. It is also getting late.
For Western civilization as a whole, it may very well be "the
evening of the day." Small wonder that we are sad.

What Paula has been through, in *Made in USA,* is in her own
words, "something to make one vomit"—political kidnappings,
political assassinations, torture, treachery, the whole seamy and
sadistic web of secret-police machinations in a state that disguises
its fascism in publicity slogans of old-fashioned patriotism. It has
been a narrow and constricting world—a world in which the word
liberté has literally been plastered up against the wall and riddled
with machine-gun bullets. But the very fact that it is getting late,
that we are moving toward the end of something, seems in Godard's view to be a source of hope. In the final sequence of *Made
in USA* there comes a moment when the camera shows us a book
jacket with the words "Gauche, Année Zéro" (year Zero of the
Left), while we hear on the sound track the beginning of the
beautiful Largo movement of Schumann's Fourth Symphony.
"Unless you're blind and deaf," Godard asserted in an interview,
"it's impossible not to see that this shot, this mixture of image
and sound, represents a movement of hope."

Moreover, in that final sequence, the horizon begins to open
up for the first time in the film and the soft, natural morning light
is a dramatic contrast to the bright, sharp splashes of violent
color we have seen all through the film. Paula leaves the corrupt
world of "Atlantic City" and begins to extricate herself from the
constricting morass of the past, which unravels itself like a giant
ribbon as we watch the auto route spin out behind her through
the rear window of the Europe #1 radio-car in which she is riding.

"Fascism will pass away," she says to journalist Philippe Labro, the driver of the car: "It's just a fad, like miniskirts. But the struggle for a real viable Left will be long and difficult." The conversation continues, punctuated intermittently by the long, flowing lines of the Schumann. "The Right and the Left are both the same," objects the journalist. "They'll never change: the Right because it's as stupid as it is vicious, the Left because it's sentimental. Besides," he adds, "the Right and the Left is an equation completely out of date; one can't put the problem in those terms anymore." "Well, how?" asks Paula, looking straight ahead at the future in front of her as the film comes, characteristically, to an end that is only a beginning.

3

Weekend, *or the Self-Critical Cinema of Cruelty*

Weekend, in more ways than one, equals "dead-end": not for Godard, and not for the cinema, but for a particular type of cinema—the cinema of spectacle—which is pushed to its limit. Future generations (if there are any) may even look back upon *Weekend* as the terminal point of a particular phase in the development, or, more literally, the disintegration of Western civilization. The point seems clear: "civilization," as it exists in *Weekend,* is doomed to devour itself.

But *Weekend,* in spite of its searing insights and its sense of the general movement of history, offers a very selective view. Godard, in this film, concentrates almost exclusively on two of the most flamboyant aberrations of contemporary life—the bourgeois materialist in his most aggravated fever of accumulation and consumption; and his double, the antibourgeois, antimaterialist drop-out from society, whose only alternative to the horror of the bourgeoisie is more horror still. "This is a helluva film," remarks the male lead in *Weekend,* "the only people you meet in it are sick!" The remark is crucial to the understanding of the film, for clearly *Weekend* is the negative and destructive side of the same social revolution that is depicted in a more positive and constructive side in Godard's previous film, *La Chinoise.* But *La Chinoise* only becomes positive and constructive by means of a dialectical process of trial and error and by a lucid acknowledgment of the negative and destructive tendencies which revolution contains within itself, but which are gradually overcome and transcended; whereas *Weekend* presents a view which seems so overwhelmingly negative and destructive that one can hardly come away from the film without a feeling of profound despair at the spectacle of man's inhumanity to man.

Still, on closer examination, it is not altogether true that everyone in the film is sick, but simply that either the few relatively healthy exceptions (in the film or, for that matter, in society) are not given much to say or do, or when they do speak out or act they seem irrelevant and insignificant amidst the spectacular carnage all around us—and appear flat, dull, and uninteresting compared to the grotesque, Ubu-esque bourgeois characters and the bizarre freak-out types of the hippie guerilla-band. That the healthy and reasonable should appear flat, dull, and insignificant (again, both in the film and in society) is an integral part of the theme, for *Weekend* is, first and foremost, a spectacle which examines civilization's ritual of the spectacle.

One might call *Weekend* a primer on civilization in much the same way that Godard called *Les Carabiniers* a primer on war; moreover, Godard, in *Weekend,* takes up and develops many of the insights and ideas he introduced in *Les Carabiniers,* perhaps the most important being the linking of the passage from barbarism to civilization with the transition in the human psyche from concern with *things themselves* to concern with *images* of things. As an illustration of this transition, there comes a moment in *Weekend* when Corinne (Mireille Darc) takes a bath—a classic example of the voyeur-spectacle aspect of cinema; but Godard does not show us her breasts (just out of sight below the frame) but shows us instead the breasts of a woman in a Renaissance portrait hanging on the wall behind Corinne: thus we are twice-removed from direct physical experience: the movie image we are viewing is only a flickering shadow-play of light and darkness; and, second, even the breasts that are photographed are not the breasts of the real woman who, at least at the moment of being photographed, was physically present, but instead the flat, two-dimensional breasts on a painted canvas.

The real irony of this scene, however, is that within the ground rules of our society's ritual of the spectacle, we have seen what we paid our money to see and we are satisfied. The image, no matter how far removed it may be from the real thing, has somehow become more important than the thing itself. In our modern civilization we don't want sex, we want the spectacle of sex.

The bathtub sequence in *Weekend* is a subtle refinement of the memorable bathtub movie-sequence in *Les Carabiniers,* in which Michel-ange, who was not yet initiated into the ritual of the cinema (not yet civilized), responded naturally and directly to the sight of a nude woman taking a bath, and, unsatisfied with the mere image of the woman, wanted to touch her and to possess her physically—an impulse quite natural and healthy, and yet an impulse which, in our society's ritual of the spectacle, appears as a biological anachronism that produces only comic results: the unsuspecting Michel-ange falls through the movie screen. One will recall, however, that by the end of *Les Carabiniers* Michel-ange has learned his lesson, he has been civilized through war and can now take his place in our society's ritual of the spectacle and be content with images. Witness the famous sequence with the post-cards.

But in *Weekend* the nature of the spectacle is intimately related to the phenomenon of language: the first "image" may have been a word, and perhaps the ultimate refinement in the passage from the thing itself to an image of the thing is the "spectacle" of the spoken word. Corinne's remarkable description, at the beginning of the film, of a three-way sex orgy provides a perfect illustration of the magnificent spectacle that is the word. Corinne herself, while she describes what took place, is clad only in bra and pants and she sits on the edge of a table in front of a window. Now, normally, the opportunity to take a good, long look at one of France's leading sex-kittens *déshabillée* might very well qualify as a spectacle of sex par excellence. But Godard plays it down, photographing the scene in a soft half-light that utilizes only the natural daylight filtered through the yellow curtains which are pulled closed over the window. Thus, with the only light source in back of her, Corinne is photographed in half shadow which does not reveal the contours and proportions of her body. If this scene is to be a spectacle of sex, as it assuredly is, then the spectacle has got to come from something other than the visual image. And indeed it does: the spectacle, in this scene, is the word.

It is interesting to compare Corinne's description of her sexual activities in *Weekend* with the sex anecdote related without flashback in Bergman's *Persona*, which inspired Godard to conceive a similar anecdote (two females and one male, with ambiguous and constantly shifting relationships among the three) while letting the words tell the story. Moreover, Godard clearly intends the word to be more stimulating, more exciting, more capable of arousing the sexual appetite of the audience than the image. It is important to note, however, that Godard (mistakenly perhaps) does not let the words and their incantatory powers work alone, but chooses instead to supplement the words with intermittent passages of string music of a suggestive nature, always building in intensity, then waning, then building again. It is "movie music" of the kind often used to accompany (or to substitute for) torrid sex scenes; and its use here by Godard, although it still calls attention to the blatant manipulation that invariably goes into an audience's response to sex on the screen, also erodes somewhat the power of the words, which, if left alone, might have done the job by themselves. Still, the use of the music is so obviously contrived that it calls forth on the audience's part a very healthy critical awareness of how each individual element works, and makes it clear that from then on if you are the slightest bit aroused by the scene, it is due to the power of the word. Finally, the preeminence of the word as an instrument of eroticism is emphasized again and again in Corinne's account, not just of what was done at the orgy, but also of what was said.

She recounts, for example, that when feeling each other in the car before the orgy began, she and a man named Paul (whom we never meet) kept telling each other that what they were doing was "vulgar and dirty" as a means of getting each other aroused. Then, during the orgy itself, as we learn from Corinne's account, much of the excitement was generated by one person's describing in detail to a second person a part of the anatomy of the third person. Moreover, when Corinne is asked what she was doing at a particular moment in the orgy, she explains that her role was to describe in words exactly how everything felt—"in order to excite them." In the final analysis, then, in spite of the obvious preoccupation with feces of the orgy's climax (one woman squatting nude on top of the refrigerator with her *derrière* in a bowl of milk while the man slowly shoved an egg between the *fesses* of the other woman until the egg broke and oozed out), this entire sequence, instead of being called "ANAL-YSE," might more accurately have been called "ORAL-YSE."

Let us consider now, however, the very different form of sexual behavior practised by the hippie band in the latter part of the film. For the hippies, too, sex is a ritual; not, as for the bourgeoisie, a ritual of words but rather a ritual of deeds. One might be tempted to infer that hippie sex brings man back into direct physical contact with things and is therefore more healthy. As the film suggests, however, this is not exactly the case. Words, it is true, are reduced to a minimum (a few shouted commands: "Take off your sweater . . . skirt . . . bra . . . pants!"), but there is no real contact between sex partners: instead of lying down with a nude woman, the hippie (in this case, a girl) dances around her; instead of embracing a nude woman, the hippie (this time a boy) takes a paint brush and paints psychedelic colors on her body; and in the climax of the hippie ritual of sex, a phallic *symbol* (a large live fish) is used to penetrate the woman's body rather than the phallus itself. In short, far from providing direct physical contact with the *thing itself*, hippie sex in *Weekend* provides no direct contact at all between one human being and another; in many ways it is more cruel and inhuman than the verbal sex of the

Weekend: "The only people you meet in this film are sick."

Weekend: the courtesies of the road

Weekend: a primer on "civilization"

Weekend: two-dimensional titillation

Weekend: frantic orgies of consumption

bourgeoisie. Ultimately the hippie mode of sex is outright destruction, for the victim is ritually violated and then sacrificed, and
finally eaten—thus revealing that hippie life, just as much as
bourgeois life, rests on the capitalist's fundamental obsession with
consumption. One doesn't *live* life, one *consumes* it.

Weekend's juxtaposition of the bourgeois ritual of consumption
with the hippie ritual of consumption points to a dead-end in
which the only movement is in vicious circles of endless exploitation and destruction. The hippies feed off the bourgeoisie and the
bourgeoisie nourishes within itself the future hippies. The bourgeoisie fails to recognize the internal contradictions of its existence, but so do the hippies fail to recognize the internal
contradictions of their existence. Moreover, the hippie way of life
ironically seems to attract the most blatantly fascist of the young
bourgeoisie, as is illustrated by the fact that the mod girl (Juliette
Berto) who invokes class priorities, and who indignantly berates
and despises the peasants early in the film, eventually turns up as
a member of the hippie band engaged in guerilla warfare against
the bourgeoisie. Finally, just as the members of the bourgeoisie
inevitably exploit and destroy one another, so do the various
hippie groups turn against and destroy one another. An exchange
of women hostages near the end of the film turns into an in-
ternecine shooting match between the hippie gangs of "Uncle
Ernest" and "Arizona Jules."

The ultimate identity (or at least interchangeability) of the
bourgeoisie and the hippies is brilliantly suggested by Godard in
a long-range group shot of the hippie band on maneuvers, peering
out from behind the ferns and foliage of a forest scene reminiscent
of the tableaux of Henri Rousseau. The irony and insight of this
shot is that the hippie *fauves* are no more *sauvages* than the stolid
bourgeois and *bourgeoises* of the Douanier Rousseau's compositions. (We might also turn the comparison around and say that
the impeccable middle-class citizen in capitalist society is actually
no tamer, no less barbaric than the bizarrely dressed hippie.) In
Weekend they are, each of them, unhealthy aberrations of a sick
society.

Because the notion of ritual is so important in this film, we should look for a moment at ritual and its functions, and, in particular, at ritual's relation to the drama. Antonin Artaud, the famous theorist of the Theater of Cruelty, saw in primitive ritual man's highest form of expression, and he sought to create a new theater that would reverse the nineteenth-century trend toward psychologizing melodrama and bring the theater back to its essential nature—ritual. For Artaud, the word as an instrument of rational dialogue was deadly and stultifying; its place in the drama had to be eliminated, the only saving grace of the word being the magic of its incantatory powers, which Artaud sought to incorporate into a total theater of ecstatic communion. Ritual, for Artaud, was essentially cathartic: the community came together to act out its destructive impulses and to express its deepest fears, and, in the acting, to purge them. The most destructive impulses —murder, crimes of blood, and sex—were to be pushed to the paroxysm of intensity, to the very brink of action, to that instant just before the point where the impulse would spill over into direct rather than symbolic action: but at that brink the tension was to be sustained. The ritual, then, and hence the drama, function as a release valve for the society to blow off steam and return to its normal level.

The problem with this view of ritual, however, is that it ignores and excludes the larger context within which primitive ritual operates—a context which can only be described as *revolution;* a context in which *change,* not perpetuation of the status quo, is the goal. Theodore H. Gaster, in his exhaustive study of ritual and its relation to the drama, points out that the purgative aspect of ritual is only one phase in a seasonal cycle whose ultimate goal is to prepare the community for a transition from one phase of life-experience to another.[8] The Year Festival ("Out with the Old and in with the New!") and the *rites de passage* are basic examples of this function of ritual. In brief, the wider view of ritual advanced by Gaster and others recognizes that while preservation of the society is implicit in ritual, it is a preservation of society *through its ability to transform itself,* often radically, and through its ability not just to adapt to changing conditions but to bring the changes about, willfully and lucidly.

In terms of the modern theater, then, whose theories and traditions are constant preoccupations of Godard, we can see how the cathartic spectacle provided by Artaud's so-called total theater falls considerably short of providing a total picture of the function of ritual. Artaud's theatrical techniques need to be placed in a much larger context of social change in which theater also functions as a stimulant—as a sort of Socratic gadfly, which, by engaging society in a dialogue, manages to sting society into looking at itself in new ways. In short, if Artaud's Theater of Cruelty is one phase of the ritual cycle, Brecht's Dialectical Theater is another; and the Brechtian notion of theater as a stimulant comes closer to the ultimate function of ritual than does the merely purgative theater of Artaud.

Weekend, Godard's Artaud-style spectacle, seems to concentrate almost exclusively on what might be termed the purgative phase of the ritual cycle. In order to be seen as truly constructive it may have to be considered within the larger context of social change introduced by Godard in *La Chinoise.* That Godard intends both *La Chinoise* and *Weekend* to be considered as interrelated parts of a larger whole seems quite clear. Chronologically, it can even be established that *Weekend* is a sequel to *La Chinoise,* not simply because Godard made it after *La Chinoise,* but because *Weekend* picks up Jean-Pierre Léaud's character (Guillaume, the committed actor) at the very point where he left off at the end of *La Chinoise:* where, dressed up in eighteenth-century garb, he went out into the world to shake up people's notion of the theater and, at the same time, shake up their notion of society.

That Guillaume doesn't seem to be having much success in *Weekend* is perhaps to be expected, since *Weekend,* as the title implies, is a hiatus within the productive cycle, a period given over to idling or, among Parisians, to mad dashes out into the countryside and to frantic orgies of consumption. Nonetheless, Guillaume perseveres in his task, declaims aloud a text from Saint-Just with his only audience the bourgeois husband-and-wife team, and places poignant singing-telephone calls *"dans le vide."* That Guillaume's efforts seem ineffectual, to say the least, may simply indicate Godard's own modest admission that the artist's chances of really establishing communication with his audience are small indeed, especially when, as in *Weekend*, the spectacle aspect of his art is so diverting.

Still, Guillaume's activity in *Weekend*, although ineffectual, can be considered an instructive lesson in his "theatrical apprenticeship" undertaken at the close of *La Chinoise*. Moreover, something that Guillaume says in *La Chinoise* seems to look forward to *Weekend* and to suggest that Godard, when making the very Brechtian *La Chinoise*, may already have been thinking of the very different sort of film that would be inspired by Artaud, and thinking as well of the inconsistencies and limitations in Artaud's notion of the theater and its function in society. In *La Chinoise* Guillaume reveals that his father worked quite closely with Artaud in the days when Artaud's notions were considered the most revolutionary movement in the theater; but Guillaume goes on to point out that something was obviously lacking in that notion of revolution, for his father now works as social director of a vacation site run by the Club Méditerranée—a bourgeois travel organization given over to blatant consumption of all the appurtenances of sex and leisure, and whose vacation camps, Guillaume asserts, are sealed off from the rest of the world just like the Nazi concentration camps.

In any case, the point seems clear: even if Artaud's theater could accomplish what it sets out to do, it would still not be enough; for the result, as we see in the example of Guillaume's father, is merely reintegration of the individual within the existing social institutions and preservation of the status quo. Moreover, it is questionable if Artaud's theater, as he envisioned it, could ever even exist. What we usually attribute to Artaud is often nothing other than garish spectacle: instead of evoking total involvement on the part of the spectator, it simply provides him with a wider range of sensory phenomena to divert him, to entertain him, and even to flatter his sense of self-importance by the extravagant dissipation of energies that has gone into the task of providing him with such a magnificent spectacle.

Fittingly enough, *Weekend* itself seems vulnerable to some of these accusations; and it is ironic that Godard seems likely to receive more acclaim from the general public for *Weekend*, in which, by pushing spectacle to its utmost, he attempts to demonstrate the inadequacies of spectacle, than for previous films such as *Les Carabiniers, Masculin-Féminin,* or *La Chinoise,* from which the element of spectacle is rigorously excluded—or in which what spectacle remains is clearly subordinated to the critical awareness the film calls forth on the part of the spectator. This is not to imply that *Weekend* is *merely* spectacle or that the film does not seek to call forth critical awareness; quite the contrary; but the immensity of the spectacle in *Weekend* may make it too easy for the audience to remain at the level of spectacle instead of critically questioning both the ritual of the spectacle and the society that has produced this form of ritual.

Consider, for instance, some of the critics' reactions here in America to the "Third World" sequence in which a black and an Arab (those who are forced to do the meanest tasks in our highly advanced society—like collecting our garbage) stand alongside their garbage-truck, eat their meager meal of unbuttered bread, and deliver rather formal little speeches about the plight of the oppressed and the need for revolution. Renata Adler, in *The New York Times,* advises people to walk out on this sequence, get themselves a cup of coffee and a cigarette, and come back in when the "unprofessional invective" is finished and the spectacular carnage is resumed. Pauline Kael, in *The New Yorker,* admits to "blanking out" on this sequence, rebukes Godard for its "directness," and asks "who can assimilate and evaluate this chunk of theory thrown at us in the middle of a movie?"

Assimilating and evaluating this sequence is precisely the task we must undertake, not by treating the Third World sequence as a chunk of theory alien to the film, but rather by understanding how this particular chunk (not of theory but of images and sounds) fits into the film and relates to the other sequences and to the film as a whole. The Third World sequence is not an interjection; it is not an aside; it is an integral part of an artistic whole. To dismiss it or to walk out on it because it seems too direct and unspectacular compared to the rest of the film is to miss the main point. Both of these critics, while praising *Weekend* as a spectacle, refuse to rise to the film's level and to do what the film itself does: namely, to question the ritual of the spectacle.

Of course the Third World sequence is unspectacular: and of course it is direct. The underprivileged and oppressed peoples cannot afford the luxury of spectacle and they are not nearly as interested in the symbolic image of a thing as in the thing itself. Things, we should realize, are precisely what they lack. The mass media, penetrating even into the darkest corners of the Third World, provide them with plenty of *images* of things and arouse their hopes and desires; but the things themselves remain forever out of reach. Even the things which we in our affluence take for granted, like bread, are the things which they have to struggle for and which are often denied them.

Godard could have made this point in a spectacular way—by photographing some of the Third World's emaciated victims of malnutrition—but that sort of spectacle works so powerfully on our emotions that it leaves little opportunity for constructive reason. By eschewing spectacle and letting the black and the Arab look directly into the camera while they deliver (in a voice-over) lucid and unemotional statements calling for revolutionary awareness, Godard places the Third World sequence in dramatic contrast to the spectacular sequences devoted to the bourgeoisie and the hippies. But when critics denounce the Third World sequence for failing to sustain the spectacular frenzy of the rest of the film, they are falling into the very trap *Weekend* attempts to expose. When wisdom and calm are rejected in favor of the greater spectacle offered by violence and destruction, we can only agree with Guillaume's conclusion, quoted from Saint-Just, that "it seems as if humanity, tired of calm and wisdom, preferred to be miserable and mad." And we in the film medium (whether directors, producers, actors, critics, or moviegoers) are certainly just as guilty of this charge as anyone—perhaps even more guilty. Wisdom, apparently, is not what we want; but with spectacle we're very much at home, the more violent the spectacle the better; but in *Weekend* the spectacle spills over into life. Only up to a certain point are we still safe and secure in our knowledge that the dead bodies on the screen are not really dead, that the carnage is not real, that it's all a game, that it's cinema. Godard's films, we recall, are often full of what looks like blood but is really only ketchup or paint. Even when the bourgeois husband in *Weekend* kills his mother-in-law and pours her blood over the flayed carcass of a skinned rabbit, we may flinch a bit but only because it's such a grisly *image*. But when we see one of the hippie band slaughter a live pig and a goose, the props are knocked out from under us. Suddenly we don't know where we stand: it was all such wonderful spectacle a moment ago, and now, well, the *image* and the *thing itself* are one; *the cinema is real life*.

We laughed earlier in the film when the characters kept insisting that cinema was real life; but we don't laugh anymore. Spectacle has been pushed to its limits and has brought us down abruptly. In the cinema, as in the Roman Coliseum, the ultimate spectacle has turned out to be the taking of a life. But getting angry at Godard and blaming him for this death, as Pauline Kael did, is only bad faith, an evasive tactic to enable us to retain our self-respect by washing our hands of any complicity and foisting all of the blame upon the film-maker. All Godard has done, after all, is to film an act which we in our society have others commit for us thousands of times each day. What this shot accomplishes, if we are honest with ourselves, is to shatter one of our most cherished illusions—the illusion of the innocence of the spectacle. For all our talk about total theater and audience involvement and ecstatic communion, we have obviously refused to accept any responsibility for what takes place in the theater: it has all been a spectacle and we have considered ourselves innocent, untouched, and uninvolved.

Once again, as in *La Chinoise*, we see that the artist's way of contributing to the revolution is to revolutionize the way people look at art and the relation between art and life. The killing of the pig and the goose is only one of many attempts in *Weekend* to help us step out of our habitual ways of looking at things. The Emily Brontë sequence, for example, illustrates both the artist's attempts to stimulate people to look at things in new ways and society's rigid resistance to having its illusions shattered. To the bourgeois couple, a blade of grass is a blade of grass and a pebble is a pebble; no further thought is required. The name suffices. But to the poet or to the scientist, these things have more meaning: they are even called by different names. The poet, who long ago placed a word between us and things, now realizes the need to bring us back to direct experience of things. Emily Brontë holds up a pebble for us to look at and we suddenly begin to understand what the poet Francis Ponge has called *"le parti pris des choses."* Moreover, the poet helps us, too, to look more closely at words, to see how they work, and to see their limitations. Emily Brontë's reading of the nonsense riddles points out what the laborer's non-sense phrases in *Made in USA* pointed out: namely, that words are a system unto themselves and that words do not necessarily have any relation to the world of things.

In the final analysis, then, it is not ecstatic communion, but *critical awareness*—of things, of words, of ourselves and our society—that is for Godard the goal of art. Nor is it awareness for its own sake, but rather, as Marx and Freud, among others, have pointed out, because awareness enables us to master situa-tions instead of being mastered by them. Unfortunately, however, we still have with us members of society who, instead of working with their fellow men and women for the common good, strive only to master other men in order to retain and augment their own position of power and privilege. To this type of person the true artist is a threat that must be removed—even, like Emily Brontë in *Weekend*, burned at the stake. But another poet steps forth to speak the eulogy and to carry on the artist's task of helping us to comfort ourselves and the world.

And, in a way, this is the task being carried out in *Weekend* by the pianist who plays Mozart in the farmyard. Like Guillaume at the end of *La Chinoise*, he is taking art to the people. Moreover, his is a very human art, a modest art, an art, like that of Mozart, "too simple for beginners and too difficult for the experts"; and his art is an art of dialogue. The pianist does not offer his recital as a spectacle; he breaks into the music to talk, to explain, to point out his own inadequacies as an artist. His art, like Godard's, is unafraid of self-criticism; in fact, it makes self-criticism an integral part of the artistic whole.

While the pianist plays and talks, the camera executes a 360° pan shot around the courtyard of the farm, encompassing the tractors, trucks, plows, onlookers, sheds, farmhands, and the pianist himself. Even the cameraman and his camera, although they are not shown, are encompassed within the circle of the 360° pan. In this shot the artist acknowledges that he is in the same boat with his audience.

How different this self-encompassing pan shot is from the long, comic apotheosis of the tracking shot, which, earlier in the film, moved relentlessly ahead, past stalled cars, lions, monkeys, a llama, and who knows what else, straight ahead to destruction, but with the camera remaining serenely Olympian in its complete detachment! How different, too, is the modest and human art of the pianist from the strident ultra-Romantic art of the hippie drummer, whose chant (from Lautréamont), instead of seeking a human dialogue, addresses itself to the Old Ocean and would pridefully wrest from nature the very secrets of the universe.

If there is an image of hope in *Weekend,* it lies in that farmyard circle, self-contained within its limited circumference and yet open to those who care enough to attempt to establish a dialogue between one human being and another. There, in the eye of the storm, in the middle of *Weekend*'s nightmarish cataclysm of violence and destruction, Godard has depicted a haven of wisdom and calm. Like the Third World sequence, the scene in the farmyard is unspectacular, to say the least; but one of the things *Weekend* seems to be trying to tell us, in its own spectacular way, is that if it is to continue, our civilization could use a lot more wisdom and calm—and a lot less spectacle.

4

Le Gai Savoir: *Critique Plus Auto-Critique du Critique*

Critique (AUGUST 1969, MUNICH)

In *Weekend* Godard pushed spectacle to its limit, and, in so doing, revealed the inadequacies and pitfalls of spectacle. In his next film, *Le Gai Savoir,* Godard switches tactics and approaches the problem of cinema from the other end. Experimenting with his own distinctive brand of "minimal cinema," Godard here dissolves not only the traditional appurtenances of the cinema of spectacle—action, plot, characterization, local color, and the preeminence of visual rather than aural stimuli—but he attempts to dissolve as well the very composition of image and sound as we generally encounter them in the cinema.

As the film's young protagonists point out, to solve a problem in chemistry or in politics one has to "dissolve" the component parts. "In chemistry, they dissolve hydrogen, for example; in politics, they dissolve parliament. Here, we've got to dissolve images and sounds." And what few elements of spectacle Godard carefully builds into *Le Gai Savoir*—elaborate lighting and color contrasts, for example—are designed more to change our notion of spectacle than to satisfy our expectations and demands.

For the most part, the only "action" in the film is two radical film-students (played by Jean-Pierre Léaud and Juliet Berto) talking before the lights and cameras of a television studio; the only "plot" is what they talk about (the uses and abuses of image

61

and sound in bourgeois capitalist society); the only "character insights" we get are from hearing them talk; and the "local color" (due to the TV spotlighting) is a pervasive inky blackness which envelopes the young couple and seems to set their conversations in a void. Furthermore, the visual stimulation in *Le Gai Savoir* is pointedly subservient to the aural stimulation and edification from the sound track.

Interspersed with the long, wordy discussions in the TV studio are a couple of equally wordy "direct interviews," which are actually word-association experiments carried out by the film-students—first on a very delightful seven- or eight-year-old boy (who is identified as one of the "Afranics," which, it is explained, means the "français" of the year 2000); then on a colorful and touching old *clochard*, who is both puzzled and delighted by the tape recorder's ability "to speak" when part of the word-association experiment is played back for him. Finally, throughout the film there are innumerable intercut shots of Paris sidewalk scenes and intercut stills of newspaper photos, drawings, book-covers, and printed passages from books and articles—nearly all containing various handwritten marginal comments (mostly enigmatic) by Godard. The intercut material sometimes seems intended to demonstrate a point made by the young couple in their discussion; but generally the film as a whole proceeds far more by association and allusion than by actual demonstration and comes dangerously close to deteriorating into a mere enumeration and aberration of all of Godard's cinematic tricks (and tics), divorced this time from any larger narrative structure.

But in *Le Gai Savoir* it is clear that Godard seeks to free the cinema as much as possible from traditional narrative structure and to explore and develop, instead, the cinema's *educational* resources, especially its ability to *demystify itself* through an analysis of the praxis of its basic cinematic means. Ultimately *Le Gai Savoir* is very much in the vein of an "educational film" (it was commissioned by French television, which indignantly refused to show the finished product and, instead, filed suit against Godard for having failed to produce the sort of "educational film"

—supposedly a "loose" adaptation of Rousseau's *Émile*—he was commissioned to make); and one might say that *Le Gai Savoir* is an educational film on the subject of education—especially, but certainly not exclusively, on film education.

In a sense it is Godard's own cinematic education which is presented in *Le Gai Savoir;* and the film might easily be subtitled "How I Studied Image and Sound and Discovered Marxism," for Godard, in pursuing what he calls the "scientific experiment" aspect of cinema, has increasingly questioned the nature of the cinematic image, and has come to a recognition that just as there exists no such thing as a "neutral" science, there is likewise no such thing as a "neutral" image. To paraphrase Eldridge Cleaver, "an image which is not part of the solution is part of the problem." Or, as Patricia (Juliet Berto) declares in *Le Gai Savoir,* "In each image one must find a method . . . and the discourse of that method . . . . In each image, one must know *who* is speaking. . . . Our task is to discover images and sounds which are *free.*"

The question of what constitutes a "free image" is obviously a difficult one—perhaps analogous to and as difficult as the question Jean-Paul Sartre faces in calling for an ethics based on total freedom. For both Godard and Sartre, however, the first task is to reveal and "unveil" the freedom that is presently covered up and hidden by the ideology of bourgeois capitalism and its concomitant exploitation. One of the first tasks, then, for those concerned with *notre civilisation de l'image* is to demonstrate how so many of the images which surround us today in the mass media are not at all as innocuous as they might seem, but are, in fact, carefully calculated to inculcate bourgeois values that serve to perpetuate the privileged position of the capitalist ruling class.

Le Gai Savoir addresses itself to this problem, but in a way that is unfortunately both cryptic and allusive. There is, for example, a shot of a magazine-cover depicting a well-built, bikini-clad young woman cavorting in the sea. The title of the magazine is ACTION; and Godard has penciled in words to make it read *"Plaisir de la Ré-*ACTION.*"*

Here, as usual, Godard makes his point simply, sharply, and

ironically; but it is worthwhile to ask whether the point itself can be grasped and appreciated by someone who has not already understood the insidious nature of the mass media's twin cults of leisure and sex as instruments of repression. In other words, one should seriously question whether simply alluding, cryptically and ironically, to exploitation and repression constitutes in any useful sense an *unveiling* of that exploitation and repression. (There are quite a few members of the radical movement in both America and France who even accuse Godard—unjustly, I think, but not without raising some important questions—of doing far more *veiling* of issues than *unveiling*.)

Granted, however, if one misses the point here about leisure, sex, and capitalist ideology, one can later read—that is, *if* one looks carefully at the penciled-in (vertical) handwriting which Godard has added to a series of briefly held stills of various advertisements, posters, and pictures of nude women—the statement that "le . . . capitalisme . . . bourgeois . . . a . . . transformé . . . la . . . technologie . . . et . . . la . . . sexualité . . . en . . . instruments . . . de . . . répression." Even here we are not presented with an *unveiling*, but simply an *assertion*. To demonstrate *how* bourgeois capitalism has transformed technology and sexuality into instruments of repression would constitute an unveiling of the situation. And this task, I would maintain, is done far better by Godard in films like *Une Femme Mariée* or *Deux ou trois choses que je sais d'elle*, for example, than in *Le Gai Savoir*.

But in making *Le Gai Savoir* a far more avowedly militant film than any of its predecessors, Godard has made this film far more vulnerable to the two most serious criticisms directed at radical films in general: first, that they often make assertions without demonstrating the truth of their assertions; and, second, that the films seem to be addressed to an intramural club of initiates who already assume that the assertions are true, with the result that the film-maker has only to flash the appropriate key word or image on the screen in order to elicit from his well-trained audience the appropriate revolutionary salivation.

Perhaps the reason *Le Gai Savoir* is much more vulnerable

to these criticisms than, let us say, *La Chinoise*, *Une Femme Mariée*, or *Deux ou trois choses* is simply that Godard's cryptic allusions and verbal and visual puns lose a great deal of their subversive power when they are not integrated within the richly woven narrative tapestry of an "adventure" Godard can both utilize as a sort of demonstration model, and, at the same time, criticize and subvert.

But Godard seems worried these days that films like *La Chinoise* and, especially, *Weekend* may have been "absorbed" by the bourgeoisie without the subversive dose of social criticism ever taking effect. When reminded recently that *Weekend* was doing well at the box-office in America, Godard replied: "Yes, but possibly in the wrong way. That's why I'm sorry I didn't make it dirtier." Behind this remark lies an interesting and provocative hypothesis. There are two basic ways, he apparently believes, to guard against a film's being "absorbed" by the bourgeoisie: first, by reducing drastically the element of spectacle; and, second, by making the film insolent to the point of offensiveness. In the case of *Weekend*, where the basic conception of the film required a heavy dose of spectacle, Godard now regrets that he didn't make the treatment of sex still more provokingly insolent in order to offend the bourgeois sensibility.

Providing a sort of formula for his film-making projects since *Weekend*, Godard recently said:

> The idea is to make the script [by "script," of course, we can assume he means either "treatment" or simply his working notes rather than a full-blown scenario] out of a political analysis, and then to convey that, sometimes in poetry, sometimes science, sometimes all it takes is film. The film itself is less and less spectacular because I think very strongly now that the more spectacular you are, the more you are absorbed by the things you are trying to destroy. You don't destroy anything at all, and it's you who are destroyed because of the spectacle.[9]

In *Le Gai Savoir* not only is spectacle reduced to a minimum, but also what remains of spectacle is transformed from a diverting aspect into a teaching device; and the film's "educational exercises" (which delve not so much into the ontology of the cinematic image but rather more into its sociology) make up the entire film and provide its sole *raison d'être*. The title itself, which suggests both the medieval troubadors' "gay science of love" and Nietzsche's *Die Fröhliche Wissenschaft* (best rendered in English as "Joyful Wisdom"), seems to imply that the individual's self-development, when guided by love and concern for his fellow man, constitutes life's most joyful adventure. The cinematic correlative of this notion—upon which Godard has built *Le Gai Savoir*—seems to be that in going to the cinema, we should neither expect nor demand any "adventure" other than that of learning—about cinema, and then through cinema, about society. The joy, as well as the adventure, should be in the harmonious development of the individual and society.

In *Le Gai Savoir,* however, it is difficult to say what we are supposed to be learning, and it is questionable whether most people will find the film very joyful. There are, of course, some joyful moments in *Le Gai Savoir:* for example, Patricia Lumumba (Juliet Berto) telling Émile Rousseau (Jean-Pierre Léaud) that she has taken a job posing in bra and panties for a radical publication *(Humanité-Dimanche)* because she thinks it's a shame the way radical publications always use the same sort of sexy photos as the reactionary press, whereas she hopes to prove that a girl can show her underwear in a "revolutionary" way; or Patricia standing in front of Émile and serving as his *masque* while he uses foul language to vituperate against the Gaullists, the police, and the "Establishment shits," then dares the censors (the police) to determine who should be charged with obscenity. But there are also long stretches where Godard's usually wry humor and sharp irony seem to miss their mark completely and the film keeps droning on as the "educational" exercises are simply strung together *en vrac*.

Given this sort of structure (as Léaud says, "even chance has structure, like the unconscious"), one is reduced to picking out isolated moments and concentrating on one or two effects. The single most striking visual aspect of *Le Gai Savoir* is the elaborate lighting effects Godard uses to photograph in as many variations of light and shadow as possible the same two people (Berto and Léaud), whose only activity throughout the film is either to *sit* and talk or else to *stand* and talk. Surrounded by inky darkness, they are lighted now from above, now from below, now from the right, now from the left, now one is lighted, now the other, and every combination thereof, in a shifting kaleidoscope of light, shadow, and color contrasts; as first the red of Juliet Berto's slacks is highlighted, then the blue of her pullover, then the brown of Jean-Pierre Léaud's jacket, then the bright red plaid of his scarf, and so on throughout the entire film.

In a way, *Le Gai Savoir*'s lighting effects recall those of the well-known "love ritual" sequence in *Alphaville,* where Lemmy (Eddie Constantine) and Natasha (Anna Karina) were alternatively lighted as they stood together, embraced, and took the first hesitant steps of love. The first hesitant steps taken by Émile and Patricia are those of revolution rather than love, but, as a handwritten note asserts in *Le Gai Savoir,* "the true revolutionary is guided by great feelings of love." In any case, the effect the lighting has on the viewer in both films is a thoroughly hypnotic one. The slightest gestures—the movement of a hand or the turning of a head—seem to be beautifully choreographed dance movements and the "action" seems somehow set apart from reality in a sort of ritualistic dreamworld. However, this effect in *Le Gai Savoir* certainly leads one to hold some grave doubts about the practical efficacy of these "revolutionary" discussions which seem to take place in a void.

In cinematic terms, however, the elaborate lighting seems designed to demonstrate that a certain intrinsic element of spectacle exists in any cinematic image, but that one can, and perhaps *should,* eliminate from cinema those extrinsic elements of spectacle which cinema has more or less inherited from the novel and the drama in order to retain only what is fundamentally cinematic: the varying degrees of light and shadow, the way in which the image is framed, the movement within the frame, and the way in which the film proceeds from one shot to another. These elements alone, *Le Gai Savoir* attempts to demonstrate, can hold the viewer's attention without being so obtrusive that they divert his attention away from the learning process and the issues being explored.

Le Gai Savoir also attempts to demonstrate that these cinematic elements can be used to focus one's attention on a specific issue. Unfortunately the occasional attempts too often simply lead the viewer to say "so what?" For example, a statement that "since Freud, we know that perversions are the result of sexual repression" is accompanied by the cinema's equivalent of a "perversion"—a *faux raccord* in which the camera shows Jean-Pierre Léaud turn his head toward what is for the viewer the left-hand border of the frame, followed by a panning camera movement to the left which halts momentarily on Juliet Berto, who likewise turns her head to the left-hand border of the frame, followed by a second panning movement to the left which reveals Jean-Pierre Léaud, who, by all "normal" cinematic expectations, should not be there at all. This little exercise may be rather charming and the pun on "perversion" rather cute, but that's as far as it goes. Neither the subject of perversions nor the subject of faux raccords in the cinema is developed any further, and the viewer is left wondering whether Godard really intends anything by the "cinema-logical" implication that faux raccords, like all "perversions," are the result of sexual repression. And if so, then what?

A general and not inconsiderable fault throughout *Le Gai Savoir* is that it raises issues—or, all too often, merely alludes to issues—without ever really exploring them. Finally, at the end of the film Godard, using Léaud as his *porte-parole,* acknowledges that quite a few issues have been left unexplored: like, for instance, "demonstrating that there are no problems which cannot be fruitfully analyzed from a Marxian or a Freudian point of view"; or, for a second example, "analyzing the problem of taboos in a bourgeois family"; or, for a third issue, "depicting the ecstasies of looting in the Third World." But these tasks, Léaud assures us, will not be left undone. "Bertolucci will do the first in

Le Gai Savoir: the ABC's of image and sound

Le Gai Savoir: ''Not representation, presentation . . . not spectacle, struggle!''

Italy; Straub will do the second in Germany; and Glauber Rocha will do the third in Brazil."

And what, we might ask, will Godard do in France, in England, in America, or wherever he chooses to make his next films? Will *Le Gai Savoir* mark a turning-point in his development, or will it simply stand a bit apart from the mainstream of his work—a compendium of possibilities put together for educational purposes? It is hard to tell. As Godard himself whispers at the very end of *Le Gai Savoir*, "this film cannot describe nor embody cinema, but, more modestly, it can suggest some practical means of making film; and, in any case, cinema must follow *some* of the paths shown."

True. But that covers a lot of ground. The question—for Godard as well as the others—is *which* paths?

Auto-Critique du Critique (OCTOBER 1969, PARIS)

> Bien que les nombreux intellectuels
> révolutionnaires jouent un rôle
> d'avant-garde et servent de pont,
> tous ne sont pas révolutionnaires
> jusqu'au bout.
> (Although the numerous revolutionary
> intellectuals play a role of avant-
> garde and serve as a bridge, not all of
> them are revolutionary all the way.)

>> (*The above statement is part of a
>> handwritten epigraph which appears
>> at the very beginning of*
>> Le Gai Savoir.)

Unfortunately, the critique you have just read seems to me to be an illustration of the way in which even those intellectuals who seek to affirm and advance the cause of a revolutionary transformation of society have great obstacles to overcome and a long way to travel if they are to succeed in being revolutionary all the way. Moreover, as a statement from the voice-over sound track of *Le Gai Savoir* puts it: "To apply a bourgeois work-style to the study of Mao's thoughts, is to apply a bourgeois politics."

What I suspect, then, is that my original critique of *Le Gai Savoir* also illustrates just how difficult it is for intellectuals in general—and particularly those of us concerned with art—to throw off bourgeois notions and a bourgeois work-style, which, whether they are applied to Mao's thought or Godard's films (and the two have much in common), add up, albeit unintentionally, to a bourgeois politics.

But this auto-critique is not meant to imply that I *disown* the views expressed in the original article (as if such a thing were possible; as if a product of thought were a product like any other —a possession to be owned and disowned). What I want to put in question, however, is what *Le Gai Savoir* itself puts in question —a notion of art which in the long run is a bourgeois reactionary notion—and I have decided that the best way to do this is to let the original critique stand, but to point out the limitations of its argument and to demonstrate that this sort of argument is perhaps all the more dangerous precisely because it is often put forward with the best intentions of serving to advance the revolutionary praxis, a task it does not necessarily fulfill, and may even impede.

At the base of my article on *Le Gai Savoir* there lies a fundamental principle (one which I continue to uphold) that a "revolutionary work of art" must be effective in a revolutionary way in both its art and its politics. Perhaps the best articulation of this principle is the following well-known statement by Mao himself, often quoted by Godard:

> What we demand is the unity of politics and art, the unity of content and form, the unity of revolutionary political content and the highest possible perfection of artistic form. Works of art which lack artistic quality have no force, however progressive they are politically. . . . On questions of literature and art, we must carry on a struggle on two fronts.[10]

In the name of this principle, then, and in seeking to advance this struggle on two fronts, I attempted to strike a balance between the task of delineating the very urgent practical and theoretical issues which *Le Gai Savoir* raises concerning the relations between film and society; and, on the other hand, the task of pointing out, regretfully, that the "art" of *Le Gai Savoir* seemed, on the whole, annoyingly "artless." In short, it seemed to me that since so much of what usually works in Godard's films this time seemed not to work—or simply worked more equivocally than in the earlier "narrative" films—the end result was a film which, in spite of having a most laudable revolutionary politics, failed much more than it succeeded, *both as politics and as art,* precisely because it seemed to fail as *art.*

But here, I think, is where I overlooked the real revolutionary action of *Le Gai Savoir,* which is the action of *applying the revolution to art itself.* In criticizing *Le Gai Savoir* for failing to be effective as art, I either did not fully realize or perhaps was simply not ready to accept the degree to which Godard had moved beyond mere *subversion of the narrative* as his contribution to revolutionary consciousness, and that he now sought to lay the foundations of a truly revolutionary art which would no longer conveniently neglect the much needed task of making the revolution *chez soi;* of sweeping away all of the dust, dirt, and intellectual bric-a-brac of that bourgeois duplex we honor as the House of Art and Culture; of destroying the accepted bourgeois notion of art, the *mystique* of art, all that we have come to *worship* in art—in short, the *religion* of art.

Like any other religion, the religion of art is an "opiate of the masses," a mystification which covers up and diverts attention away from the very real repression that exists within society. And like any other religion, the religion of art is a powerful weapon in the arsenal of the Establishment; and that is why the power elite not only tolerates this form of religion but actually cultivates it. As André Malraux, the self-proclaimed apostle of the religion of art, expressed it more than a decade ago, "we have transformed our churches into museums; there remains only the next step of transforming our museums into churches"—a step which Malraux accomplished by aligning himself with DeGaulle's mystification and elitist policies, and, as France's "Minister of

Culture," by setting up a *Maison de la Culture* in towns all over France.

Moreover, the more the Establishment "domesticates" art by cultivating the religion of art, the less it has to fear from art, even from would-be "revolutionary art." As Marcuse has pointed out, the increasing permissiveness in the arts in modern industrial capitalist society is by no means a sign that the Establishment is weakening its hold; on the contrary, it is rather the case that the more the Establishment is secure in its position of power and privilege, the less it needs to exercise any *overt* censorship over art—simply because the task of emasculating the potentially subversive elements in art is accomplished more efficiently and painlessly by letting these elements be expressed within the Establishment-controlled and therefore easily absorbable context of the religion of art, than could ever be accomplished by overt repression.*

What Godard has gradually come to realize (partly as an outgrowth of the May 1968 events in Paris and partly as the very natural outgrowth of his own development as an artist) is simply that, given the fact that even the most uncompromising artistic experiments are compromised in the end by being absorbed within the bourgeois religion of art; and given that even a work of art with a high dosage of potentially subversive elements (like *Weekend*, for example) is all too easily emasculated, absorbed, and co-opted by the simple bourgeois reflex of hailing it as a masterpiece and placing it on the altar of art as still another object of worship; then the time has come when the only way for art to be revolutionary is to destroy itself, to destroy even the most advanced artistic values, to break down the cult of the "masterpiece," to produce purposely flawed works of art which the bourgeoisie will not even recognize as art, and which will

---

* *Le Gai Savoir* also points out that, where film is involved, a great deal more censorship—especially politically-motivated censorship—goes on than the public hears about; not the least of the censor's work involves censoring public dissemination of information on just what and how much does get censored.

therefore escape being absorbed and emasculated, and will preserve intact their revolutionary power.

But how can we reconcile this destruction of artistic values
with our own already stated position of demanding the unity of
politics and art, of form and content, of revolutionary political
content and the highest possible perfection of artistic form? And
if we agree with Mao when he states that "works of art which
lack artistic quality have no force, however progressive they are
politically," then we are entitled to question (as I did) exactly
what subversive power is preserved intact when Godard (or anyone else) creates a deliberately "artless" work of art.

The answer, it seems to me, is provided by *Le Gai Savoir*—
namely, that the creation of a revolutionary work of art must be
an act of simultaneous destruction and creation; that revolutionary art must destroy the accepted artistic values (and, consequently, appear "artless" by even the most avant-garde standards)
at the same time that it creates, out of the rubble and debris of
the old, new artistic values which will be truly revolutionary
because they will challenge the prevailing mystification and repression in art itself.

Godard's films have always sought to attain some sort of
balance between creation and destruction, between creating
within a tradition of "adventure" and "spectacle," and, at the
same time, criticizing and undermining that tradition; but *Le Gai
Savoir* marks a crucial shift of weight to the side of destruction
and seems to mark a realization on Godard's part that balance
between two poles is not necessarily attained by equal portions
of each; that when the fulcrum is off-center, then a much heavier
weight must be placed on the short side to counteract the greater
leverage it is up against; that when the bourgeois religion of art
holds such overwhelming leverage over the would-be forces of
change, then it no longer suffices (if indeed it ever did) merely to
construct a more or less traditional narrative of adventure within
which there would be traps, mines, and holes inviting the spectator (but often only the very sophisticated spectator) to subvert
and destroy the traditional pattern; and that, instead, what is

urgently needed today is a revolutionary art which will completely reject and eschew the traditional pattern, will decompose one by one all of the individual elements that went into the old pattern, will refuse to put these elements back together in any of the ways we have come to expect them to be put together, and yet will hold these decomposed elements together by demonstrating—as *Le Gai Savoir* does—how each formal element in a film can and *must* be related to the class struggle and to the struggle for the means of production—in short, to the revolution in art and society!

In other words, in *Le Gai Savoir* Godard has almost entirely done away with the traditional apparatus of the bourgeois cinema (and that includes the "art-cinema"); and, instead of holding the film together by means of even a "fractured" narrative (like that of *Vivre sa vie, Pierrot le fou,* or *Masculin-Féminin*), Godard holds *Le Gai Savoir* together in just the way that the children's alphabet-primer (read aloud by Émile and Patricia) is held together: that is, by running through the ABC's of image and sound; by giving examples of how they are used—and abused; and by pointing out how each formal element in a film necessarily engenders questions other than merely formalistic ones, questions which imply and involve a certain view of the world and our own situation in that world—questions, in other words, which force us to confront the fundamental structures of society and to recognize that behind every cinematic image, in capitalist society there lies a class struggle and a struggle for the means of production; and that any image which does not address itself to solving the problem of exploitation and unequal distribution of capital automatically serves to perpetuate the problem and to strengthen the stranglehold of the exploiting "haves" over the exploited "have nots."

If the destructive element seems much greater in *Le Gai Savoir* than the constructive element, this is because—as the film itself tells us—the revolutionary dream of "starting again from zero" can never be realized unless we first get back to zero. But it is important to understand the sort of destruction that *Le*

Gai Savoir performs and to distinguish this sort of destruction—which destroys the old pattern by systematically breaking it down into its individual component parts, which are then analyzed to determine how they can be used in the future in new and revolutionary ways—from the sort of mindless destruction that simply smashes everything to shattered and unusable smithereens. For Godard, getting back to zero means destroying the existing structures by taking them apart, not by blowing them up. And once back to zero, the task, as the film itself acknowledges, will be to look around at whatever traces are left and to see how we can use them to build something new.

And the task, it seems to me, is performed by *Le Gai Savoir* itself—particularly the way Godard decomposes the spectacle, analyzes it, reduces it to its essentials, then puts it to use in a new and revolutionary way in which spectacle is no longer the diverting aspect of film, but rather becomes the cinematic means of focusing our attention on social problems and issues, and, at the same time, becomes the cinematic means by which the analysis of these problems is carried out. As for my own discussion of the function of spectacle in *Le Gai Savoir,* while it was probably the most insightful point in the original critique, it did not go far enough and did not prevent me from falling, at one point, into the very trap the film warns against: the trap of the *idéologie du vécu* (a term Godard and the *Cinéthique* theorists are using to designate the bourgeois cinema's emphasis on the illusion of the *lived,* emotional, "you-are-there" aspect of film).

When I pointed out that *Le Gai Savoir's* elaborate lighting (like that of the "love ritual" in *Alphaville*) had a hypnotic effect on the viewer and seemed to set the "action" (in this case, the "revolutionary" discussions of Émile and Patricia) apart from reality in a sort of ritualistic dreamworld, I then proceeded to question the advisability of creating such an effect in *Le Gai Savoir* on the grounds that it leads us to hold grave reservations about the practical efficacy of those "revolutionary" discussions "which seem to take place in a void." However, implicit in this remark (although I didn't realize it at the time and wouldn't have made the remark if I had) is an assumption that if Émile's and Patricia's revolutionary discussions had taken place in a different setting (not even necessarily in a more "revolutionary" setting, like in a factory or in the street, but simply in a more "realistic" setting, like an ordinary room lighted in an ordinary way), then we might be more likely to believe in the practical efficacy of these discussions.

But practical efficacy for whom? In the latter case, if it is true that we would be more likely to believe that the revolutionary talk would lead somewhere, to some revolutionary action, it is only because we would be better able to believe in the cinematic fiction of Émile and Patricia, and, consequently, in the practical efficacy of these discussions *for them.*

But this is beside the point. *They* don't exist. There are no Émile and Patricia outside of *Le Gai Savoir;* and from the very beginning, where Émile and Patricia make a point of introducing each other *to us,* the film preserves only enough of the conventional pretense of fictional characters to unmask this pretense, to demonstrate to us that the pretense of *representation* is simply a tool in the task of *presentation;* and at the end of the film, when the task has been accomplished and the tool has served its purpose, then the pretense itself is dropped and the actor and actress make a point of addressing each other by their real first names. In short, for Godard (as for Brecht), the actor's task is not to make us *believe* that he *is* the role he is playing, but rather (as Brecht insisted Charles Laughton should do in playing Galileo) to force us to *understand* that he is an actor who does not *represent* a certain character so much as he *presents to us* through the words and actions of that character certain *issues* and certain *problems,* which the artist does not pretend to solve and which require our participation, our give and take, both during and after the *presentation,* which, far from being a reenacting of something that happened in the past, is itself only a *prelude* to the work which, after the film, awaits all of us.

As Patricia/Juliet Berto says in *Le Gai Savoir,* thereby providing a definition of Godard's notion of revolutionary cinema:

"Pas représentation, présentation . . . pas spectacle, lutte!" ("Not representation, presentation . . . not spectacle, struggle!")

It is interesting to notice, moreover, that if there is such a thing as "ontological realism" in the cinema, then Godard has both been faithful to it and at the same time located it more precisely —not in the mere verisimilitude of the *representation*, but rather in the demystified reality of the *presentation*. Furthermore, in shifting the accent away from the *representation* (whose basic dynamic lies in the tension between the actor and the role he seeks to incarnate) over instead to the *presentation* (whose basic dynamic lies in the tension between, on one hand, the *issues* and *problems* the actor *presents* and, on the other hand, the *minds* (and not the mere credulity) of the audience; Godard thereby succeeds in demonstrating the truth of his oft-repeated assertion that ultimately the *reality* of the cinema lies not in what takes place on the screen but rather in what takes place in the give and take between the screen and the spectators' minds.

In conclusion, then, we discover that those revolutionary discussions in *Le Gai Savoir* do not take place in a vacuum. The dialogue between Émile/Jean-Pierre Léaud and Patricia/Juliet Berto constitutes only one-half of a much more important dialogue, the other half of which must come *from us*—and the real question we must ask is whether these revolutionary discussions have any practical efficacy *for us*.

But we should realize (as I originally failed to do) that if we couch our response to this film in the language of even what may heretofore have been the most advanced notion of art, then we not only run counter to the real revolutionary praxis of *Le Gai Savoir* (which applies the revolution to the art itself) but we may also find ourselves, albeit unwillingly, in the position of counterrevolutionaries in relation to the revolution as a whole. Unless we who are concerned with art have the courage and perseverance to look our art in the face and to recognize the counterrevolutionary visage which often lurks there, then I'm afraid that for people like us—as Bertolucci's Fabrizio says—it will *always* be "before the revolution."

5

One Plus One, *or*
The Praxis of History

In Godard's *One Plus One* (distributed in America as *Sympathy for the Devil*) the operation, the *process of drawing a relation,* is an end in itself. Results, after all, depend on relations —that "plus" between the "one" and "one." And in *One Plus One* the result is simply what is at stake in the relations: History. More than any other film, perhaps even more than any other "work of art," *One Plus One* concentrates so intently on the *praxis* of History, and repudiates the *exis* so thoroughly, that History itself is almost freed from the distortions of art, emerging as what it has always really been: *a free play of relations* (that undefined but not undefinable "plus"), the result of which ("makes two") can be left unsaid because it is re-created at every moment.

One Plus One is composed of ten sequences of roughly ten minutes duration apiece. Each sequence, or, technically, each *plan-séquence,* is a single continuous shot complete with synchronous sound, the camera sometimes remaining fixed, sometimes moving about quite freely. Each of them is interrupted momentarily from time to time either visually, by intercut shots of a young girl (Anne Wiazemsky) painting various political graffiti, or aurally, by a voice-over reading of a sordid "political novel," the characters of which are named after world leaders or international figures.

There are two clearly distinct sets of sequences in the film: "Stones sequences," in which the Rolling Stones are shown rehearsing in a recording studio, and "other than Stones sequences," among which are two sequences depicting black militants in an automobile junkyard, an interview in a forest with a young girl named Eve Democracy, a sequence in a pornography bookstore, and, closing the film, a sequence on the beach which depicts the symbolic death of Eve Democracy. These two sets of sequences are equally weighted structurally: there are five "Stones sequences" and five "other than Stones sequences" alternating throughout the film in an AB AB AB AB AB pattern.

Even disregarding for a moment the intercut material (which embroiders upon the film's basic structure without altering it), let us note Godard's paradoxical structural achievement of a *film de montage* composed of raw material that would seem to be the essence not of montage but of what is usually considered its polar opposite—*mise-en-scène* shooting. In fact, the *plan-séquence* was heralded by André Bazin, the prophet of *mise-en-scène*, as the royal road to the salvation of the cinema; while montage, for Bazin, was forbidden as the domain of the damned. And in *One Plus One* Godard even ventures into the terrain of Hitchcock, the master of *mise-en-scène* shooting, whose film *The Rope* was composed of eight *plans-séquence*, each of which advanced the narrative by a complicated, continuous traveling movement of the camera. But while Godard pushes the potential of the *plan-séquence* to the point of creating a feature film out of ten shots of nearly ten minutes duration apiece, unlike Hitchcock (and the Bazin school), Godard refuses to utilize the *plan-séquence* for *narrative* purposes, and, instead, he utilizes it solely for its simplicity and insistent presence; while montage—although reduced to an elementary juxtaposition of disparate, seemingly unrelated long takes—is nonetheless reaffirmed as the basic combustion element that creates intellectual relations and *sense*. Or, as Eisenstein put it, "By the combination of two 'depictables' is achieved the representation of something that is graphically undepictable."

In *One Plus One* this preeminence of montage is further accentuated by the opposition and interplay between the ten *plans-*

séquence, on one hand, and the aural and visual intercut material mentioned earlier. Through the use of synchronous sound the *plans-séquence* are all presented in a unity of image and sound; the intercut material, however, is presented now in image alone, now in sound alone, and often with the intercut aural material *over* the intercut visual material. But in no case is the intercut material presented in the synchronous unity of image and sound that we find in each of the *plans-séquence.*

Thematically, the opposition (set up by the montage) between the intercut material and the material of the ten *plans-séquence* presents a dialectic between two different faces of contemporary reality—and of History itself. *One Plus One* is characteristic of Godard's work in that it presents one of the faces of reality in the mask of fiction and sets up a subtle dialectic between fiction and reality. Sometimes in Godard's films it is a character, or group of characters, who confuses fiction and reality: in *A bout de souffle* Michel Poiccard (Jean-Paul Belmondo) imitates Humphrey Bogart, and even dies à la Bogie; so does the group of would-be outlaws in *Bande à part*—with Arthur (Claude Brasseur) even out-dying Bogie; in *Le Mépris* the scriptwriter Paul Javel (Michel Piccoli) becomes the victim of a fiction, the story of Ulysses, which is superimposed above the real action of his wife's growing contempt for him; and in *Pierrot le fou* the lead character is called by two names, Pierrot and Ferdinand, and admits to feeling like "un homme double" who is unable to sort out the real from the fictional self. In still other Godard films the split between fiction and reality is implicit in a split between two distinct "worlds": in *Alphaville* the world of logic (the city of Alphaville) is cut off from the world of the emotions ("les pays extérieurs"); in *Masculin-Féminin* the world of youth is cut off from the world of adults; and in *La Chinoise* the world of the youthful communards is cut off from the day-to-day realities of the society they seek to change.

In *One Plus One* the sordidness of political intrigue which in *Made in USA* was the reality of contemporary life has passed over into the world of fiction. Further, it has moved from the synchronous unity of image and sound to the sound track alone: it is no longer the labyrinth in which we are forced to grope, but only a disembodied voice—a *récit* that is no longer even a *récit filmique* but purely and simply a *récit parole*.

"Power politics," the comings and goings (especially the comings) of presidents, prime ministers, popes, and princesses, the "news" we have been conditioned for so long to regard as momentous events shaping contemporary history—all of this is suddenly seen to be nonessential, negative, of no real significance: it is all a cheap novel that can be read just the way cheap novels are usually read—at random, by skipping back and forth from one scabrous passage to another. The novel in *One Plus One* is, in fact, read at random; and the voice-over interruptions seem to occur at random. There is, however, a significant pattern of these interruptions: the frequency with which the sordid "high society" world of the voice-over novel breaks in upon the Stones sequences seems to suggest an affinity and overlapping between these two elements; while there is only one brief aural interruption of each of the black sequences, suggesting that there is very little these two elements have to do with each other, and that the blacks, because they are excluded from white society, are relatively immune to the viruses of the power elite and its parasites. Moreover, far from being random in their intrusions, the words of the voice-over novel are carefully timed to coordinate with a particular word or image (or both) from the *plan-séquence* material or with an image from the intercut material. Thus, Godard sets up a subtle audio-visual interplay of connotations from one element to another, with these connotations serving as the transitional *raccords* between two different shots or two fragments of the sound track. In addition, Godard's use of hand-printed inter-titles to introduce each *plan-séquence* is designed to enrich the printed words—through selective underlining, suggestive typography, and the use of different colored crayons for the lettering—so that they, too, like the other elements of the film, can generate a multiplicity of relations.

On one hand, then, the film presents the conventional reality of power politics in the form of a fragmented and disembodied fiction—and Godard's systematic undermining of the old tyranny of narrative has now reached the point of demonstrating, as a parting blow, that the narrative is such an authoritarian structure that even fragmented narrative is actually a perfect vehicle for the sordid smut of fascism. On the other hand, the film presents staged material (all of the *plans-séquence* are made up of staged material—including the Stones' rehearsal, since even a "real" rehearsal is transformed into a performance by the simple presence of the camera) in straightforward documentary fashion, without the slightest recourse to narrative. In short, an important dialectical reversal is involved here, for the real becomes fictional and the fictional becomes real.

As Hegel pointed out, reality is two-faced: there is a negative, nonessential face of reality, as well as a positive and essential face; and History inevitably passes through a phase wherein what will ultimately prove to be positive and essential appears to contemporary observers to be negative and nonessential. But as History unfolds, the real truth of a situation surfaces; the negative, nonessential face of contemporary reality begins to recede (is sublated); and through this process of reversal, the positive and essential face of History comes to the forefront.

In *One Plus One*, and specifically in the central sequence entitled "The Heart of Occident," we can see even the moment when the major currents of *our* reality come together, that instant when the changing tides of History bump up against each other; when the old outgoing tide seems to retain just enough of its former strength to dominate for one last moment the first swellings of the new incoming tide. For once in the film the fascism of the Word is reflected in the Image, where we see the myriad images of sadism, perversion, war, crime, and violence on the covers of row upon row of sex magazines, scandal sheets, and cheap novels—plus some film magazines as well, to remind us that we too get co-opted by the oppressors (that is, unless we too are not already one of them ourselves). "The Heart of Occident" is nothing other than a porno store where the customers give the

Nazi salute to the proprietor (played, appropriately enough, by the youthful, mod producer of the film, Iain Quarrier), who reads aloud passages from *Mein Kampf* and, instead of demanding cash for the purchases, directs the customers to render payment in the form of slaps in the face administered to two long-haired young men who are kept sitting in the corner as ritual scapegoats for fascist frustration and aggression.

But the youths do not keep silent: at each slap in the face they shout out the call for a new reality, a new truth, a new history. "Vive Che!" "Victory to the NLF!" "Long live Mao!" At first, their words seem like empty slogans spewed out mechanically, as if the youths were willing accomplices in the fascist order that oppresses them. But if we watch the development of this sequence carefully, as the camera moves restlessly back and forth from long-haired radical youth to over-thirty fascist proprietor, there comes an instant when, without anything seeming to happen, all is changed. The development of this sequence is like the development of the famous "pendulum" camera movement sequences in *Vivre sa vie* and *Le Mépris:* the camera records the instant when fate hangs in the balance, when a soul is damned or saved, when a lovers' quarrel reaches the point of no return. Only this time it is History itself which hangs in the balance, until the new tide moves to the forefront.

The camera—here embodying the objectivity of History—suddenly stops its endless lateral panning and moves, for once, in depth—singling out the two long-haired youths and moving in slowly to focus on them in full close-up as they lift their heads and turn slightly to look directly into the camera. Suddenly the tide has turned: and everything changes its sense, dialectically, to adjust to the new sense of History. As the Hitler text (read by Quarrier) closes by exalting the triumph of the individual, we understand not the triumph of the individual-as-demagogue—the Hitlerian "great magnetic force to attract the masses"—but rather the triumph of the nameless individual who is a part of the masses and whose revolutionary vigor and determination are turning History inside-out, even at the "Heart of Occident."

One Plus One: Eve Democracy, turning more and more inward . . . or opening up to others?

One Plus One: "outside" . . . on the fringes of society

One Plus One: The Rolling Stones rehearse "Sympathy for the Devil"

One Plus One: To what extent is the black militant's act of militancy just an "act"?

One Plus One: "The Heart of Occident"

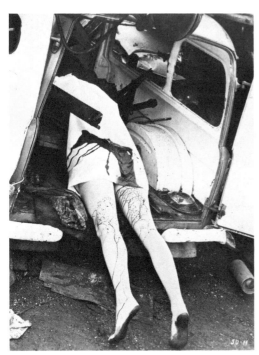

One Plus One: meanwhile . . . back at the junkyard

One Plus One: Godard at work (left): "It's no longer a question of self-expression."

One Plus One: radicalization as a rite of passage

One Plus One: The cinema is dead. *Vive le cinéma révolutionnaire!*

The turning-point of contemporary history having been reached and passed, it is at this point that Godard presents to us, for the only time in the film, the full equation that is his metaphor for History:

$$1 + 1 \text{ makes } 2.$$

Simple enough. As simple as "one plus one." But look at it closely. It is not a static equation. It does not say $1 + 1$ equals 2. Instead it emphasizes the action, the praxis, of *making* a result. History, after all, is *made;* and it is made by one individual *relating* to other individuals.

Even at the interpersonal level, *One Plus One* suggests the all-important need for the making of a relation. Failure to relate—as in the case of Eve Democracy, whose isolation and inability to communicate symbolize the involuted rigidity of the Western individualist—ultimately leads to a form of spiritual death. And the artist is by no means exempt from this need to relate; quite the contrary, but its exigencies are manifested in him more problematically than elsewhere. The Rolling Stones may play music together as a group, but the claustrophobic recording studio with its isolated booths for each musician highlights the fundamentally self-absorbed, even narcissistic quality of artistic creation. Ultimately, *One Plus One* suggests that for the artist, but by no means only for the artist, the first revolutionary task is to stop retreating further and further inside oneself as so much of the Western world, particularly the intelligentsia, still does. We must perform our first revolutionary act on ourselves by relating more freely and openly with men and women and things than we have since the rise of industrial capitalist society. This opening-up of ourselves to the world and to each other, helping us to recognize and to begin to rectify the injustices we have inflicted on the blacks and the rest of the world, is an urgent task for us in the "Heart of Occident" if we are not to be left behind by the new tide of History.

In *One Plus One*, the turning-point having been passed, History having turned itself inside-out, the blacks, who in the first half of the film were introduced by the word "Outside," are now introduced by the word "Inside." In short, then, *One Plus One*'s dialectic of History unfolds like a Moebius ribbon, with the transformation of the blacks (as well as the militant youth) from a marginal, peripheral phenomenon existing "outside" the mainstream of Western civilization, into a vital force working away at the "inside" and playing a leading role in the revolutionary reshaping of History.

But even armed with Hegelian dialectics, how does one get at "truth"—especially in the cinema? Can there really be such a thing as *cinéma-vérité*? And, if so, we might well ask (as Godard has) just *which* truth is it talking about? Godard has expressed his view of cinema's search for truth in the following way: "You can start with fiction or documentary. But whichever you start with, you will inevitably find the other."

For example, look at the Rolling Stones in *One Plus One*. Filmed in the "nitty-gritty" of a recording studio session, the Stones are for real and at the same time they are a fantastic put-on. (Role-playing, posturing, putting on an act, and concern for one's "image" are not, after all, merely theatrical conventions; they are part of our behavior.) Conversely, the blacks in *One Plus One* are filmed in the "act" of a big theatrical put-on, yet they are in dead earnest.

Elaborate camera movements notwithstanding, Godard in *One Plus One* works much like Lumière and Méliès, the founding fathers of cinema and the two poles of cinema's dialectic of fantasy and the real. Godard films the Rolling Stones the way Lumière filmed *La Sortie des Usines:* he brings his camera to where the action is, he sets it up, turns it on, and captures a "slice of life." He films the blacks the way Méliès filmed *Le Couronnement du Roi Édouard VII*, with the greatest artifice and theatricality. As Guillaume (Jean-Pierre Léaud) says in *La Chinoise*, one might argue that the real documentary films of the turn of the century are Méliès's tricked stagings of events like Edward's coronation (acted out, in costumes, by a butcher's apprentice and a laundry girl as King and Queen), or the explosion of the battleship *Maine*

(filmed with toy boats in the pond of the Tuileries), or the erup-
tion of Mont Pelé (filmed with miniatures); while, on the other
hand, the films of Lumière, by heightening the minutiae of everyday life—a train entering a station, workers leaving a factory,
women playing backgammon—constitute the very stuff of fiction.

Similarly, in *One Plus One* the "slices of life," the recording
sessions with the Rolling Stones, lead ultimately to a form of the
fantastic, aptly designated by an inter-title as "Hi Fiction Science," while the filming of that elaborately staged and acted bit
of theater in the automobile graveyard becomes a "documentary"
presentation of one of the key developments taking place in the
world today. (Think of the way *La Chinoise*, also an "acted" and
elaborately staged piece of theater, can be considered a documentary on student militancy and, specifically, on the French
student uprising of May 1968—which it *preceded*. Might one not
be justified in concluding that ultimately history decides what is
a documentary?) And the theatricality of the black sequences
simply makes them all the more faithful as documents of what
the Black Power movement is all about, for no one is more aware
of the theatricality of his position, and no one is more deeply concerned with the effect of his performance, than a black militant.

The Black Panthers, with their black-leather jackets and
berets, the clenched-fist salute, the rifles and cartridge-belts, are
involved in "street theater": they are revolutionary *non*-actors
acting for the revolution. And the Panthers' act is not even primarily for the audience, especially not the white audience—
although they do want to shake us up a little, and to keep us
guessing. In the first black sequence of *One Plus One*, for example, shots are fired, but the framing prevents us from seeing
what is shot. We know, of course, that a number of white girls
have been brought in as hostages or as prisoners of war, and later
we see their bodies lying on the ground covered with blood. Were
they shot? Cinema-logically, yes; but then it's only cinema. It's
only an "act." But what about black militants in "real life"? To
what extent is the black militant's act of militancy just an act?

The answer is, of course, that his militancy is by no means

just an act. When the black militants in *One Plus One* call for blacks to go out into the streets, to run up and down, to take what they want, to kill the white men who get in their way— it corresponds to a reality of looted cities and sniper activity, which, for better or worse, cannot be passed off as mere play-acting. And when the blacks in the film shout out the magic words —"Up . . . against . . . the . . . wall . . . mother . . . fucker"—we would do well to remember that more than one motherfucker has already gone up against the wall.

The only difference perhaps (and for the white man, the only consolation) is that today's black militants see the possibility of reaching their goals with a maximum of symbolic activity and just enough real violence to keep people shook up. But this does not mean that the black man's "magic dance" of militancy is essentially a cathartic ritual in which he gets out of his system his aggressive impulses; on the contrary, like a primitive hunting or war dance, it is a means of preparing himself to do in reality what he does first in art.

And what today's black militant is readying himself to do, if things don't change radically for the better, is to bring down white society, even killing the white man if he gets in the way. The ritual militancy thus serves to prepare the black man for the real hunt, while, at the same time, it is an attempt (which does involve a calculated risk) to accomplish his goal without having to resort to killing—by pressuring, by scaring, even by shaming the white man into recognizing his oppression of the blacks and then into sharing with the blacks in the dismantling of the oppressive power structure and the building of a new, more just society.

Perhaps this is utopian (though Marcuse, among others, has argued that the hope for a new society, free of repression, can no longer be termed utopian, since it is now, perhaps for the first time, technologically realizable), but we must not shrug off as mere playacting a movement with the appeal of the Panthers to the ghettos and the Third World, and which even reaches white youth in our own "Heart of Occident."

Ultimately, then, *One Plus One* presents Black Power as a theatrical fiction which leads to the real, while the rock music phenomenon is presented as a chunk of reality which leads to a theatrical fiction. This is not to imply, however, that the rock music world, especially when seen as a part of the global "implosion" triggered by electronic mass media, is not itself one of the important contemporary phenomena. On the contrary, in a film that explores the shaping of contemporary history, Godard's filming a recording session with the Rolling Stones at such length suggests its potential importance. But as part of that exploration, Godard is certainly questioning where all these different phenomena lead.

At the most elementary level, we wonder where the song "Sympathy for the Devil" will lead—we want to hear it all the way through. Like the film itself, it is a sort of paeon to history; and as it changes in tempo from one "take" to another, the transformation from the cool version at the beginning to the double-time rhythmic holocaust the last time the Stones sing it seems to parallel nicely the dizzying effect of the contemporary world's vastly accelerated rate of social change. Nonetheless, with the song, as with history, we wonder where it all leads.

But by refusing to let us hear the song in its polished, definitive entirety, Godard insistently focuses our attention on the action (praxis) of making either a work of art or history. And where the Stones are concerned, we can't help but be aware, I'm afraid, that there's an awful lot of *money* involved. This is not to imply that Godard thinks the Rolling Stones or other rock groups are simply out to make as much money as they can. Obviously the Stones enjoy the creative process of making music. They spend a great deal of time and effort experimenting with various tempo changes and trying out various instrumental and vocal arrangements. Like Godard, in fact, they are artists who enjoy working out the technical possibilities of their art. But they are also, again like Godard, artists whose medium of expression requires an enormous outlay of money for equipment and for distribution of the finished product. Moreover, like Godard, the

Stones had to break into a highly competitive industry financed by capitalist investment, an industry where your career as an artist depends, above all, on whether or not your art *sells*.

Granted, an artist can attempt—as both Godard and some of the rock musicians have done—to subvert the traditional bourgeois notion of art while remaining inside the tradition. But *aesthetic* subversion is all too easily absorbed and co-opted by contemporary society, which has developed sophisticated mechanisms for emasculating art by cultivating it; and these mechanisms are particularly well-adapted for emasculating the avant-garde in art because they cultivate an ever greater *demand* for novelty, provocativeness, and even scandal. In our culture the avant-garde in art ultimately serves the *institutions of scandal*, which is to say, the emasculation of scandal, and so brings about the *transformation of artistic subversiveness into market value*.

There is no doubt, for example, that much of the appeal of rock is its subversive aura—which is, of course, carefully played up by record-jacket designers, poster designers, and publicity agents, who make sure their protégés wear the most far-out clothes, sport the longest and fuzziest hair-styles, and strike belligerent poses whenever they're in camera range. And if their songs contain allusions to drugs, street fighting, free sex, and revolution—all the better, the songs will *sell* better! (In movies, of course, we have the same thing: films like *The Trip, Revolution, More!, Easy Rider, Katmandu, RPM, Getting Straight, The Strawberry Statement*, with others apparently in the making—all of them trying desperately to cash in on the market for revolution.)

In an interview in *Rolling Stone*, Godard talked about rock: "There is some invention, but it should be politicized. The Stones are more political than the Jefferson Airplane, but they should be more and more so every day. The new music could be the beginning of a revolution, but it isn't. It seems more like a palliating to life. The Stones are still working for scientific experiment, but not for class struggle or the struggle for the means of production."[11]

In the same interview, using Mao's language, Godard described his own position as an artist: "What is social *praxis*? There are three kinds. There is scientific experiment; there is class struggle; and there is struggle for the means of production. And I discovered, at about the same time as the May 1968 events occurred in France, that I myself have to be related to class struggle and struggle for production, though scientific experiment is still necessary."

The real task, then, for the "revolutionary artist," is to avoid remaining exclusively or even primarily on the easily co-opted level of aesthetic subversion (which merely qualifies as "scientific experiment") and to apply his intelligence and his aesthetic skills to the urgent task of *politicizing* the constantly growing mass of people who have dropped out culturally from bourgeois capitalist society, but who have not yet begun to take an active part in the political struggles necessary to break down and destroy that society.

For Godard the days of the *auteur* polemics, the cult of self-expression, and the mystique of Art and Culture are all left behind; and when he was asked not long ago whether the cinema of Antonioni and some of his other peers interested him as much as it used to, Godard responded negatively, expressed his horror at Antonioni's making *Zabriskie Point* for MGM, and then pointed out that, for himself, unlike Antonioni or the others, it was no longer a question of self-expression or of turning out another "work of art." His own position, he explained, is now more like a militant worker; and what concerns him now are problems that can only be solved by relating to others and working together in a more collective way.

In *One Plus One* it is possible to see in the film's intercut shots a sort of demonstration of the differences between Godard's new revolutionary aesthetic and the old aesthetic of Antonioni and Godard's other former colleagues. Quite often the young girl (played by Anne Wiazemsky, Godard's wife) is seen painting her political slogans over just the kind of strikingly colored walls that Antonioni ordered painted to serve as backdrops for his filming of *Blow-Up* in London. But whereas Antonioni painted buildings, even whole city blocks (and trees) in order to obtain a certain beauty and psychological mood, Godard comes along and defaces that mystique of beauty which hides its own praxis from the public, presenting only the clear, bright façade of the finished product; and Godard creates a revolutionary form of art which calls attention to its praxis—a

MAO

R

T

(as one of the painted slogans puts it) that is both art and an appeal to go beyond art; or (as another puts it) a

CINEMARXISM

wherein our task is not simply to understand either art or society but to change them both radically. In short, Godard's new revolutionary art takes the old art apart, demystifies it, even defaces it, but then uses the best of the old art (like Antonioni's sense of the color and texture of a wall) as a base, as a point of departure from which to get people thinking about the society in which they live, and hopefully to bolster their readiness to transform that society.

And for Godard, as an artist, this means giving up both the old aestheticism and the fascination with metaphysics (the search for the Absolute) that characterized some of his earlier films, *Le Mépris* and *Pierrot le fou* in particular. It is no coincidence that the final scene of *One Plus One*, with its panorama of sea and sky and its association with death, is reminiscent of the final scenes of both *Le Mépris* and *Pierrot le fou*. But in *One Plus One* the death that is associated with the film's closing image is a symbolic rather than a physical death. It is both a death and a rebirth, a *rite de passage* to a new and "higher" form of existence.

The death that is ritually enacted is the death of Eve Democracy and, through her, the death of the old Western idealist notions of society and of the function of art in society. And for Godard as film-maker, it is the death of the old bourgeois cinema and the birth of the new cinema of revolution. The last shot of *Le Mépris* showed Ulysses getting a first glimpse of his homeland after years of metaphysical wandering—a fulfillment denied in that film (and in *Pierrot le fou*) to alienated modern man. The last shot of *One Plus One,* however, gives us a first glimpse of the new revolutionary order we must build on the ruined shores of the old. The film closes on the image of a huge Hollywood camera crane, with its lifeless cargo of a limp body and an inoperative camera swinging effortlessly in free abandon, first right, then left, with the red flag and the black flag waving briskly in the wind that blows in from the sea. The *rite de passage* is achieved. The cinema is dead. Vive le *cinéma révolutionnaire!*

6

"See You at Mao": Godard's *Revolutionary* British Sounds*

Introduction: Ideology

A fist punches through a paper Union Jack. Smashing through from behind, the fist seems to smash right through the screen as well. A voice declares: "The bourgeoisie created a world in its image. Comrades, let us destroy that image." From its opening shot, Godard's *British Sounds* aims its critical thrust at *ideology*— at the world view secreted by the mass media purveyors of images and sounds that reflect and serve to perpetuate the bourgeois capitalist mode of production and its concomitant exploitation.

Louis Althusser has reminded us that although Marx's conception of the structure of society placed ideology at the uppermost floor, so to speak, of the cultural superstructure, nevertheless, in Marx's own terms, ideology (like all social phenomena) was determined in the final analysis by the infrastructure or economic foundations on which society was based.[12] And Althusser points out as well the extremely important *economic function of ideology* in assuring the reproduction of the labor force. Just as factory owners must constantly maintain and replenish their supply of raw materials, machinery, and the physical plants, so must they also maintain and replenish the supply of workers willing and

---

* *British Sounds* was the original title—and as far as I can ascertain still is the "official" title—of the film Godard showed on several university campuses in America billed as *See You at Mao*.

qualified to carry out the work expected of them. The terms "willing" and "qualified" are key ones, for in order to ensure that the potential labor force actually continues to render itself at the factory gates, ready to work, each morning from now till eternity, the ruling class must carry out a pervasive, permanent propaganda campaign aimed not only—or even primarily—at rational persuasion, but rather at *unquestioned, unconscious* acceptance and reinforcement of the existing social system and the values which are useful to that system. In other words, people must be trained to know what "society" (the ruling class) expects them to do and to be willing to do it. And this is where ideology comes in.

Cinema and television are of course by no means the only or even the most important vehicles of ideology. (Althusser lists, in addition to these, the schools, churches, courts, political parties, labor unions, the press, and—perhaps most important of all—the family.) But cinema and television have proved particularly useful ideological weapons in the past few decades, both because of the vast audiences they reach and because, as photographic media, they lend themselves so well to the ruling class's need to present the status quo as if it were *reality* itself. Photography, after all, is said to reflect reality. There's an old adage that "the camera doesn't lie," and whatever shows upon the photographic image— barring obvious tampering—is automatically raised to the stature of "reality."

As Godard states the problem of ideology in cinema and television, "the bourgeoisie creates a world in its image, but it also creates an image of its world that it calls a 'reflection of reality.'"[13] What he is pointing out here is the insidious confusion of terms perpetrated by the bourgeois image-makers. The image they create is an image of their own bourgeois capitalist society, but they seek to pass off this image as a "reflection of reality." Why? What is gained in this switch of terms?

If the bourgeois image-makers admitted that the image they present was merely a reflection of their own bourgeois capitalist ideology, this would be to admit the subjective, partisan, arbitrary, and mutable aspects of that image—and, by extension, of that *society*. Instead, they seek to inculcate a belief that the image they present is an objective one, that it is not partisan, that it is not arbitrary; that, in fact, it could be no other image precisely because "that's the way things are in reality." The ideological sleight of hand that substitutes "reflection of reality" for "reflection of bourgeois capitalism" not only seeks to make bourgeois capitalism disappear as an *issue*, but also to ensure that bourgeois capitalism will perpetually reappear *in the guise of reality*.

And in the guise of reality it is far less vulnerable: we can ask questions about how best to accommodate ourselves to reality; but we certainly can't ask "reality" to go away. Reality, after all, is considered a *given*. We are told to confront reality, to look reality in the face—and we are left only the choice of coping with the given as best we can. Ideology, then, in a class society, is a weapon used by the ruling class to inculcate in the masses the acceptance as a given of the existing social system which privileges one class at the expense of another. Ideology serves to suppress the asking of questions about the social system and to assure that what few questions do get asked are questions of *how* rather than *why*, of *reform* rather than *revolution*, of how to accommodate ourselves to "reality" rather than why this particular social system should exist at all, much less be elevated to the status of "reality" and accepted as a given.

The aesthetics of the photographic media also serve to reinforce this attitude of respect—almost of religious veneration—for "reality." The clear, untampered-with photographic image is considered sacrosanct: and using the myriad possibilities of the photographic process for anything other than a straightforward "reflection of reality" is invariably denigrated by our aestheticians, if not actually proscribed.

In cinema, the aesthetics of André Bazin effectively codifies (for whose benefit we shall see in a moment) all the realist rationale of photography. In "Ontology of the Cinematic Image," the opening essay of Bazin's *What Is Cinema?*,[14] he sets forth a whole series of "thou shalt nots" in which such devices as superimposition, multiple exposures, slow motion, fast motion, expressionistic sets or décor, theatrically stylized action—and even most types of montage—are rendered suspect under any conditions and are downright *forbidden* under most. Their "sin": tampering with "reality," interfering with the "clean," "pure," "virgin," *reflection of reality.*

The religious terminology in Bazin's writings is by no means coincidental or even merely metaphorical. Bazin's entire aesthetic system is rooted in a mystical-religious (Catholic) framework of transcendance. The faithful "reflection of reality," for Bazin, is a prerequisite—and ultimately merely a *pretext*—for finding a "transcendental truth" which supposedly exists in reality and is "miraculously" revealed by the camera. Reality, if one reads Bazin carefully, sheds very quickly its *material* shell and is "elevated" to a purely metaphysical (one could justifiably call it a *theological*) sphere.

For Bazin, all roads lead to the heavens. Even when writing about a film like Buñuel's *Las Hurdes (Land Without Bread)*, which is a scathing documentation of the *material* condition of a specific people (the inhabitants of the Valley of Las Hurdes) in a specific country (Spain) under a specific economic system (capitalism) with a specific ruling-class coalition (between the bourgeoisie and the Catholic Church)—all of which is pointed out with bitter emphasis in the film itself—nonetheless, Bazin manages to sweep the *material* dust under the table so fast you can hardly see it and immediately takes off for the stellar dust of the heavens.

Not once, it has been pointed out,[15] does Bazin in his article on *Las Hurdes* even mention the words "class," "exploited," "rich," "capitalism," "property," "proletariat," "bourgeoisie," "order," "money," "profit," etc. And what words do we find in their place? Large ones; broad generous concepts that are the staple of a long tradition of bourgeois humanist idealism—words like "conscience," "salvation," "sadness," "purity," "integrity," "objective cruelty of the world," "transcendental truth," "cruelty of the human condition," "unhappiness," "the cruelty in the Creation," "destiny," "horror," "pity," "madonna," "human misery," "surgical obscenity," "love," "admiration," "*dialectique pascalienne*" (it would have to be *pascalienne!*), "all the beauty of a Spanish *Pietà*," "nobility and harmony," "presence of the beautiful in the atrocious," "eternal human nobility in adversity," "an infernal earthly paradise," etc. And this is no unique case, either in Bazin's aesthetics or in bourgeois ideology in general. The broader, more general, and more generous the concepts, the easier it is to cover up the *absence* of a materialist, process-oriented analysis of human society that, if undertaken, would reveal some hard, unpleasant facts that could cause people to start rocking the boat. (As I indicated earlier, ideology functions at least as much in what it does *not* say—in what it *keeps quiet*—as in what it does say).[16]

With this background, let us turn now to *British Sounds*, Godard's first serious attempt to break bourgeois ideology's stranglehold on the cinema, to free the cinema from a misguided and mystifying aesthetics, and to construct a *cinematic dialectical materialism* that will unveil those hard, unpleasant facts the ruling class seeks to conceal.

As Godard defines the basic premise of this new, analytical approach to images and sounds: TELEVISION AND CINEMA DO NOT RECORD MOMENTS OF REALITY BUT SIMPLY MOMENTS IN THE DIALECTICAL PROCESS, AREAS/ERAS OF CONCENTRATION THAT HAVE TO BE EXAMINED IN THE LIGHT OF CLASS STRUGGLE.

Let us do this with *British Sounds*.

Analysis: The Dialectics of Image and Sound

In the first sequence—roughly ten minutes in length—the camera tracks slowly down the assembly line of a British Motor Corporation "model" factory where MG sportscars are being assembled. Meanwhile, on the sound track, there are at least three distinct elements: a man's voice-over reading of various passages from the *Communist Manifesto* fulminating against the alienation and exploitation of workers under the capitalist wage system; a little girl's voice-over memorizing of a Marxist catechism of important dates in the history of working-class struggle in England;

and factory noise, which itself seems to consist of two distinct elements—a base of synchronous sound that records the actual hammerings and machine noises of the assembly-line activity we see in the image, and very loud, harsh, and grating machine noise that seems to be overlaid on the sound track. The voice-over text is only intermittently audible even without the high-intensity machine noise; and, of course, when the latter is on, its shrieking metallic whine is all we hear.

We can begin to understand Godard's method in this film by asking why he might resort to sound mixing for the high-intensity machine noise. After all, if one of the points he is trying to make in this sequence is that factory workers labor under excruciating conditions of noise, wouldn't this point be made more effectively if Godard simply documented the noise of an assembly line instead of making the point intellectually by manipulating the sound track? Well, perhaps, but only if you subscribe to the realist canons of those who insist that cinema must be a reflection of reality. It is, I think, precisely because this aesthetic attitude has proved so useful to the capitalist ruling class in disseminating bourgeois ideology that Godard, who wishes to unveil and combat that ideology, rejects its realist aesthetics and openly flaunts its rules.

Moreover, by playing with the relations among different elements of the sound track in this sequence, Godard makes a much more subtle and telling point. The physical alienation through harsh, intensive noise gets in the way of our understanding, in the film, the Marxian explanation of the economic alienation and exploitation of the worker under capitalism. Analogously, we can appreciate how, for the worker in the factory, the physical alienation through noise (combined with other factors, such as repetitious, mechanical gestures, fatigue, constant danger of injury, etc.) can be so brutalizing and benumbing that the worker (during working hours, at least) has no opportunity—or, for that matter, inclination—to ponder anything so seemingly abstract and complex as Marxist theory. If he's going to complain about anything, it's not capitalism; it's noise. He's going to demand better

British Sounds: "The bourgeoisie created a world in its image. Comrades, let us destroy that image."

working conditions, or shorter hours, or higher wages, or medical plans, or all of these; but with all these immediate evils to lessen or eliminate, his attention will not be drawn to the greater evil—capitalism itself—which is the root of the problem.

And precisely because Godard imposes that machine noise on the sound track and calls attention to the way it serves to block out or impede Marxian political awareness, we are better able to understand not only the effects of that factory noise but also what may well be one of its causes. Factory workers today may be laboring under alienating conditions of noise, among other things, *not* because technology is incapable of reducing machine noise, but because (a) noise-reduction is expensive and would cut into the ruling class's profit margin, and (b) because, in any case, noise in the factory is useful to the ruling class in maintaining the alienation of the workers as a means of preventing them from focusing their critical attention on the capitalist system as a whole, and, instead, deflecting their attention to petty grievances which the ruling class can handle.

And unlike a straightforward, synch-sound documentary sound track of factory noise (in which the noise would simply be a given for us to experience), Godard's manipulating of the relations among various sound-blocks and levels of intensity enables us both to *experience* just how excruciating machine noise can be, and, more important, to *analyze* some of the more subtle effects—as well as a possible cause—of that noise by analyzing the relations among factory noise, the worker, and the worker's ability to gain an awareness of his own alienation.

In the second sequence, unlike the first, issues are raised not so much by the relations among the different elements of the sound track as by the relations between image and sound. What we see in the image is a nude young woman; what we hear on the sound track is an impassioned voice-over reading of a text on Women's Liberation. The nude is not shown doing anything interesting—just walking back and forth from one room to another, standing idly, talking on the telephone, or—in a visual pun on Marcel Duchamp's famous painting—descending (as well as ascending) a staircase.

The shots of her walking up and down the stairs are fairly long-range shots; those of her sitting on a chair and talking on the phone are middle-range shots; and the visual *pièce de résistance* of this sequence is a two-minute frontal close-up, as she stands idly, that frames from just above the navel to mid-thighs, with pubic hair up front and center in what has to be the boldest—and some would say most boring—"beaver" shot in the brief history of that budding genre of cinematic experience. But what Godard is exploring in this entire sequence is not the ways of sexually titillating the film-goer, nor the beauty of the unadorned female body, but rather the complex and ambiguous relations among nudity, sex, and liberation—especially as these concern women. And, as always, Godard's exploration is on "two fronts" simultaneously, for while he explores certain issues (in this case, nudity, sex, and liberation), he is also exploring different cinematic possibilities for dealing with these issues.

Take nudity and sex, for instance: they are hardly new to the movie screen. Movies have always toyed with suggestions of nudity, if not nudity itself—giving us fleeting, peekaboo glimpses of starlets in bubble baths, or, as sexual mores became less rigid, of starlets popping in and out of bed, but popping so fast that one hardly saw a thing. Slower, longer looks at nudity (almost invariably female nudity) were carefully contrived through elaborate camera angles and framing to avoid full frontal shots. Until roughly five years ago, the unwritten law in most European as well as American productions was "you can't show pubic hair." Lately, however, coming in the wake, I suppose, of nudity onstage, the movies have, for the moment at least, relaxed their vigilance on pubic hair—and on a lot of other things as well—with the result that there is now a rash of "erotic" films that show anything and (preferably) everything, and there is also a freer, franker acceptance now of frontal nudity in the traditional "art film" and "mature adult film."

But to Godard, it is clear, the question of what or how much is shown is only part of the issue where nudity is concerned—and the question of *how* is really far more important. If nudity is simply used as a come-on, then it serves to exploit both the audience and the actors and actresses concerned. Moreover, if the undraped female body is simply offered up as a sex object for male-chauvinist consumption, then the exploitation of women is perpetuated and reinforced.

Here again, seeking to combat the prevailing ideology, Godard rejects its conventions and flaunts its rules. He systematically excludes from this sequence all the usual appurtenances of sex-on-the-screen. Instead of showing the woman undressing (the old striptease routine), Godard has the woman appear in the nude from start to finish. And she is alone throughout the entire sequence: her nudity is casually, unself-consciously for herself, for her own free-and-easy feeling of liberation; it is not, as movies invariably have it, female nudity for a man's waiting lust or for any form of sexual activity whatsoever—be it hetero, homo, or auto. In fact, at no point are we the audience given the voyeuristic titillation of watching even the old "frustrated longing" bit (heavy sighing, restless tossing, etc.) of the woman-at-home-alone scene (like the one that awkwardly opens *Bonnie and Clyde*)—a scene which always functions as the cinematic correlative of that archetypal male-chauvinist cliché, "All she needs is a good fuck!"

Godard's nude young woman may assert that fucking can help some of her problems, but she's talking of taking the initiative, liberating herself from dependency relationships, of "fucking around" whenever she feels like it and with whomever she chooses. Not letting herself get in the situation where "all she needs is a good fuck" might mean doing just what males have always done or had the right to do, and that is "fucking around"— an activity which the double standard (another male-chauvinist ploy) has always declared off-bounds for women.

And as for cinema's hypocritical attitudes toward pubic hair, Godard not only shows us pubic hair in the two-minute close-up, one could almost say that he rubs our noses in it—if it weren't for the fact, however, that he simultaneously distances us from this shot by the dialectical interplay he sets up between image and sound. Throughout this sequence image and sound serve to call each other into question and to raise questions in our minds concerning the relations between the nudity and potential sex content that we see in the image and, on the other hand, the struggle to eliminate exploitation of one sex by the other that we hear advocated on the sound track. Ultimately, of course, this dialectical interplay transcends the immediate issue of Women's Liberation and raises questions concerning the relations between sexual behavior and political behavior in general—with cryptic interjections (both aural and visual—male voice-over and hand-written placards) that suggest parallels between "sex perversion and Stalinism," or "concealing one's sex and keeping secret the decisions of workers' councils," or, finally, to sum up what this particular sequence is all about, "Freudian revolution and Marxist sexuality."

As usual, Godard doesn't spell out what might be meant by these terms; but within the context of this sequence in the film it is not difficult to grasp the point that political liberation must also be conceived in the light of psychosexual liberation, and vice versa. And, as for the way these issues are presented to the public, it is clear that sex and nudity on stage and screen, while promoted as vehicles of liberation (and undoubtedly helping to liberate our society from old puritanical attitudes toward sex), are nonetheless very likely to be working counter to the liberation of women from the male-chauvinist attitudes that limit women's free development and maintain them in a situation of exploitation. Moreover, with sex being used to sell us everything from a toothbrush to an automobile, there is every reason to fear that the much-touted sexual revolution, in spite of its positive aspects, is actually the trump card of the reactionary ruling class which seeks to develop a hedonistic, pleasure-seeking society that will buy ever greater quantities of the sexual status symbols so many consumer products have become. Taking the complexity of the situation into account, unveiling the female body is only a small part of the struggle for liberation—and it is only truly liberating if it helps to unveil the ideology that exploits even women's nudity.

Although the issues in this Women's Lib sequence are raised primarily through the relations between image and sound, nonetheless, some important questions are raised through the relations among the various elements on the sound track. In fact, a number of questions are raised through the use of what might be called *unheard sound*. I am thinking here of the telephone conversation, of which we hear only the half spoken by the nude young woman we see in the image. We wonder not only what the voice on the other end of the line is saying (and perhaps whose voice it is), but also what the relation is between the words we do hear and those we don't hear. Partly because of the way the nude young woman speaks, and partly because of our past experience of the way people in recent Godard films repeat words that are fed to them by someone else (especially through an electronic communications medium—in this case, the telephone), we are drawn into

a suspicion that the nude is repeating or improvising on words
that are being fed to her by the voice (Godard's perhaps?) at the
other end of the line.

And if this is the case, what is the relation of the words the
woman is saying to her own thoughts on the subject of Women's
Liberation?* And, finally—to be ultra-skeptical—what is the relation of the words the nude young woman is saying not just to
her own *thoughts* on the advisability of "fucking around," but also
to her *actions?* In short, synch-sound may be used to record the
nude young woman's voice, but it's at least a possibility that the
words might be out of synch with either her own thoughts or
actions, or both. And this possibility creates a certain healthy
distance from the very simplistic "fucking around" solution which
the girl so blithely advocates.

In the next sequence as well, the notion of synch-sound is
somewhat problematic, for although there is no manipulation of
the sound track during the crude, ranting, ultra-right-wing speech
of the TV news-commentator, questions arise. "Whose words are
these?" . . . "Who is speaking?" . . . and "For whom?" There is a
strange incongruency between the words that are spoken and the
young man who speaks them. Not that he doesn't look like the
type to assert such racist and fascist opinions (on the contrary,
with his football-player shoulders, large close-cropped head, narrow gap between his eyes, and wide gap between his front teeth,
he seems all too perfectly typecast for the role)—but simply that
the words seem too strong and too overtly fascist to come from an
ordinary (supposedly objective) TV news-commentator.

As we watch and listen to his ravings, we wonder if perhaps
he's a politician making a campaign speech on television, but
throughout the entire sequence there is no indication that he is
anything other than your usual friendly TV news-commentator.
So, because this film is "set" in England, we wonder if perhaps to

---

* An unsubstantiated rumor suggests that the nude girl herself wrote the
text delivered out of synch (in voice-over); on the other hand, paradoxically,
the words she speaks in synch on the telephone might be out of synch with
her own thoughts.

the English this guy is a well-known, easily identifiable newscaster notorious for his right-wing views—sort of an English Fulton Lewis, Jr. But nothing ever gives us any clues to his identity or indicates what interest he has personally in expounding these views. So we start to wonder just who is behind him, whose words he is speaking, whose interests he is serving.

And these, of course, are questions Godard wants us to ask, not just about the "information" provided in this sequence of *British Sounds,* but about all the "information" fed us by television and cinema all the time. A newscaster's voice may be in synch, but Godard wants us to realize just what his words are in synch with —the ruling-class ideology. Granted the views expressed by the newscaster are a bit more extremist than those we expect,° but the main point of this sequence is that the dissemination of information is not in the service of the people, but in the service of the ruling class, which controls the mass media and utilizes these resources to impose bourgeois ideology on the masses as a means of perpetuating control over them. And if the views expressed in the media are not normally so overtly and crudely fascist, it is simply because a cool, calm veneer of objectivity serves far better to lull the audience and to inculcate bourgeois ideology than would an aggressive harangue. But the goals are the same: to perpetuate the power and privilege of the ruling class and the exploitation and fragmentation of the working class.

By occasionally cutting away from the face of the newscaster to intercut shots of isolated workers going about their tasks, Godard graphically suggests the fundamental opposition between the working class and the mass-media lackeys of the ruling class, and suggests as well that what little coverage the mass media give to the working class is calculated to depict only the individual worker and to strictly avoid any depiction of the working class *as a class.* As for the sound track in this sequence, it is given over almost entirely to the ranting voice of the ruling class: no dissent-

°Program notes prepared by Godard (including his auto-critique on the film) indicate that the words spoken by the newscaster in this sequence are excerpted from speeches by "Wilson, Heath, Pompidou, Nixon, etc."

ing voice can get a word in edgewise; and even at the very end of the newscaster's harangue, only the barest whisper is heard—as if it were spoken by a gutsy studio technician who nevertheless was afraid of getting caught—asking for the workers to "unite and strike."

And in the very next sequence it is made clear—*by a worker*—that the workers' interest lies *not* in striking merely to win this or that concession from the capitalist owners and managers, but in using general strikes as a political weapon to help overthrow the capitalist system itself. As a small group of English Ford workers discuss their problem, Godard finds a new way to dramatize what is out of synch and what is in synch—he keeps the camera aimed away from whoever is speaking, except toward the end, when one worker (who seems to have the most highly developed political awareness of the group) articulates a clear analysis of the situation and formulates a firm proposal for action. The rest of the time, as the workers gropingly discuss some of their general grievances or speak resignedly of their plight, the camera pans around the room from one silent listener to another, boycotting whoever is speaking at that moment, as if to say "No, we're still groping around in the dark; we're still not speaking to the point; we're not yet in synch with the situation."

But when the camera finally focuses on the young worker who denounces demands for better deals within the capitalist system and calls instead for political organization and united struggle to overthrow capitalism, then, finally, for the first time in the film, everything really comes together in an authentic synchronous unity. There are no aural or visual interjections, no manipulation of the sound track. At this moment, image and sound are completely in synch. Moreover, this time the words are clearly in synch with the convictions of the person speaking and with his actions as well. He is involved at this very moment, among his fellow workers, in the very political organization he is talking about. And for once the speaker's words, thoughts, and deeds are all really in synch with his *needs*—not with the ersatz needs inculcated by capitalist ideology, but with his urgent need for creative, nonalienating, nonexploitative work-relations among his fellow men.

Structurally as well as thematically (thematically *because* structurally), this is the moment the film has been building up to —this is the moment that gets it all together and points out the path to be taken toward human wholeness. And, significantly, that way is pointed out to us by what Marx (as well as Lenin) considered to be the real guiding light of humanity—the avant-garde of the proletariat, the worker who matches a concrete experience of the situation with a concrete analysis of the situation.

From this point on—now that we know where the film's basic movement has been leading (as well as where a class-based political movement must lead)—*British Sounds* takes on a more joyful and lyrical tone, as we see in the final two sequences ways in which students and practitioners of the various arts can contribute to the struggle for a new and more wholesome society. In the next-to-last sequence, a group of Essex University students are seen and heard making radical posters and discussing how to combat the bourgeois ideology of popular songs by rewriting their lyrics in a politically militant spirit. (The Beatles' song that goes "You say yes, I say no" is changed to "You say Nixon, I say Mao," then changed again to the more punning line "You say US, I say MAO.") Meanwhile, during the synch-sound presentation of the students' activities, there is also a running voice-over commentary which raises theoretical questions on the ways of creating images and sounds that will oppose the images and sounds of capitalism.

This voice-over commentary—unlike most of the previous overlaid material—does not blot out or let in only a few fragments of the synch-sound material, but rather serves as the theoretical complement to the social praxis of the students and artists whose activities are presented in a new, enriched synchronous unity which takes care not to neglect the urgent theoretical considerations that must be dealt with if we are to succeed in building new, nonalienating relations in society.

In this commentary three types of films are distinguished:

imperialist films, revisionist films, and revolutionary films. In an imperialist movie, the speaker tells us, the movie screen sells the voice of the boss to the viewer: the voice lulls the viewer or it hammers away at him, but in either case it seeks to inculcate bourgeois ideology. In a revisionist movie the screen is a loudspeaker for a voice that represents the people without at all being the actual voice *of* the people, since they still must sit in silence watching a distorted image of themselves. Finally, in a revolutionary film the screen is merely a blackboard on which is presented a concrete analysis of a concrete situation: it is a learning device for both teacher and pupil and contains a healthy dose of self-criticism.

In the film's final sequence we see in the image a close-up shot of a hand (Godard's)—covered with red paint, writhing along in a patch of mud and snow until it reaches out to grasp a stick with a red flag attached to it. Getting a firm grip on the stick at last, the hand raises the red flag and waves it triumphantly in the air while, on the sound track, extracts from revolutionary songs from different countries ring forth. It is a lyrical finale—a piece of cinematic agit-prop theater that gives us the *feel* of revolutionary militancy as a necessary complement to the analytical *rationale* for revolutionary militancy that is provided by the body of the film. Finally, fist after fist is seen punching through a succession of paper Union Jacks, as voices on the sound track assert their solidarity with various British radical movements, and, in a parting shot at ideology, denounce the "Gestapo of the old humanist university."

Conclusions: Pour ne pas conclure

Just as the conclusion of Godard's *British Sounds* does not seek in any way to sum up the film as a whole, but rather to provide us with a "send-off" (*envoi*) which brings us back out of the internal structure of the work of art and into our own everyday realm of social praxis; so, too, the conclusion of this chapter seems to me to demand not a conclusion in the sense of a summing up, but rather conclusions (plural) to be drawn for future use in that part of our social praxis that we carry out as film-goers, film-critics, or film-makers.

And in this sense I think there are a few striking conclusions to be drawn from *British Sounds* that deserve our attention—and, more important, our *use*. I don't claim that these conclusions are new or that they are uniquely to be drawn from *British Sounds,* but I do consider them grossly neglected in our general practice of cinema. I simply enumerate them here; they are presented, quite literally, for our future use and development:

(1) Relations between image and sound do not by any means have to be "realistic" to bring us to grips with "reality."

(2) Relations among various sound elements do not by any means have to be "realistic" to bring us to grips with "reality."

(3) "Reality" itself is a much-abused concept (inside the cinema as well as out) and should give way to a more *dialectical* concept. ("Don't say *nature,*" wrote Engels, "say the *dialectics of nature.*")

(4) Cinema and television have a vast potential not merely for "reflecting reality" (which potential has always been tapped) but also for *analyzing* it (which potential has been tapped far too little).

(5) Cinema and television, like all social praxis, are imbedded within class struggle. They must be analyzed in the light of class struggle because, in any case, they are a product of class struggle.

7

Godard and Rocha at the
Crossroads of Wind from the East

Near the middle of *Vent d'Est (Wind from the East)*, Godard has filmed a sequence in which Brazilian film-maker Glauber Rocha plays a brief but symbolically important role. As Rocha stands with arms outstretched at a dusty crossroads, a young woman with a movie camera comes up one of the paths—and the fact that she is very evidently pregnant is undoubtedly "pregnant" with meaning. She goes up to Rocha and says very politely: "Excuse me for interrupting your class struggle, but could you please tell the way toward political cinema?"

Rocha points first in front of him, then behind and to his left, and he says, "That way is the cinema of aesthetic adventure and philosophical inquiry, while this way is the Third World cinema— a dangerous cinema, divine and marvelous, where the questions are practical ones like production, distribution, training three hundred film-makers to make six hundred films a year for Brazil alone, to supply one of the world's biggest markets."

The woman starts off down the path to the Third World cinema, hesitates, takes a half-hearted kick at a red ball she finds lying on the path, and then reverses her steps. The ball comes rolling back behind her, however, as if it were insisting on following her—like Lamorisse's famous "red balloon," which it resembles slightly. In any case, she ignores the ball, which comes to a stop at the side of the road, and she doubles back behind

Glauber Rocha, who is still standing at the crossroads with arms outstretched like a scarecrow or a crucified Christ without a cross. And finally the pregnant woman with the movie camera sets off anew along the path of aesthetic adventure and philosophical inquiry, proceeding slowly, checking out the bushes alongside the path, leaving no leaf unturned in her search for clues regarding "political cinema."

I choose to begin an analysis of Godard's *Vent d'Est* by describing this brief sequence and suggesting some of its tongue-in-cheek symbolism because I believe it to be of critical importance not just for an understanding of what Godard is trying to do in this film, but also for an understanding of the way certain very important issues are shaping up in the vanguard of contemporary cinema. The issues involved certainly go beyond just Godard and Rocha—and ultimately it may well be cinema itself which now stands at a critical crossroads.

To get at these issues and to delve more deeply into the significance of the crossroads sequence, I think it best to take first a brief detour and explain a little of how *Vent d'Est* came into being and of Glauber Rocha's problematical association with this film at various stages of its development. Shortly after France's "May Events" in 1968, Godard contacted one of the May movement's leading militants, Daniel Cohn-Bendit, and suggested that the two of them collaborate on a film project that would explore the deadly ideological malaise at the root not only of French politics but of the, post-Cold War political situation in general. Godard also indicated his desire to make the film in such a way as to draw parallels between the repressiveness of traditional political structures and the repressiveness of traditional film structures, particularly those of the standard Western.

Cohn-Bendit agreed, and Godard contacted Italian producer Gianni Barcelloni, who had previously worked with directors like Pasolini and Glauber Rocha and the young French underground film-maker Philippe Garrel. Barcelloni jumped at the chance to produce a film by Godard and he persuaded Cineriz to advance him $100,000 for "a Western in color, to be scripted by Daniel

Cohn-Bendit, directed by Jean-Luc Godard, and starring Gian-Maria Volonte" (Italy's current box-office favorite).

What the producer and distributor apparently were expecting was something on the order of a "*Cohn-Bendit le fou.*" In any case, shooting took place in early summer 1969 in Italy. Godard, who by this time had committed himself to collective creation, assembled his three-man Dziga Vertov Group (which at the time included Jean-Henri Roger as well as Godard and Gorin),* enlisted his actress-wife Anne Wiazemsky, numerous Italian actors and technicians, and a number of French and Italian left-wing militants of diverse leftist persuasions. Cohn-Bendit, who had discussed with Godard the overall conception of the film, showed up for only a portion of the shooting, apparently argued with Godard and Gorin, and does not appear in the finished film.

Exit Cohn-Bendit. Enter Glauber Rocha.

In Rome for talks with producer Barcelloni, Rocha encountered Godard, who, as Rocha tells it, suggested that the two of them should coordinate efforts "to destroy cinema"—to which Rocha replied that he was on a very different trip, that his business was to build cinema in Brazil and the rest of the Third World, to handle very practical problems of production, distribution, etc.

This disagreement seems to have given Godard the idea of shooting a "Rocha at the crossroads" sequence to include in *Vent d'Est* as a way of delineating different revolutionary strategies.

---

* The nucleus of the Dziga Vertov Group has always been a working relationship between Godard and one other person—first with Jean-Henri Roger (a young militant from Marseilles) for *British Sounds* and *Pravda,* then with Jean-Pierre Gorin (a twenty-nine-year-old former journalist and student activist) for the last five films the Group has made—but the collective planning and making of the Group's films have involved many other individuals and militant groups as well. (Incidentally, some Godard filmographies list *Un film comme les autres* [*A Film Like All The Others*] as the first of the Dziga Vertov Group's films; however, although this film on the French riots of 1968 grew out of Godard's participation in some of the loosely organized militant groups that sprang up during that time, the film was finished in late 1968, which, to my knowledge, antedates by at least several months the founding of the Dziga Vertov Group. It should, I think, be considered a precursor of the Group's work rather than a part of it.)

Rocha agreed to play his part, although not without indicating his reluctance at "joining the collective mythology of the unforgettable French May-Gang."

In the summer, then, the sequence was shot, and Godard and Rocha parted amicably, but with each man apparently feeling that the other had failed to understand his position. Godard went to work on the editing of *Vent d'Est*, and he and Gorin completed the film early in the winter of 1969–70. Rocha happened to be in Rome again at the time of the producer's private preview screening of *Vent d'Est*, saw the film, and found himself—and everyone else—in such bewilderment and consternation at the path taken by Godard that he decided to write an article about the film for the Brazilian magazine *Manchete*.[17]

At Cannes in May 1970 *Vent d'Est* was given a midnight showing. (Godard, by the way, didn't want the film shown at Cannes at all: it was entirely the distributor's doing.) A few people admired the film; most hated it. Ditto for the September showing of *Vent d'Est* at the New York Festival. Ditto again for the showing a few weeks later in Berkeley. But that kind of reaction is more or less to be expected whenever a new Godard film is first released. What is unusual and a bit more complicated is the controversy over whether *Vent d'Est* can be considered a "visually beautiful" film and whether or not visual beauty is an attribute or a liability given Godard's revolutionary aims.

Much of the controversy over the visual quality of *Vent d'Est* may arise simply from the fact that both 35mm and 16mm prints of the film are being shown; and that visually these two are very different films. Although the film was shot in 16mm (entirely outdoors, by the way), it is the 35mm print (blown up from 16mm) which is by far the better of the two (especially because of the lush greens of the beautiful Italian countryside near Cinecitta and the lovely rose red wall of an old half-ruined peasant dwelling). The 16mm print, on the other hand, is extremely dark and murky, with very false, somber color.

But the controversy really gets thick when people start debating the relative merits and demerits of visual beauty (or its absence) in *Vent d'Est*. One argument has been that because the film is "too beautiful," it remains in the realm of bourgeois aesthetics and doesn't really function as a politically militant film. Godard, however, turns the argument around to assert that "if *Vent d'Est* succeeds at all, it's because it isn't beautifully made at all." Rocha, in his *Manchete* article, comes out against *Vent d'Est* not because the film remains in the realm of aesthetics, but rather because he sees Godard as trying to destroy aesthetics. Rocha praises the film for its "desperate beauty" but reproaches Godard for feeling so desperate about the usefulness of art. Rocha laments that such a gifted artist as Godard (whom he compares to Bach and Michelangelo) should no longer have faith in art and should seek instead to "destroy" art.

For Rocha, a Brazilian, the present intellectual crisis in Western Europe over the usefulness of art is senseless and politically negative. He sees the European artist—best exemplified by Godard—as having worked himself into a dead end; and Rocha concludes that where cinema is concerned, the Third World may be the only place where an artist can still fruitfully go about the task of making films. Godard, on the other hand, reproaches Rocha for having "a producer's mentality," for thinking too much in so-called practical terms of production, distribution, markets, etc., thereby perpetuating the capitalist commodity structures of the cinema and extending them to the Third World . . . and thereby neglecting in the process urgent theoretical questions that must be asked if Third World cinema is to avoid merely repeating the ideological errors of Western cinema.

What sorts of ideological errors might Godard have in mind? Well, let's go back to the crossroads sequence in *Vent d'Est*, which, with its obvious association of the woman with a movie camera as a symbol for the cinema itself, reads something like this: at a very pregnant stage of creative development, the cinema turns to the Third World for direction regarding the proper relation between cinema and politics. (The question "Which way to the 'political cinema'?" is actually a question of "What ought a socially responsible, *liberating* cinema to be like?") Given a somewhat equivocal answer by Glauber Rocha, but sufficiently impressed by what he says—or, more accurately, by what he *sings* —regarding the "divine and marvelous" Third World cinema, our woman with the movie camera starts off down the path Rocha has identified as the path of Third World cinema. But a few steps along the way she has some misgivings, takes a half-hearted kick at a red ball inexplicably lying on the path, and changes her direction to double back behind Rocha and to set out on the path of aesthetic adventure and philosophical inquiry.

Now, as I said earlier, the fact that the red ball comes rolling back to her after she kicks it reminded me of Lamorisse's famous red balloon, which also doggedly followed its "master." I can't say, of course, whether Godard had the red balloon in mind when he put the red ball in the path of the woman with the movie camera; but the more I thought about it, the more I realized that certain ideological misconceptions inherent in Western cinema are manifested in Lamorisse's charming film about a little French boy and a red balloon that follows him wherever he goes.

André Bazin, one might recall, devoted one of his more important essays,[18] "Montage interdit," to *The Red Balloon* and to Lamorisse's other popular short film, *Crin Blanc (White Mane)*. Bazin's argument, a basic stepping stone in the development of his realist aesthetics, was that even in a film of such imaginative fantasy as *The Red Balloon,* what was essential *(ontologically essential)* was the cinematic faithfulness to reality, "the simple photographic respect for spatial unity." The fact that a trick was used to enable the balloon to appear to follow the boy didn't matter to Bazin just so long as the trick was not a cinematic trick —like, in his opinion, montage. What mattered was simply that whatever we saw on the screen had been photographed as it really happened in time and space. What we didn't see (like an imperceptible nylon thread which enabled Lamorisse to control the movements of the balloon) didn't matter to Bazin so long as what we did see really took place, was *pris sur le vif* (captured alive) by the camera, and was untampered with in the laboratory or on the editing table.

And it mattered not a bit to Bazin (in fact, it fitted in perfectly with his bourgeois humanist idealism) that this faithfulness to "reality" served as a jumping-off point for simplistic metaphysical pretensions and sentimental moralizing—as, for example, in *The Red Balloon*, where the struggle between the little boy and a gang of street toughies symbolizes the struggle between Good and Evil, with Evil winning out here on Earth as the balloon gets popped, but Good winning out in another, "higher" realm, as thousands of other balloons miraculously descend from on high, lift up the little boy, and whisk him up to the heavens.

Bazin's reality, as I have pointed out in the "Introduction: Ideology" section of Chapter 6, sheds very quickly its *material* aspect and is "elevated" to a purely metaphysical (one could justifiably call it a *theological*) sphere. And Bazin's realist aesthetics, with its insistence on cinema's supposed "reflection of reality," makes cinema a very useful ideological tool for the ruling bourgeoisie, which, in the cinema as elsewhere, attempts to pass off as reality (and thereby elevate to a metaphysical *essence*) the status quo of class society.

Perhaps, then, these are the sorts of ideological errors Godard would like to see the Third World cinema avoid, for Godard clearly deplores the way in which Western cinema from its birth has been disfigured by a bourgeois capitalist ideology that permeates its very theoretical foundations. In *Vent d'Est*, therefore, Godard systematically takes apart the traditional elements of bourgeois cinema—especially as exemplified by the Western—and reveals the sometimes hidden, sometimes blatant repressiveness that underlies it.

What Godard attacks in *Vent d'Est* is what he calls the "bourgeois concept of representation," which encompasses not only a certain acting style but also the traditional relations between image and sound—and, ultimately, of course, the traditional relationship between the film and the audience. Godard accuses the bourgeois cinema of overemphasizing and playing upon the deep-seated emotional fears and desires of the audience at the expense of their critical intelligence. And Godard seeks to combat this tyranny of the emotions not because he is *against* emotions and *for* rationality, nor because he is opposed to people's attitudes and actions being influenced by their experience of art, but because he believes very strongly that the film-goer should not be taken advantage of the way he is in bourgeois cinema, that he should not be manipulated emotionally but should instead be addressed directly and forthrightly in a lucid dialogue which calls forth *all* of his human faculties.

The way things now stand, however, every element of a bourgeois film is carefully calculated to invite the viewer to indulge in a "lived" emotional experience of a so-called slice of life instead of assuming a critical, analytical, and ultimately *political* attitude toward what he sees and hears. Why should one's attitude toward a film be political, one might ask? The answer is, of course, that the invitation to indulge in emotion at the expense of rational analysis already constitutes a political act on the part of the people who produce and make and distribute the film, as well as constituting a political act and attitude on the part of the viewer-listener—without the viewer-listener's usually being aware of it.

For one thing, by letting himself be emotionally moved by the cinema—and even demanding that the cinema should be emotionally moving—the film-goer puts himself at the mercy of anyone who comes along with a lot of money to invest in seeing to it that film-goers are moved. And the people who have that kind of money to invest also have a vested interest in making sure that the film audiences are moved in the right direction, that is, in the direction of perpetuating the investor's advantageous position in an economic system that permits gross inequities to exist in the distribution of wealth. In short, cinema (as well as television) functions as an ideological tool or weapon used by the ruling-owning class to extend the market for the bourgeois dreams it sells, and, at the same time, to divert people's attentions away from any serious questioning of the economic system which privileges one class at the expense of another.

Moreover, as Godard asserts in *Vent d'Est,* cinema tries to pass off bourgeois dreams as reality, and even plays on the heightening and enhancing effect of cinema in an effort to make us believe that the bourgeois dreams depicted on our movie screens are somehow larger than life, that they are not only real, but somehow more real than the real. In bourgeois cinema all conspires to this effect: the acting style is at the same time "realistic" and larger than life; the decors are "realistic" (or, if filmed on location, simply real), but they are also carefully selected for their beauty and their larger-than-life aspect. Likewise the costumes, clothing, jewelry, and make-up worn by the actors and actresses, who, themselves, are carefully selected for their beauty and their larger-than-life aspect. Finally, even sound in the bourgeois cinema is used to give us the illusion that we are eavesdropping on a moment of reality where the characters are oblivious to our presence and are simply living out their real-life emotions.

Since *Weekend* Godard has rejected conventional film dialogue because he finds that it contributes to this misguided illusion of reality and makes it all the easier for the viewer-listener to imagine himself right up there with the people on the screen, present yet safe, in a perfect position (that of an eavesdropper and a Peeping Tom) to participate vicariously in the emotion of the moment. In short, the bourgeois cinema pretends to ignore the presence of the spectator, pretends that what is being said and done on the movie screen is not aimed at the spectator, pretends that cinema is a reflection of reality; yet all the time it plays on the viewer-listener's emotions and capitalizes on his identification-projection mechanisms in order to induce him subtly, insidiously, unconsciously to participate in the dreams and fantasies that are marketed by bourgeois capitalist society.

There is an excellent sequence in *Vent d'Est* where Godard demonstrates and demystifies what takes place behind the façade of bourgeois cinema. On the sound track we are told that "in a few seconds you will see and hear a typical character in bourgeois cinema. He is in every film and he always plays a Don Juan type. He will describe the room you are sitting in." We then see a close-up of a very handsome young Italian actor standing at the

Wind from the East: Rocha at Godard's crossroads

Wind from the East: the repressiveness of the Western movie

Wind from the East: With a hammer and sickle they enact the symbolic destruction of bourgeois culture.

edge of a swift-running stream and looking directly at the camera. Behind him—but photographed so that depth perception is greatly reduced and the image as a whole is markedly flat—rises the muddy embankment of the opposite side of the river.

The young man speaks in Italian, while voices on the sound track give us a running translation in both French and English. The translation, however, is rendered indirectly: the voice tells us, "He says the room is dark. He sees people sitting downstairs and also up in the balcony. He says there is an ugly old fogey over there, all wrinkled; and over here he says he has spotted a good-looking young chick. He says he would like to lay her. He asks her to come up on the screen with him. He says it's beautiful up there, with the sun shining and green trees all around and lots of happy people having a good time. He says if you don't believe him, look . . . ," and at this point the camera suddenly pulls back and upward, keeping the young man in focus in the right-hand corner of the frame while it reveals on the left side—and what seems like almost a hundred feet below the young man—a breathtakingly beautiful scene of a waterfall spilling into a natural pool in a shaded glen where young people are diving and swimming in the clear water.

It's a magnificent shot. The image itself is extremely beautiful, and most amazing of all is the very complex restructuring of space accomplished by such a simple camera movement. But if we think about this sequence and its dazzling denouement, we realize that everything in it is a calculated come-on aimed at the dreams and fantasies of the audience. The man is young and handsome. When he speaks, he disparages age and ugliness, and glorifies youth and glamor. What he wants is sex, what he offers is sex, inviting the audience to come up on the screen and have sex with him. On the screen, he assures us, everything is beautiful and people are happy.

And that sudden restructuring of space literally invites us into the image all by itself. Like bourgeois cinema in general, it presents the bourgeois capitalist world as one of great depth, inexhaustibly rich and endlessly inviting. And the bourgeois cinema's predilection for depth-of-field photography (see Bazin) emphasizes the you-are-there illusion and thereby masks its own presence—and its own act of *presenting* this image—behind a self-effacing false modesty calculated to make cinema appear to be the humble servant of reality instead of what it really is—the not at all humble lackey of the ruling class.

In short, the bourgeois cinema is nothing other than a sales pitch monologue aimed (indirectly, to keep us off guard) at the audience, which is flirted with, coaxed, and cajoled into coming up onto the screen to join the "beautiful people" for a little sex and leisure amid beautiful surroundings! And the thing that really clinches the deal is the stunning virtuosity of the cinema in providing visual thrills.

Once again this raises the problem of visual beauty in political cinema; but it also demonstrates how Godard uses visual beauty in new ways that serve to demystify (and make us less vulnerable to) the old uses of visual beauty in the bourgeois cinema. After all, if beauty (like language) is one of the arms the ruling class uses to pacify us and keep us in our place, then one of our tasks is to turn that weapon around and make it work against the oppressors. One way to do this is to demystify beauty and to show how it is used against us; another way is to effect a "transvaluation of values" in which we make a vice of the bourgeois concept of beauty while making a virtue of a different concept of beauty (e.g., "Black is beautiful"). In his films since *Weekend,* especially in the films made collectively with the Dziga Vertov Group, Godard has been utilizing both of these tactics. His films now have a very different look about them which a lot of people are unable to consider beautiful because it doesn't conform to their bourgeois standards of beauty. And when individual shots or sequences do have a visual quality that most film-goers would consider beautiful, there is always some cinematic element or juxtaposition of elements that calls our attention to just how this beauty is achieved and how it is used as an ideological weapon.

Whatever the pros and cons where beauty in a militant film is concerned, it certainly does no good to criticize Godard's use of visual beauty in *Vent d'Est* without having understood just how and why he uses it—or to assume that Godard is trying to move people emotionally as the bourgeois cinema does, but that he fails in this effort because his images have a very formal, austere beauty which somehow turns the viewer off instead of turning him on. Writing in *Manchete*, Glauber Rocha criticizes the fact that the shot of the American cavalry officer roughing up the girl-militant (Anne Wiazemsky) is not really frightening at all, but only beautiful. What Rocha fails to appreciate is that Godard does not want this shot to be frightening and that he makes it beautiful in precisely such a way as to ensure that it won't be frightening. While the officer (Gian-Maria Volonte) wrings the girl's neck and shouts at her, someone offscreen throws thick gobs of red paint that catch in her auburn hair and occasionally splatter the officer's dark blue coat. The visual effect, with its rich interplay of colors and textures, is quite striking, and it serves to distance us from the action and the potential emotion it might otherwise arouse.

A few moments later Godard gives us another, similar shot, only handled this time more in the emotive style of bourgeois cinema. Instead of shooting from behind the girl's right shoulder as he did in the previous "torture" shot (with torturer and victim face-to-face, but only the face of the torturer seen by the audience), Godard now has the torturer holding the girl from behind so that the scene can be shot to reveal both of their faces in frontal close-up, with the framing and composition and lighting drawing our attention particularly to the girl's grimaces of pain. This time, however, no paint is thrown in and there are no overtly theatrical elements of the distancing kind. There is only a very good acting performance by Anne Wiazemsky, who really seems to be wincing with great pain. In a bourgeois film this shot might be quite frightening for the audience (especially if the girl screamed, as the bourgeois cinema loves to have actresses do), but in this film, coming after the earlier torture shot with the paint thrown in, the painful or frightening effect of the shot is minimized (notice that I do *not* say it is eliminated) and our critical intelligence is alerted to analyze the differences in handling between the two shots. We are shown the differences again in a later sequence where the cavalry officer rides around on horseback clubbing the recalcitrant prisoners—another scene which Rocha finds extremely beautiful but which he criticizes for not turning out to be brutal in the way he (and even Ventura, who was the sound man for *Vent d'Est*) thinks the scene was intended. What Godard does in this sequence is to utilize a few of the common place technical devices for this type of violent action sequence: turning the sound volume way up and continually making abrupt camera movements. The effect of these devices is usually a high emotional intensity and a very visceral sense of violence and confusion. (Remember their use in *Tom Jones.*) But Godard has made one major variation on these elements which completely changes our relation to this sequence.

His camera does continually make abrupt movements, but it also traces a very precise formal pattern—swinging about 35° left, then 35° right, back and forth several times, then swinging about 35° up, then 35° down, and so on, exploring in a very formal way the closed space of the lush ravine where the action takes place. The purely formal quality of these camera movements (Rocha proclaimed them "unprecedented in the whole history of film") effectively distances us from the action and prevents us from reacting emotionally to it. In short, this sequence is not meant to be brutal, but it is meant to call our attention to the way bourgeois cinema would make the sequence brutal—and, in so doing, brutalize us.

What's wrong is not what Godard does with image and sound; it's the tremendously strong habit we have of demanding that a film fulfill our bourgeois expectations of what a film should do. What's wrong is that even politically militant films are expected to express their militancy in the same language that bourgeois films use to inculcate the dreams and fantasies of bourgeois capitalism. What's wrong, in short, is that even among the world's leading film-makers—and even among those who are seeking a revolutionary transformation of society—not nearly enough thought is given to theoretical questions of the uses and abuses of image and sound and of the ways to build new relations between images and sounds that will no longer exploit the viewer-listener by manipulating his emotions and his unconscious fears and desires, but will instead engage him openly and forthrightly in a lucid dialogue, the other half of which must come from him.

But the way things stand now, the film-goer rarely seems to look upon the cinema as a dialogue between himself and the film, and he relinquishes all too readily his own active part in that dialogue and hands over the tool of dialogue exclusively to the people in the film. And the more emotionally charged the dialogue in the film, the more the viewer-listener is moved by it. In *Vent d'Est*, however, this habitual passivity is challenged from the outset, as Godard gives us an opening shot that arouses our curiosity (a young man and woman are seen lying motionless on the ground, their arms bound together by a heavy chain) but he systematically thwarts our expectations by simply holding the shot for nearly ten minutes without any action (the young man does stir enough to gently touch the face of the young woman at one point) and without any dialogue. In fact, when the voice-over commentary finally breaks in (on the forest murmurs we have been hearing), what we get is not dialogue but the critique of dialogue.

Ostensibly talking about strike tactics in some labor dispute, the speaker states at one point that what is needed is dialogue, but that dialogue is usually handed over to a "qualified representative" who translates the demands of the workers into the language of the bosses and in so doing betrays the people he supposedly represents. This voice-over discussion of the failure of dialogue clearly refers to the bargaining dialogues that go on between labor and capital; and a few minutes later, in the next sequence, there is a demonstration (in the style of a Western movie) of the way the "qualified representative" (the union delegate) distorts the real demands of the workers (for revolutionary overthrow of the capitalist system which exploits them) by translating those demands into terms the bosses can deal with (higher wages, shorter hours, better working conditions, etc.). But in a strange and insightful way, this discussion of the failure of dialogue in the hands of a "qualified representative" also refers to the failure of dialogue within the "bourgeois concept of representation" in the cinema.

"What is needed is dialogue"— this statement in the voice-over commentary seems to echo our own thoughts as we watch this exasperatingly long, static, and dialogue-less shot. We are impatient to get into the movie, we are impatient to get on with plot. We wonder why the young couple are lying on the ground and why they are chained together. We wish they would at least regain consciousness enough to start talking to each other so that we could find out, from their dialogue, what is happening—that is, what is happening *to them*. As usual, in the cinema we don't ask ourselves what is happening *to us*. We don't ask ourselves why a film addresses *us* in a particular way. In fact, we rarely think of a film as addressing us, or, for that matter, anyone at all. We sit back and accept the tacit understanding that a film is a "reflection of reality" captured in the mirror of that magical "eye of God" that is a movie camera. We sit back passively and wait for a film to lead us by the hand or, more literally, by the heart.

What is to be done, then, to get us out of this situation? As the voice-over speaker in *Vent d'Est* puts it,

> Today the question "what is to be done?" is urgently asked of militant film-makers. It is no longer a question of what path to take; it is a question of what one should do practically on a path that the history of revolutionary struggles has helped us to recognize. To make a film, for example, is to ask oneself the question "where do we stand?" And what does this question mean for a militant film-maker? It means, first but not exclusively, opening a parenthesis in which we ask ourselves what the history of revolutionary cinema can teach us.

Then follows a capsule history on some of the high points and weak spots of what could qualify as revolutionary cinema, beginning with the young Eisenstein's admiration for D. W. Griffith's

Intolerance. Certainly Griffith was a decisive influence on Eisenstein and, through Eisenstein, on the first great chapter of revolutionary cinema—the Russian silent film. But the commentator in *Vent d'Est* asserts that from a revolutionary standpoint this borrowing of technique from the expressive arsenal of a "North American imperialist" (Griffith) eventually did more harm than good and represents a defeat in the history of revolutionary cinema. As a consequence of this initial ideological error, it is affirmed, Eisenstein confused primary and secondary tasks and, instead of glorifying the ongoing struggles of the present, glorified the historic revolt of the sailors of the battleship *Potemkin.* As a second consequence, in 1929, when he made *The General Line* (also called *The Old and the New*), Eisenstein managed to find new ways of expressing Czarist repression, but could only utilize the same old forms to express the process of collectivization and agrarian reform. In his case, it is asserted, the "old" ultimately won out over the "new"—and, as a consequence, Hollywood found no difficulty in hiring Eisenstein to film revolution in Mexico, while at the same time in Berlin Dr. Goebbels asked Leni Riefenstahl to make "a Nazi *Potemkin.*"

All of this may sound somewhat heretical and perhaps arbitrary, but there is actually a very perceptive argument here if one follows it closely. The same techniques that Griffith used to glorify in retrospect the old racist cause of the Southern whites in the American Civil War were taken over and developed by Eisenstein to glorify in retrospect an already twenty-year-old episode (the mutiny of the battleship *Potemkin* took place in 1905)—and not a particularly important one at that—in the history of the Russian Revolution. Later, when confronted with the task of dealing with issues of contemporary urgency (agrarian reform and collectivization), Eisenstein could only trot out the same though now somewhat older techniques. Still later, those same techniques were perfectly compatible with the fascist propaganda of the Nazis; and Eisenstein himself was not altogether unjustifiably considered to be "co-optable" by Hollywood.

The problem is that the cinematic forms which Eisenstein inherited from Griffith and which he then developed were not flexible enough to deal with the complexities of the ongoing present but were very well suited to emotionalized, reconstituted documentaries of past history. Moreover, precisely because they emphasized the emotional, "lived," "you are there" aspect of history, it was all too easy for these cinematic forms to be used to stir up people's emotional involvement in even such aberrant doctrines as Hitler's "racial purity" and blind obedience to the Führer.

Next in line for critical scrutiny is Dziga Vertov, in whose name Godard founded his militant film-makers' collective. Vertov is credited with achieving a victory for revolutionary cinema when he declared that "there is no cinema which stands above class, no cinema which stands above class struggle," and that "cinema is only a secondary task in the world struggle for revolutionary liberation." But Vertov is faulted for having forgotten that, in the words of Lenin, "politics commands the economy"—with the result that his film *The Eleventh Year* does not sing the praises of eleven years of sound political leadership at the hands of the dictatorship of the proletariat, but glorifies instead Russia's surging economy and rapidly developing industry in exactly the same emotional terms that capitalist propaganda uses to glorify its own economic growth. "It is at this point," the commentator of *Vent d'Est* asserts, "that revisionism invaded the Soviet movie screens once and for all."

Next in the rundown of revolutionary cinema is the "false victory" of the early sixties, when progressive African governments, having achieved their revolution and kicked out the imperialists, "let them back in through the window of the movie camera" by turning over the production of films to the old European and American movie industry—"thereby giving white Christians the right to speak on behalf of blacks and Arabs." Finally, a victory is claimed for revolutionary cinema in the recent report of Comrade Kiang Tsing[19] (wife of Mao), in which the theory of "the royal road of realism" was denounced, along with a denunciation of most of the canons of the old Stalinist "socialist-realism" aesthetics.

Throughout this brief bird's-eye view of revolutionary cinema there runs the unifying thread of the necessity of thinking through very thoroughly the theoretical foundations of one's cinematic praxis. If we (along with Godard) can learn anything from the history of revolutionary cinema, it is clearly that constant self-critical vigilance is necessary if a film-maker is to avoid playing unwittingly into the hands of the oppressors. And if a film-maker's commitment to revolutionary liberation is more than just an emotional identification with the oppressed, then his cinematic practice must address itself to more than just the emotions and identification-projection mechanisms of the audience. Moreover, if he is firmly convinced (as Godard is) that the process of revolutionary liberation involves far more than just the revenge of the oppressed and that it offers the concrete possibility of putting an end to all oppression—in other words, of creating a more just society in which the free development of the individual works for rather than against the free development of his fellow man—then it is the film-maker's urgent task to create cinematic forms which themselves work for rather than against the free development of the viewer-listener, forms which do not manipulate insidiously his emotions or his unconscious but which engage him directly and openly, in a way that calls forth *all* of his human faculties—*rational and emotional*—in a lucid dialogue that can help both film-maker and film-goer to forge a revolution in the way man relates to his fellow man and to things.

And self-criticism is an integral part of Godard's cinema, as witnessed by the fact that the second half of *Vent d'Est* is given over to an implicit critique of Godard's own previous efforts. The first and most serious criticism brought forth is his own lack of contact with the masses. (Since he began working collectively with the Dziga Vertov Group after May 1968, Godard has made increasingly frequent and fruitful contact with militant workers' groups.) Second, Godard criticizes the bourgeois-sociology approach to cinema, in which the film-maker shows the misery of the masses but does not show their struggles. (While this criticism is made in the voice-over commentary, we see a number of shots of shantytown houses and of modern high-rise apartment buildings like the ones Godard photographed for *Deux ou trois choses que je sais d'elle,* which film he has referred to as "a sociological essay.") The trouble with this approach, as well as with *cinéma vérité,* it is asserted, is that by not showing the struggles of the masses one weakens their ability to struggle; and the implication is that the cinematic image of their misery simply reinforces their own self-image of misery, while the cinematic image of their struggles conversely reinforces their ability to carry on the struggles. Finally, it is pointed out that contemporary cinema in Russia ("Brezhnev-Mosfilm") is perfectly interchangeable with contemporary cinema in America ("Nixon-Paramount"), so pervasive is the bourgeois ideology of cinema; and, moreover, that the two of them together are perfectly interchangeable with what passes for "progressive" cinema at the avant-garde film festivals throughout Europe. These so-called "liberated" films, it is asserted, are revisionist because they do not question the bourgeois cinema's relations between image and sound, and because, although they have broken the old bourgeois taboos on sex, drugs, and apocalyptic poetry, they have continued to uphold the most important bourgeois taboo of all—that which prohibits the depicting of *class struggle.* (Self-criticism is clearly implicit in this statement too, since the same reproach could be made—and has been made by Godard himself—to all of his own films up to and including *Weekend.*)

But Godard's self-criticism does not arise out of morbid self-doubt, defeatism, or an urge for self-destruction, as Glauber Rocha argues in his article on *Vent d'Est.* On the contrary, self-criticism plays a large part in Godard's current cinematic practice (and, for that matter, it always has—at least implicitly) for the simple reason that Godard (along with Mao) considers self-criticism a *constructive* activity of the highest order. Self-criticism is a way of opening ourselves out of a competitive, self-assertive approach to problems that concern us all, of helping to assure that we do not simply impose our views on others by the sheer force of personality or the power of office. (And in the cinema, as we have seen, this kind of check on the almost unilateral power wielded by the film-maker over his audience is urgently needed.)

Godard's recent films are politically pointed, to be sure; but although the verbal commentary is prominent, if not preeminent, the films are not exhortatory. There is nothing demagogic in Godard's approach either to cinema or to politics. A film like *Vent d'Est* is at the opposite pole in cinematic method from either Riefenstahl's *Triumph of the Will* or Eisenstein's *Potemkin*. And for that matter, Godard's *British Sounds, Pravda,* and *Vent d'Est* are far removed in cinematic method from Glauber Rocha's *Black God and White Devil, Land in a Trance,* and *Antonio das Mortes*. There is a strong messianic tone in Rocha's films that is very alien to Godard's way of constructing a film. (It is quite clear, by the way, that Rocha's outstretched arms in *Vent d'Est*—suggesting a parallel between Rocha and Christ—constitutes Godard's ironic comment on the messianic aspects of Rocha's film style.)

And while both Rocha and Godard are committed to the worldwide struggle for revolutionary liberation, they clearly differ about how revolution can develop and how cinema can contribute to that development. Rocha takes the spontaneous approach and largely discounts the importance of theoretical concerns, which he considers mere "auxiliaries" to the spontaneous energy of the masses. He has expressed his belief that "the true revolutionaries in South America are individuals, suffering personalities, who are not involved in theoretical problems . . . the provocation to violence, the contact with bitter reality that may eventually produce violent change in South America, this upheaval can come only from individual people who have suffered themselves and who have realized that a need for change is present—not for theoretical reasons but because of personal agony."[20] And Rocha emphasizes his belief that the real strength of the South American masses lies in *mysticism*, in "an emotional, Dionysiac behavior" that he sees as arising from a mixture of Catholicism and African religions. The energy that has its source in mysticism, Rocha argues, is what will ultimately lead the people to resist oppression—and it is this emotional energy Rocha seeks to tap in his films.

Godard, on the other hand, rejects the emotional approach as one which plays into the hand of the enemy, and he seeks to combat mystification in any form, whether it comes from the right or the left. While there is no indication that Godard underestimates the importance of the agonized personal experience of oppression as a starting point for the development of revolutionary consciousness, he takes the position that solidly developed organization on sound theoretical foundations is urgently needed if the revolutionary movement is to advance beyond the stage of abortive, short-lived, "spontaneous" uprisings (like the May 1968 events in France).

And in emphasizing the theoretical struggle, Godard follows in the path of no less a practical revolutionary than Lenin himself, who, in his pamphlet entitled *What Is To Be Done?* (echos of which abound in *Vent d'Est*) roundly castigated the "cult of spontaneity" and pointed out that "*any* cult of spontaneity, any weakening of the 'element of lucid awareness' . . . *signifies* in itself—*and whether one wants it this way or not is immaterial*— *a reinforcing of the influence of bourgeois ideology*" (Lenin's italics).[21] Or, as Lenin puts it a few lines further, "the problem poses itself in these terms and in no others: bourgeois ideology or socialist ideology. There is no middle ground (for humanity has never set up a 'third' ideology; and, in any case, where society is torn by class struggle, there could never be an ideology above and beyond class)."[22] And, later, "but why, the reader asks, does the spontaneous movement, which tends towards the direction of the least effort, lead precisely to domination by bourgeois ideology? For the simple reason that, chronologically, bourgeois ideology is much older than socialist ideology, that it is much more thoroughly elaborated, and that it possesses infinitely more means of diffusion."[23] And, finally, "the greater the spontaneous spirit of the masses, and the more the movement is widespread, then all the more urgent is the necessity of the utmost lucidity in our theoretical work, our political work, and our organizing."[24]

(This latter statement comes closest to Lenin's later qualification of the position set forth above and adopted in *What Is To Be Done?*, which position, as Lenin indicated, was a tactical response to a concrete situation—the 1902 squabbles among diverse factions of the Russian left. Later, when the potential dangers of the spontaneous position were no longer so much of a threat to the revolutionary cause, Lenin toned down the attack on spontaneity and called for a more dialectical approach of "organized spontaneity and spontaneous organization.")

Lest anyone be tempted, however, to jump to the conclusion (which Rocha seems to encourage in his *Manchete* article on *Vent d'Est*) that the differences of opinion on revolutionary strategy between Godard and Rocha are simply the result of cultural differences between the European situation and that of the Third World, it should be pointed out that even in Latin America—and in the Latin American cinema—there is nowhere unanimous support for the spontaneous approach espoused by Rocha. In fact, Latin American film-makers are increasingly, it seems, following the lead of Argentine film-maker Fernando Solanas *(La Hora de los Hornos)* in calling for an intensification of the organized and lucid theoretical struggle at the level of ideology. (See Chapter 9.)

By way of a conclusion, let us pick up once more the crossroads metaphor. Godard's path—which, as he points out, is simply the path that study of the history of revolutionary cinema has helped him to recognize—is the path of creating the theoretical foundations of revolutionary cinema within the day-to-day practice of making films. In short, the real dilemma for film-makers today is not a choice between theory and practice. The act of making a film necessarily combines both—and this is true whether one makes films in the Third World, in Russia, or in the West.

In the crossroads sequence in *Vent d'Est*, there is even a strong visual suggestion that the threeway intersection is simply the point where two paths—that of the Third World and that of the European cinema—converge and join together in what is really one big ongoing path of "aesthetic adventure and philosophical inquiry," which, by necessity, combines both theory and practice.

8

Godard / Gorin / The Dziga Vertov Group: Film and Dialectics in Pravda, Struggle in Italy, and Vladimir and Rosa

Critically injured in June 1971 in a near-fatal *quartier latin* motorcycle accident, Godard pulled through six anxious months of hospitalization and was almost literally pieced back together in the course of several operations and skin grafts.

Appropriately, the film he and Jean-Pierre Gorin made following his convalescence bears the title *Tout Va Bien (All's Well)*—a title which they originally intended, long before Jean-Luc's accident, as an ironic comment on the self-satisfied optimism of bourgeois society. But the title has also picked up a very literal sense of well-being now that Godard has successfully recovered from his injuries and is back to work. For Godard, now in his forties, *Tout Va Bien* is his twenty-fifth feature film in thirteen years and the seventh film he has made collectively under the aegis of the Dziga Vertov Group.

With Godard and Gorin indicating that they plan to do a number of projects individually in the immediate future (although still planning to do certain other projects collectively), it would seem useful to undertake a retrospective look at the previous body of work issued by the Dziga Vertov Group.

Let us try to determine, then, what characterizes the films of the Dziga Vertov Group? Since I have already dealt with the first, *British Sounds* (in Chapter 6), and the third, *Vent d'Est* (in Chapter 7), I shall here concentrate on *Pravda, Struggle in Italy,* and *Vladimir and Rosa*—the second, fourth, and fifth. Before discussing these films, however, a word should be said about *Till Victory,* Godard and Gorin's film on the Al Fatah liberation struggle in Palestine, which, had it been released, would have been their sixth and most ambitious film to date. Unfortunately, however, a number of problems have arisen which have caused Godard and Gorin to hold grave reservations about their film's analysis of the Palestinian situation—and, consequently, they have decided to withhold release of the film in its present form. Shot in Palestine during spring 1970—at a time when the collapse of King Hussein's rule in Jordan seemed imminent and Yassir Arafat's Al Fatah organization seemed to have consolidated its position of leadership in the liberation struggle—*Till Victory* was to have been a *défense et illustration* of how the Fatah movement's thorough, patient, and systematic planning and organization made it a model of revolutionary preparedness. The sudden turn of events which saw Hussein's troops rout the Palestinian guerrillas in fall 1970 and decisively in spring 1971, however, came as a great surprise and disappointment to Godard and Gorin —as well as to many international observers.[25] When I spoke with Gorin about *Till Victory* in Paris in summer 1971 he acknowledged that this setback at the practical level of revolutionary struggle was forcing him and Godard to take a long self-critical look at the theoretical analysis which led them to ally themselves with the Al Fatah position. Pending this auto-critique —which, of course, had to await Godard's recovery from the accident—*Till Victory* was to remain in limbo. Their present plan is to transform the Palestinian film into a critical and self-critical analysis of how (and how *not*) to film history in the making.

All the films of the Dziga Vertov Group are fairly difficult to get to see. Even in America, where distribution rights have often been sold in advance as a means of raising the money to make each film, the Group's films have had very short commercial runs and have been limited for the most part to the university circuit. In France it has been even more difficult to get to see them, for Godard has refused to release them commercially, and outside of an occasional screening at the Cinémathèque, the only opportunities to see these films have been screenings set up for groups of militant workers or militant students' organizations. (The arrangements for such screenings have been handled by the editors of *Cinéthique*, the highly influential journal of Marxist-Leninist film theory in France.)

The reason for this relative exclusiveness is fairly simple, and it is related to Godard's reasons for deciding to work collectively in the first place: in bourgeois capitalist society, art, like everything else, is above all a *commodity*—and the reputation of the artist is largely what determines the value of a work of art. But this value based on the artist's reputation is almost solely an *exchange value:* the art market, and, to a great extent, our art criticism (which is an appendage of the art market) do not take up the question of the *use value* of a work of art; or, if they do, it is only in terms of the decorative potential, the status potential, the investment potential, or—for the intellectuals—the work of art's potential for enabling us to *see* something in a new light. The way in which art is a product of class struggle, and how in each historical period and in each of its many stylistic trends, art is useful to the ruling class as an ideological tool that disseminates values (e.g., contemplation rather than action) that serve to perpetuate ruling-class power and privilege—such considerations of *use value* are taboo. What is emphasized instead, and what builds an artist's reputation, is *a distinctive personal style.*

Originality, novelty, uniqueness, and individuality are the highest goods of bourgeois art; and these qualities, when conspicuously or flamboyantly displayed, are taken as emanations of genius. Moreover, since Marcel Duchamp, it is not even necessary that these qualities be manifested in the *execution* of a work of art; for Duchamp, though seeking to destroy the cult of the artist as creative genius, merely shifted our attention from execution to *selection* of a work of art. Although his ready-mades seemed to negate the values of bourgeois art by asserting mass production instead of originality, commonplace familiarity instead of novelty, easy duplicability instead of uniqueness, and anonymity instead of individuality, in the end the bourgeois values were dramatically reinforced, although shifted in their focus, by the simple fact that Duchamp's act of operating a reversal of the values inherent in a work of art could itself be reversed and turned back into a demonstration of the most brilliant originality, novelty, uniqueness, and individuality . . . *not in the work of art itself but in the mind and sensibility of the artist!* The old adage *"le style, c'est l'homme"* thus attains its apotheosis in bourgeois art: since a distinctive personal style is seen to be an emanation of the artist's unique sensibility, the bourgeois artist can flaunt his unique sensibility merely in the selection of what he chooses to designate— and has the personal flair to impose on the critics and the art market—as "art" (e.g., Duchamp's toilet and Warhol's Campbell's soup cans). In short, bourgeois art, like bourgeois society, functions on the principle of the apotheosis of the individual. To be famous, i.e., to be instantly recognized as a distinctive individual, is, as Warhol himself pointed out, the great bourgeois dream.

By working collectively and withholding his personal "signature" (the art consumer's guarantee of "originality"), Godard challenges this glorification of the individual, and by deemphasizing the exchange value of his reputation, Godard attempts to shift the film-goer's attention to the use value of a film. But what is the use value of a film? Significantly, in asking this question we run up against a train of thought which permeates bourgeois idealism's thinking on art, namely, that what makes art so special, so wonderful, is that art is the one human endeavor which has *no practical use* [sic] and thereby "frees" man from the "vulgar" material exigencies of life and allows him to function in the "higher" realm of the spirit. A correlative of this idealist contempt for man's material needs is the notion that art, true art, deals with eternal and universal values of the human spirit and that a concern for the specific issues that urgently confront us in our everyday life has no place in art, or, if it does find a place, is considered an intrusion which weakens the value of the work of art as art. (Witness, for example, the cautions, qualifications, and criticisms offered by American Brecht scholars.)

In short, the dominant idealist thinking on art has the effect of eliminating from art or limiting to a very minimal level what is disparagingly referred to as "politics." Art is treasured, on one hand, for offering man the "free" exercise of his intelligence and imagination, but he is free only to exercise his intelligence and imagination on timeless and universal values (particularly on the world of sentiments) that are untainted by politics. Is this pervasive devaluation of politics accidental? Or does the history of class society indicate that time after time and place after place art has been in the service of the ruling-class elites, of pharaohs and priests and emperors and kings and popes and dictators and presidents and philanthropic industrialists, who have held positions of power and privilege in society and who have recognized the *use value,* to *them,* of keeping people's attention diverted from questioning the existing order by providing them with *art?*

And so, interestingly enough, when we ask what is the *use value* of a film or of any work of art, we must also ask *for whom* —and also, unfortunately, *against whom*—art has use value in a class society. Where film is concerned, Godard has found it necessary to reconsider the audience his earlier films reached and to ask himself whether, realistically, that audience of "art buffs" could be expected not only to recognize the class nature of the film art but also to take a class stand *with* the exploited classes in attempting to transform film art into something that would be useful to those working actively, theoretically, and practically, for profound revolutionary social change. Obviously, Godard realized that by no means all—and most likely only a very small minority —of his old art-house audience could be expected to undergo this radicalization, so deeply ingrained were the sophisticated prejudices of idealist aesthetics. Consequently, having decided to make it difficult for the old audience to co-opt his new films, Godard started by refusing to allow the new militant films to be shown in the old temples of the art film. Moreover, Godard and

Gorin purposely have made it difficult for any carry-overs from the old audience to relate to the new militant films in the old idealist way, for they want, above all, to use art in a new and revolutionary way that will no longer cover up the class divisions of society and the struggle between the classes but instead will call attention to and aggravate class contradictions by sharpening the line of demarcation between classes and between those willing to involve themselves actively in class struggle and, on the other hand, those not willing to do so. Toward this end, *the Dziga Vertov Group's films throw out a challenge to each spectator to confront the reality of class struggle and to take a stand in it.*

And the challenge is a tough one. The Marxist-Leninist and Maoist slogans which turn so many people off are abundant in these films, and they are embedded in voice-over texts which, to many film-goers, seem to drone on tediously or to rant abrasively. Audiences accustomed to bourgeois movies which emphasize entertainment or "art" are certainly not going to dig hearing lengthy analyses of revisionism or of ideology or of the need to struggle against bourgeois individualism. And they'll couch their objections in terms of our sacrosanct aesthetics—"politics have no place in art"—or in terms of our so-called intellectual objectivity —"I'm willing to discuss these ideas rationally, but, please, no slogans!"—or, finally, on our self-indulgent demand to be entertained—"it's boring"—but all too often these attitudes merely represent some of the dodges by which the bourgeois conscience conveniently rationalizes its avoidance of issues which challenge the political status quo. Whether they are confronted with these issues elsewhere or not, they resent being confronted with them in art, of all places, and walk out—often during the film—feeling self-righteously indignant.

However, it is by no means the unpoliticized spectator who gets turned off by these films. Aware that a radical posture is fashionable these days, especially among youth, Godard and Gorin have carefully tried to avoid eliciting the facile, ego-tripping spectator response of simply shouting "Right on!" at the appropriate signal. In particular, the dogged persistence of the voice-over texts—delivered in monotone—in the Dziga Vertov Group's films presents a calculated obstacle aimed at separating the superficial, posturing radical role-player from the serious individual who is willing to do the work of exploring and acting upon the issues presented in the films.

It's the latter, finally, the actively committed Marxist-Leninist or Maoist militant, for whom the films of the Dziga Vertov Group are made.

The point is worth emphasizing, for there has been a lot of confusion over just whom these films are intended to reach. Much of the confusion has stemmed from those who assumed that since the films take a class stand with the working class they must be made for workers; and from this point discussion has degenerated into the old impasse "but will workers be able to understand these films, aren't they too intellectual for workers?" But Godard and Gorin have argued that their films are not for workers in general, for some vague "masses," but rather are for specific groups of militants, some of whom are workers, some of whom are students, some of whom are simply full-time activists, but all of whom can be expected to involve themselves in the theoretical and practical exploration of issues presented in the films. Moreover, Godard and Gorin have pointed out that it would be presumptuous on their part to make films *for* the masses or even *on behalf of* the masses. Coming from the petit bourgeois milieu, they acknowledge that they do not have the kind of working-class experience of oppression that would enable them to deal with the day-to-day experience of the worker, particularly the worker who has not yet developed a class-conscious analysis of his own oppression and alienation. Nonetheless, what they can do to help bridge this gap is to begin to work cooperatively and collectively with small groups of militant workers and students and film people who can learn from one another's experience, can exchange information, can begin to share experience by undertaking group projects, and can develop their revolutionary theory and practice simultaneously.

How has this worked out thus far? Well, the planning stages of each of the Dziga Vertov Group's films have involved lengthy discussions with various militant groups which Godard and Gorin have been in constant contact with for several years now. Moreover, the interaction has been reciprocal: the various militant groups have often discussed the planning stages of their actions with Godard and Gorin. When I asked recently if these militant groups were involved in the shooting and, particularly, the editing stages as well as the planning stages of the Dziga Vertov Group's films, Gorin replied that, yes, to a certain extent, they were, especially since he and Godard are firmly committed to Vertov's insistence that editing is a three-stage process that begins with "editing before the shooting" and includes "editing within the shooting" as well as the final "editing after the shooting." In this sense, then, even groups like the Palestinian guerrillas, who could obviously not be present in Paris for the "editing after the shooting" stage, can be said to have played a part in the editing process. And this is by no means mere playing with terms, for Godard and Gorin have repeatedly emphasized that unlike other militant film groups such as Newsreel or Chris Marker's SLON or the French CGT labor union film group of Paul Seban, the Dziga Vertov Group rejects the "reflection of reality" notion of the cinema and therefore refuses the "go out and get footage" approach (la chasse aux images) which invariably emphasizes the "you are there" immediacy quality of events at the expense of a thorough analysis of the causes, effects, relations, and contradictions of events.

Pravda: A Dialectical-Materialist Theory of Knowledge

This rejection of the facile emphasis on immediacy is most evident in Godard's Pravda (a film, by the way, which marks a transition in the Group's work, since Godard planned and shot the film in collaboration with Jean-Henri Roger, discussed and debated the editing of it with Jean-Pierre Gorin, and ended up putting the final cut together entirely on his own)—for Pravda is as much a film on how to get at truth (pravda), particularly in the

cinema, as it is a film on the post-Dubcek situation in Czechoslovakia, where it was shot in spring 1969, the year after the
Russian armed intervention there. What is ultimately at stake in
Pravda—and in the Dziga Vertov Group's work as a whole (as
well as in the work of the Group's namesake)—is the attempt to
elaborate and implement in cinematic terms *a dialectical-materialist theory of knowledge.*[26]

The first section of *Pravda* presents various images and sounds
which Godard's voice-over commentators simply refer to as "external manifestations of the Communist reality and the Communist irreality in Czechoslovakia today." The methodology of this
opening session, they acknowledge, is that of a "political travelogue," and the voice-over text is in the form of a "letter to a
friend back home." (Hence, as in Montesquieu's famous *Lettres
Persanes*, the procedure of utilizing the point of view of a complete stranger who finds himself in a foreign country has the very
constructive and ironic effect of helping us to see "as if with new
eyes" things we might otherwise take for granted.)

In *Pravda*, however, the "new eyes" with which we see Czechoslovakia are not meant to be the eyes of just anybody—and in
fact Godard clearly wants us to consider that the act of developing a point of view which will enable us to comprehend the
situations presented (in the film as in life) is above all *a mental
act* in which (despite the eminently visual metaphor of *point of
view*) the act of seeing is not necessarily the primary one and
may indeed be far less constitutive of a point of view than the act
of listening to the spoken word. Throughout his films, Godard has
continually explored combinations of visual or aural preeminence,
weighing the relative usefulness and reliability of the cinematographic image and the spoken word. Sometimes, especially
in the early films, Godard seemed to find the image more trust-
worthy than the all-too-fickle word; more recently, however, as
his investigations (starting with *Le Gai Savoir*) have led him to
probe more deeply into epistemological questions, the spoken
word has clearly asserted its preeminence in his films as the conceptualizing element in attaining knowledge.

In *Pravda,* for example, the conceptualizing point of view is established not by the image (which gives one point of view only in the perceptual sense) but by the spoken words of the man whose voice we hear addressing his letter to "Dear Rosa." His name is Vladimir, and we quickly realize that the point of view of the stranger in Czechoslovakia is that of Vladimir Ilyich Lenin returning to earth to take a look at the progress of socialism and jotting down his impressions (and the analysis of those impressions) in a letter to "Dear Rosa"—an obvious allusion to Rosa Luxemburg, with whom Lenin, in fact, carried on a famous correspondence.

And what Vladimir sees in contemporary Czechoslovakia doesn't look at all like socialism to him! ". . . TV girls wearing cashmere sweaters . . . billboards for large American corporations in the fields along the highways . . . neon signs advertising Russian trains . . . tanks, yes, tanks to watch over the peasants . . . wire fences the government puts around everything which is the private property of the people . . ."—all these are part of the concrete situation in Czechoslovakia. But, as Vladimir admits, these images and sounds are not enough: the material in this first section of *Pravda* is really just a travelogue like any other—"like Delacroix in Algiers or Chris Marker in the strike-torn factories of Rhodiaceta. *The New York Times* and *Le Monde* call it news. And I agree with you, Rosa, that it isn't enough. Why? Because it's only the knowledge perceived by our senses. Now one has to make the effort to rise above this perceptual knowledge. One needs to struggle to transform it into rational knowledge."

This task, then, is undertaken in the second section of *Pravda.* While the travelogue could only serve to present fragments of "the concrete situation in Czechoslovakia," the second section presents an attempt to develop "the concrete analysis of the concrete situation."

Vladimir tells us of renting a cart at the Prague airport—the red car we see in the images. "And guess who we rented it from?" asks Vladimir. "Just as in Moscow, Warsaw, or Bucharest, we rented it from an American company. Hertz or Avis. Two

branches of American banking or chemical trusts." And he goes
on to explain that the car is a Skoda, manufactured in Czechoslovakia at the factories nationalized in 1945 by the popular
democratic forces after their victory over fascism. "Produced in
nationalized factories, the Skoda belongs, then, to the Skoda
workers—the car should be at the service of the people who produced it. But Hertz and Avis don't rent cars out of good will;
they do it for profit. And, deviously, with the complicity of the
Czechoslovak leaders, Hertz and Avis have *appropriated* what
should rightfully belong to the Czechoslovak people. Moreover,
the appropriation of *surplus value*—theoretically eliminated in
socialist countries—makes its ugly reappearance. And, practically,
the more the socialist workers of Skoda work, the more the imperialist shareholders fill their pockets."

What we're dealing with here, Vladimir remarks, is *revisionism in practice.* But Czechoslovakia's reintroduction of various
features of capitalism is only one side of the coin of revisionism—
and the other is Russia's willingness to accommodate the capitalist
West while tightening her bureaucratic stranglehold on the socialist East. And who is always the victim of revisionism? In
Moscow, as in Prague, it is the worker who suffers the oppression
of the bureaucrats who are supposed to serve him. "Once the
people have put them in power, the revisionists devote all their
energy to keeping the people—especially the working class—out
of power. . . . The revisionist bureaucrats, like all reactionaries,
are afraid of the people, that is why they make use of police
terror. Just as in the capitalist countries, the ministry of the in-
terior becomes the ministry of oppression."

Equally unsparing of its criticism of both Moscow-style revisionism and Prague-style revisionism, *Pravda* neither justifies
nor decries the Russian armed intervention in Czech affairs in
August 1968: that is not the major issue. And what little documentary footage Godard uses of Soviet tanks in the streets of
Prague is not at all utilized for its dramatic you-are-there quality;
rather, this material, like the rest, is presented simply as "external
manifestations" which need to be organized in the editing so as

Pravda: going beyond you-are-there immediacy

Pravda: art in class society . . . For whom? Against whom?

Pravda: "The cinema is a theoretical rifle."

Vladimir and Rosa: "Find the images that oppress us in order to destroy them."

Struggle in Italy: images of consumption and production separated by ideological "black spaces"

to "establish a new contradictory relationship between them . . . and to bring into light the internal causes . . . of the present situation in the socialist republic of Czechoslovakia."

The methodology of the film, then, is to move constantly back and forth from practice to theory and from theory to practice. Following step by step the process of acquiring knowledge outlined by Mao Tse-tung in his essay "On Practice," *Pravda* begins with the practice of gathering perceptual knowledge, but the voice-over commentators *immediately* sense the inadequacy of this travelogue approach and therefore undertake *right from the start* the theoretical task of transforming perceptual knowledge into conceptual knowledge. And as soon as judgments and inferences have been drawn, theory is tested and developed . . . *in practice.* And, of course, practice constantly creates a new concrete situation which requires a new transformation of theory to produce new knowledge of each new situation. In short, as I have indicated, what is at stake here is a dialectical-materialist theory of knowledge in which, as Lenin argued somewhat crudely in *Materialism and Empirio-Criticism* and with more sophistication in his *Philosophical Notebooks,* consciousness is always "consciousness of some thing," i.e., there is no "ideal" realm of "pure thought"; and knowledge is not disembodied knowledge of the "essence" of *things-in-themselves* but is rather *a dialectical process of interaction, of work,* between man and man and between man and things. Thus, as Marx so incisively put it, man experiences the world not in order to understand it but to *transform* it.

Likewise, Godard's films are aimed not at helping us to understand the world as a *given* but to understand and affirm our inescapable role of constantly transforming it. Consequently, his films resolutely avoid the detached "eye of God" point of view, and instead openly affirm the work and struggle of the film-maker (Vertov's "man with a movie camera") who is involved himself in social practice and the relations of production just like everyone else.

Finally, as important as the epistemological concerns may be in *Pravda,* no discussion of this film is complete without a consideration of how Godard explores issues through his use of color and movement. Right from the beginning, Godard utilizes the colors and movements of Prague's streetcars as a means of calling our attention to one of the film's basic issues—the task of distinguishing the shades and nuances of different types of socialism and the different directions in which they are moving.

"We are in a socialist country," says Vladimir; "whoever says socialist says red. The red of the blood spilled by the workers for their emancipation. But there was fighting between the different kinds of red. Between the red which comes from the left and the red which goes off toward the right." And as we hear this commentary, we see in the image a busy street in downtown Prague; but suddenly a bright red streetcar comes into the frame from the left, blotting out all depth perception as it fills up nearly the entire screen. The streetcar comes to a halt, its red panels sliding slowly to a stop and revealing slightly orange areas where the red paint is chipped and fading. After a moment's pause, slowly, then quickly gathering speed, the red panels of the streetcar begin sliding off toward the right, their blemishes disappearing again as the streetcar's movement blurs the details so that one sees only the dominant red. But what is behind that unified façade? The seeds of doubt have been planted. Is there a connection between the fact that the red of socialism is beginning to look faded and blemished and the fact that this same red of socialism, here in Czechoslovakia, is moving toward the right?

Granted, of course, we are operating here at a transparently symbolic level, but Godard's artistry is such that he takes cinematic structures that are aesthetically interesting in themselves (like this shot's organization of color, line, plane, and movement) and builds out of these structures a rich cluster of connotations that both deepens the aesthetic experience and at the same time refers us back out of the internal structures of a work of art into the world of social practice. Instead of merely using the red streetcar shot for its combination of "local color" and abstract beauty (which is how Chris Marker uses an almost identical shot in his *Sunday in Peking*), Godard takes these elements as starting points—eminently cinematic ones—and links the abstract to the concrete while transforming the superficial aspects of local color into conceptual tools for probing deeper into the "red of socialism" in Czechoslovakia.

Throughout the film the color red serves as a focal point for highlighting the contradictions of revisionism: repeated shots of a lovely dark red rose—associated with the blood of the workers as well as with "red" Rosa Luxemburg and the "purists" of socialist theory—give way at the end of the film to a shot of that same rose lying trampled in the mud. And the spilling of the workers' blood in their struggle for liberation—referred to early in the film—gives way to the spilling of a glass of rosé wine carelessly poured to overflowing: a symbol of the callous betrayal of the workers (and of socialist principles) by a privileged and elitist bureaucracy. But perhaps the most telling use of color to highlight revisionism's contradictions is so *material* that it is hardly symbolic at all: over a fuzzy shot of an off-red neon sign advertising AGFA film in downtown Prague, Vladimir apologizes for the poor quality of the color, explaining that "it's West German film processed in Soviet labs."

Another recurring image in *Pravda* is a high-angle long shot of a circular tramway interchange where the streetcars of Prague come into the frame from the upper right, proceed leftward around the circle, discharge their passengers, and proceed out to the upper right again. Near the end of the third section of *Pravda* —placed in a crucial position just before the beginning of the brief lyrical coda that terminates the film—the circular interchange is seen for the last time, while on the sound track we hear the following exchange:

> Rosa: *Toi aussi, tes réponses tournent en ronds et nous n'avançons pas.* [You too, your answers are going around in circles and we're not making any progress.]
> Vladimir: *C'est en tournant en ronds que nous avançons.* [It's in going around in circles that we make progress.]

At one level, metaphorically, the circular streetcar interchange is a graphic representation of the reversal of direction in revisionist Czechoslovakia: the reversal of the red of socialism, moving left with the masses, then leaving the masses behind and moving off to the right again. But at another level, also metaphorically, Vladimir's defense of going around in circles alludes to the circular structure of the film as a whole and to the circular process of moving dialectically from practice to theory back to practice in a constant testing and development of theory (knowledge) as well as a constant transformation of the world (practice). This seemingly offhand defense of circularity—placed in the mouth of *Pravda's* Vladimir—corresponds with Lenin's own notion (it is Hegel's as well) that "human knowledge is not (or does not follow) a straight line, but a curve, which endlessly approximates a series of circles, a spiral." Or, as Mao puts it, "Practice, knowledge, again practice, and again knowledge. This form repeats itself in endless cycles, and with each cycle the content of practice and knowledge rises to a higher level. Such is the whole of the dialectical-materialist theory of knowledge, and such is the dialectical-materialist theory of the unity of knowing and doing."

Struggle in Italy: Man's Social Being Determines His Thinking

Continuing their Marxist investigations, Godard and Gorin focused their attention, in *Vent d'Est* (*Wind from the East*) and *Lotte in Italia* (*Struggle in Italy*), on the nature and function of *ideology*—an area which has recently been very fruitfully explored by French Marxist philosopher Louis Althusser. In fact, while planning *Struggle in Italy*, Jean-Pierre Gorin held frequent discussions on the problem of ideology with Althusser, who was then writing his essay "*Idéologie et appareils idéologiques d'état.*"[27] It is not surprising, then, in light of this cross-fertilization of ideas, that the Dziga Vertov Group's *Struggle in Italy* (this time, it is primarily Gorin's work) and Althusser's essay on ideology are as alike as fraternal twins.

This fraternal relation of film and essay, however, has its drawbacks as well as its strengths. Although the central protagonist of

Struggle in Italy is a young Italian girl who, at the beginning of
the film, declares herself "a Marxist and a member of the revolutionary movement," nonetheless, and in spite of its title, the film
is *not* concretely based in any specific situation in Italy or anywhere else. Indeed, it is a film that could have been shot anywhere
(much of it was shot in Paris), for it is about a situation that
supposedly exists *everywhere* in the advanced industrial capitalist
world. On the whole, then, *Struggle in Italy* is a purposely abstract
didactic film on the difficulties a young militant girl from a
bourgeois background must overcome to rid herself of the ruling-
class ideology which permeates her consciousness and behavior.

We see in the first part of the film various aspects of her daily
life, identified by a male voice-over commentator as "militancy,"
"university," "society," "family," "sexuality," etc. The various
"post card" glimpses of her handing out leaflets, going to class,
trying on sweaters in a store, monopolizing the bathroom in her
family's flat while putting on her make-up, making love, etc., all
represent, as she later acknowledges, "a bourgeois account of a
bourgeois woman who is in contradiction with herself." Inter-
spaced among these admittedly superficial images are lengths of
black leader which, we gradually realize, represent gaps in her
consciousness—"black spaces" which must be filled in with
images that reflect the true nature of her relations to the class
society in which she lives. The central problem is that man's
knowledge of "reality" is, by reason of his historical position in
class struggle, "*a necessarily distorted reflection of his relation to
production.*"

It is, of course, the essence of Marxist thought that "man's
social being determines his thinking"—and, of course, in Marxist
terms the most important constituents of "social being" are man's
relations to production. A given mode of production, like capitalism for example, will entail certain "relations of production"—
which relations must be *reproduced* constantly, day after day, by
inculcating in individual consciousness values and a world view
that "reflect" these dominant relations of production. This task of
reproducing the "relations of production," as Althusser points out,

is largely carried out at the level of *ideology,* i.e., by the State's various "vehicles" of ideology. What happens, according to Althusser, in each of these vehicles, is that the individual's real relations to the relations of production are distorted because they are short-circuited into a relation to an Absolute: in the schools, Learning; in church, God; in the courts, Justice; in politics, The Party; in labor organization, The Union; in the communications media, The Facts; in art, Truth and Beauty; and in the family, Proper Behavior. As a result of this ideological short-circuiting, then, an individual's world view is not a representation of his real relations to the relations of production which ultimately govern his existence, but rather a representation of *imaginary* relations to his real relations to the relations of production. In short, Althusser argues, "ideology equals imaginary relations to real relations."

For Paola Taviani, the student militant of *Struggle in Italy* (played by an actress of the same name), the attempts to break out of bourgeois ideology are acts of life-style rebellion: thus in the second part of the film she tries to "get to know the working class" by striking up a conversation about revolutionary politics with a young salesgirl who waits on her as she tries on sweaters; she tutors a young male worker in mathematics, hoping thereby to "serve the working class"; and she attempts to "revolutionize" her sex life, as well, by arranging with her boyfriend to make love in the afternoon instead of at night as they usually have done. But this, too, she realizes, reflects her class privilege: workers can't afford such a luxury; they have to work all afternoon.

Sensing that her efforts thus far have still been marked by a bourgeois mentality, Paola takes a job in a factory. But she is not accepted by the women who operate the other sewing machines: she obviously comes from a different background, has different manners, and is suspect. Why should a pretty young bourgeois girl want to work in a factory? Why should she want to "join the working class"? Finally, the crowning blow comes when she realizes she is not even able to keep up the crushing pace of productivity demanded by the shop foreman.

Trying to analyze these failures, Paola asks herself just what reality or aspect of reality is "reflected" in each of her acts? And she concludes that "the problem is not one of 'reflection' in general, but of *the struggle between reflections which deny the objective contradictions and reflections which reveal and express them:* the struggle between bourgeois ideology which wants the world to stay like it is and revolutionary ideology which wants to change it."

Applying this insight to her own actions, Paola realizes that the various images from the first and second parts of the film have covered up the contradictions because they have reflected only one of the two terms of the objective contradiction. The second term has always been missing—it has been a "black space," a taboo that has remained repressed and inaccessible to her bourgeois consciousness. Now, however, her increased level of consciousness—which, through practice, is more closely aligned with the class consciousness of the working class—enables her to reveal and express the contradictions by filling in the gaps. Thus the film repeats images from the first and second parts, but now a shot of Paola trying on a sweater in a boutique is not followed by "black space" but by a shot of the manufacturer's workshop where the sweater is made. Consumption is no longer something accomplished in a void; it is related to the relations of production. As other images are repeated, they too are complemented now by images of the relations of production.

These shots of factories, workshops, delivery trucks, etc. do not offer solutions in themselves; but they help Paola to understand that these "relations of production," which, as she remarks, in Italy today are "specifically capitalist relations of production," have been "reflected" in even the least suspect areas of her consciousness and behavior. And this "reflection" has been subject to the ideological distortion which substitutes *imaginary* relations to production for the real ones which have conditioned her social being and her thinking.

But now that Paola has seen through this ideological distortion, the film does not come to an end. Godard and Gorin make it clear that heightened awareness is not an end in itself. It is not enough merely to understand the world; the real task is to change it. Nonetheless, the achievement of class consciousness and the struggle to pierce the veil of bourgeois ideology play an important role in the revolutionary transformation of the world. As the male voice-over commentator of *Struggle in Italy* puts it, "We must recognize that at a certain point in the revolutionary struggle, the most important task is *theory.*" Moreover, the importance of ideological struggle must not be underestimated: Engels, one will recall, attached such importance to it that he maintained (in a famous passage of a letter to Franz Mehring) that seeing through bourgeois ideology would destroy it. For ideology to function effectively, he argued, it had to remain *unconscious.* "Otherwise," he remarked, "the whole ideology would collapse."

But in *Struggle in Italy* Godard and Gorin have dealt only with the struggle of one individual to see through bourgeois ideology. For Paola Taviani this ideology may indeed collapse; but the larger task which the film engages is that of *bringing ideological struggle out into the open* where each individual can begin to discover for himself his real relation to the process of production. In line with this task, then, Paola defines the path she must take: "To make a change in my life, to bring about a transformation in myself, means heightening the contradictions between my militant practice and the dominant bourgeois ideology. It means bringing class struggle into my personal life."

Finally, flaunting the state-owned RAI-TV network in Milan, for whom *Struggle in Italy* was made—and who subsequently refused to show it—Godard and Gorin close the film by having Paola sing the first verse of *The Internationale* while the male voice-over commentator declares repeatedly that the future will be a future *di lavoro e di lotta:* of work and struggle.

Vladimir and Rosa: Theater as Revolution, *Not* Revolution as Theater

Although at first viewing the insistent comedy of *Vladimir and Rosa* seems to set this film somewhat apart from the theoretical explorations of the previous Dziga Vertov Group films, nonetheless, in its own humorous way *Vladimir and Rosa* takes up the issues defined at the close of its immediate predecessor, *Struggle in Italy:* the necessity of heightening the contradictions between one's militant practice and the dominant bourgeois ideology by bringing class struggle into one's personal life, and thereby *changing one's life.*

There has been much talk, of course, about "life-style change" and the rise of a "counter-culture" in which each aspect of an individual's appearance and behavior can be interpreted—and is often consciously intended—as a *sign* of that individual's rejection of the "straight" life-style. Among certain segments of the counter-culture there is even a special prestige attached to being a "heavy," someone who flaunts the conventional *mores* outrageously with his or her bizarre, and often very theatrical, appearance and behavior. Indeed, the theatricality of everyday life in the polarized America of the late sixties is a subject that has been much discussed; and I suppose the prevailing attitude toward this phenomenon is a negative one: people seem to feel that theater should be clearly separated from real life.

Old prejudices against the theater, a certain moral stigma attached to the profession of actors and actresses, and perhaps a mixture of fear and envy which the ordinary individual experiences when confronted with people who have a gift for acting out the extraordinary, the full gamut of human passions—all these are undoubtedly involved, even if unconsciously, in people's attitudes on this matter. Then, too, there is a tendency to believe that the polarization of society itself is responsible for the theatricalization of everyday life—an attitude which critically fails to understand the very considerable theatricality that is involved in acting out social roles in even the most homogeneous societies.[28]

But the demand for a strict demarcation between theater and reality is expressed, very outspokenly, by Robert Brustein, who, as a man of the theater, ought to know better. (Brustein is a drama critic, a director, and dean of Yale Drama School.) Seemingly unaware of the irony of his position, Brustein bristles at any theatricality outside of the theater; and, once he has spotted any, refuses to see anything below the surface of theatricality. This leads him to think he can dismiss the Black Panthers for their "public-relations-conscious paramilitary costumes"—thus writing them off as "mere" theater. And, on the other hand, he so thoroughly misunderstands the point of the Chicago Seven's theatrical defense tactics that he offers the admittedly "terrible judicial overkill" of that trial as demonstrating that theatricality is counterproductive. In short, while justifiably indignant at the market-oriented revolutionary posturings of entertainers and the fashion-oriented revolutionary posturings of "the radical chic," Brustein utterly fails to understand, or even, it seems, to examine the various functions which theatricality can perform outside as well as inside the theater.[29]

And it is precisely such an examination that Godard and Gorin undertake in *Vladimir and Rosa,* a film which reenacts, very theatrically, the theatrical antics of the Chicago Seven. In this film Godard and Gorin take all sorts of artistic liberties with the facts of the Chicago trial—like including two young women among the defendants—but they very faithfully retain the hilarious Yippie tone of the proceedings: and in many ways *Vladimir and Rosa,* for all its levity, qualifies as a reconstituted documentary. Focusing, as it does, on a much-publicized trial, it even has an illustrious antecedent in Méliès's theatricalized reconstruction of the famous Dreyfus trial. And in this sense, *Vladimir and Rosa* is part of Godard's continuing reflection on the cinema's way of getting at truth through a dialectical synthesis of the fictional and the real.

Although the *commedia dell'arte* style of this film would seem to put the emphasis on the fictional aspect, Godard and Gorin are clearly interested in the *significance* of the Chicago trial—which they see manifested in the defendants' theatrical ways of carrying out their defense. Moreover, they sensitively distinguish a number of different defense styles in the trial: the rollicking and outrageously carefree style of Abbie Hoffman and Jerry Rubin, the more serious analytical approach of the dedicated militants among the defendants (here Godard undoubtedly has in mind Tom Hayden), the more traditional "bleeding liberal" approach taken by David Dellinger and his attorney William Kunstler (identified as "John Kunstler" in the film), and, finally, the dignified rage of Bobby Seale (identified as "Bobby X" in the film) as he stands up for his legal right to serve as his own counsel—a right denied him by Judge Hoffman (the film identifies him as "Judge Himmler"), who ordered Bobby bound and gagged for his "disorderly" refusal to give up his rights.

These different defense styles, as interpreted by Godard and Gorin, represent the respective defendant's willingness or unwillingness to make a thorough break with the system. Thus, the Yippies' break is demonstrated by their scorn for normal legal procedures and their refusal to treat the legal system with the fear and reverence which the repressive order demands of its subjects. On the other hand, Bobby Seale's break is demonstrated by his cool and courageous stand in provoking the system to reveal that in America "justice" is selective, that blacks cannot even expect the courts to let them utilize in their defense what few rights they are supposed to have. As for the dedicated militants in the trial, the film seems to understand implicitly why their actions at the trial seemed pale and insignificant compared to Abbie's and Jerry's antics and to Bobby's determination: namely, the militants' main task is *organization,* and that task requires patience and discretion rather than public flamboyance. (In the film one of the militant defendants talks of his organizing work in factories.)

Contrasted to these three positions, however—all of which demonstrate different ways of making a clean break with the system—is the William Kunstler-David Dellinger approach, which Godard and Gorin label *une mise-en-scène bourgeoise, style comédie française,* and which they liken to the stuffy, traditional legal defense put forth in France recently by the otherwise intensely militant editors of a Maoist workers' paper called *La Cause du Peuple.* "Although the people being tried in Paris had been working in ways leading to a new conception of political action," Gorin explains, "they were not acting in a new way in the trial itself." Likewise, Dellinger and Kunstler might express their criticisms of the American political and legal systems, but their courtroom procedure—polite, learned, and formal—could be seen as largely a product of their bourgeois background and their liberal humanist respect for *some* legal process, even if it was a thoroughly corrupt one. In short, as Godard puts it, "they hadn't radicalized themselves yet."

Throughout the film the emphasis is on the way one *acts,* for the film's basic thesis seems to be that our relationship to the repressive system around us is demonstrated in our way of *acting* —and the theatrical metaphor is particularly appropriate for that eminently theatrical situation known as a trial. In this sense, then, if revolution seems theatrical, it is not, as Brustein argues, because revolution has become (mere) theater, but rather because theater too is a way of making the revolution. As Brecht put it,

> We are concentrating on theater precisely because we wish to prepare a means of pursuing our affairs via the theater too. We must not be led by the urgency of our situation to destroy the means we want to make use of. The more haste, the less speed. The surgeon who has heavy responsibilities needs the little scalpel to lie lightly and easily in his hand. The world is out of joint, certainly, and it will take powerful movements to manipulate it all back again. But among the various relevant instruments there can be one that is light and delicate and needs to be handled with ease.

In *Vladimir and Rosa,* as in the Chicago trial itself, the theatrical style is predominantly one of slapstick comedy. In fact, this is a film that might well have been made by the Marx Brothers—Groucho, Chico, Harpo, Zeppo . . . and *Karl*—with the whole gang on trial not for rioting or even inciting to riot, but for "conspiracy to incite to riot." Much of the humor in this film comes from the antics of Godard and Gorin themselves, for they are on screen quite a lot either as Yippie defendants (they seem to have cast themselves as Abbie and Jerry, though Jean-Luc stands trial as "Friedrich Vladimir" and Jean-Pierre as "Karl Rosa"—whence the film's title) or in their equally humorous role as film-makers attempting to "make political film politically." Early in the film they stammer their way through a self-interview carried out on a tennis court (Jean-Luc pacing up and down on one side of the net with headphones and a directional mike; Jean-Pierre on the other side lugging a tape recorder), with both men oblivious to the tennis balls whizzing by them (and occasionally bouncing off them) from the game of mixed doubles being played on that same court.

In addition to their stammering and stuttering, Godard and Gorin adopt zany accents throughout the film that make French come out sounding like a mixture of Portuguese and German. In their self-interview on the tennis court—the subject of which, naturally enough, is how to make political film politically—they make a series of puns on the word *balles* (alternatively "balls" . . . as in "tennis balls," "bullets" . . . as shot from guns, and "balls" . . . as in the French equivalent of small round candy drops), and Godard stammers that *le ciné-mama* (that's the best pun of them all) also shoots bullets . . . sugar-coated bullets that can be deadly. But the essential problem for them, as militant film-makers, he explains, is how to render in images *la rupture*— the break with the system. And one way to do it, he suggests, is "to find the images that oppress us in order to destroy them." And in that sense, the image we see at that very moment is a good illustration of what Godard is talking about, for this shot juxtaposes the bourgeois complacency and leisure of the tennis players, on one hand, with the *work* and *struggle* (both class struggle and struggle for the means of cinematic production) of the militant film-makers. Later in the film, Godard again takes up the notion of the film-maker's break with the system, and he makes the voice-over comment that "one can't be content just to break with *narrative*"—a self-critical reference to an earlier stage of his own development on the way to making political film politically.

As the film progresses, however, the humor takes a decidedly vulgar turn (as Groucho's was known to do occasionally)—especially when Godard and Gorin detail an elaborate "shit-eating test" they recommend for determining whether prospective jurors are racists, or when they don police uniforms and do an agitprop demonstration of police brutality by having Jean-Luc unzip his fly and pull out a huge phallic billy club. Finally, there is a lame but amusing in-joke on the Dziga Vertov Group's characteristic inclusion of sections of "black leader," which they triumphantly identify in this film as signifying the involuntary absence of a real "black leader," Bobby Seale, of course, who was forcibly separated from the rest of the defendants during the Chicago trial and ordered to stand trial alone at a later date.

In spite of the rough spots, however, the comic tone of *Vladimir and Rosa* is refreshing. (As Brecht wrote, "A theater that can't be laughed in is a theater to be laughed at.") For one thing, it indicates that far from losing his sense of humor in the process of becoming radicalized, Godard has just as keen a wit as ever. Moreover, far from relegating humor to some private area of his life where revolutionary firmness might momentarily be relaxed, Godard clearly has a healthy recognition that humor can be an effective weapon in the revolutionary struggle. And that's a lesson not every would-be revolutionary has learned, I'm afraid.

And on the larger question of the function of theatricality in the struggle for revolutionary social change, *Vladimir and Rosa* demonstrates Godard and Gorin's sensitive understanding of the very significant revolutionary uses of theatricality both in the Brechtian sense, in the theater, and in the Abbie Hoffman-Jerry Rubin sense, in the streets. Whether in changing your consciousness or in changing your life-style, theatricality can have an important role to play—and, as film-makers seeking to make political films politically, Godard and Gorin clearly intend to continue their explorations into the dialectics of theater and life, art and reality.

9

Tout Va Bien *and* Letter to Jane:
The Role of the Intellectual
in the Revolution

Asking questions instead of giving answers, learning to listen to others—these are the modest, even self-effacing revolutionary virtues Godard and Gorin attempt to practice in *Tout Va Bien,* the latest and perhaps the last (at least for a while) of their collective films. Yet even as they talk of working separately (and of quietly dropping out of film-making in order to experiment with videotape), they have also collaborated on a companion-film to *Tout Va Bien*—a unique "film-letter" entitled *Letter to Jane,* which is directly addressed to Jane Fonda, who "co-starred" in *Tout Va Bien,* but is also indirectly aimed at all intellectuals and artists who seek to serve the cause of revolution.

As usual, contradictions abound in the work of Godard and Gorin. The film-makers, of course, are well aware of the contradictions; and for the most part they deal with them, dialectically, in ways that manage to be illuminating. However, somewhere in the complex set of relations between the parent film, *Tout Va Bien,* and its offspring, *Letter to Jane,* there may be contradictions that Godard and Gorin are not fully aware of, or at least contradictions they have not yet dealt with as productively as they might. In any case, some of the questions raised by these two films seem to indicate that Godard and Gorin, however insightful their films may be, are working themselves into a corner where they are more and more isolated and alienated, even from those who, perhaps with less apparent sophistication but with equal dedication, are also working to serve the cause of revolutionary liberation.

Let's start with some material concerns. After four years of making low-budget 16mm films as "theoretical exercises" for "a handful" of Marxist-Leninist and Maoist militants, Godard and Gorin decided to make a political film for a much wider audience. To obtain financial backing for such a film, they reasoned, they would have to use some big-name "stars." So they contacted Jane Fonda and Yves Montand, who not only filled the bill as stars but also as an actress and an actor who each were known for their support of liberal, even progressive political causes.

Fonda and Montand were interested; and on the basis of the box-office potential of the two international stars, Paramount Pictures put up the money to produce *Tout Va Bien*. For Jane Fonda, however, the decision to accept a role in a film directed by two men was not an easy one for her to make, as she was ardently calling for women to work with other women and to make their own films. Nonetheless, because she was sympathetic to the political concerns of Godard and Gorin (and an admirer of Godard's films), she agreed to work with them in *Tout Va Bien*.

The shooting went well, although Fonda found Godard distant and uncommunicative; while Godard's and Gorin's version of the story is that Fonda and Montand, the two big names, remained aloof from the rest of the cast, mostly nonactors who were enjoying themselves in a collective spirit of creative invention. Nevertheless, the shooting was completed, the film was edited, and Paramount Pictures decided not to take up their option to distribute *Tout Va Bien*. Godard and Gorin found other distributors, and the film was released in France, where it had a fairly good commercial run.

Invited to show *Tout Va Bien* at the New York and San Francisco film festivals in the fall of 1972, Godard and Gorin brought along with them *Letter to Jane*. They explained that they had made the 16mm film for only $300 in a few weeks of work and that they wanted it to serve as a starting point for discussion of *Tout Va Bien.*

Letter to Jane is one hour long, and for most of the film all that we see on the screen is a photograph of Jane Fonda. The photo was taken by American photographer Joseph Kraft during Ms. Fonda's much-publicized trip to Hanoi in 1972. It was released for widespread circulation by North Vietnam's government-operated news agency; and it appeared in the Paris weekly magazine *L'Express* in the first week of August 1972, accompanied by a text written by the staff of *L'Express.* The sound track of *Letter to Jane* consists of the voices of Godard and Gorin analyzing the photo and its accompanying text.

The film-makers acknowledge that an analysis of a photo of Jane Fonda visiting Hanoi might seem like a roundabout way of discussing *Tout Va Bien,* a film that deals with the political situation in France; but they argue that it's a detour that enables them to confront directly and very concretely the problems explored in *Tout Va Bien.* They acknowledge, too, that one might ask if this isn't in some way a disclaimer regarding *Tout Va Bien,* an admission of failure to confront things directly and concretely in that film. But Godard and Gorin argue at the very outset of *Letter to Jane* that they are by no means disavowing *Tout Va Bien* or avoiding discussion of its relative merits. In any case, they point out, both *Tout Va Bien* and *Letter to Jane* deal with the same fundamental question: what is the role of the intellectual in the revolution?

In *Tout Va Bien,* which is a scripted and acted fiction film with a nominal narrative "plot" ("an account for those who take no account" or "a story for those who shouldn't still need one" are roughly the twin meanings of a cryptically punning intertitle), Jane Fonda and Yves Montand play husband and wife media intellectuals. She is an American doing political commentary broadcasts for the Paris office of an American radio network. He is a French new wave movie director radicalized by May 1968: having realized that the art market for avant-garde films is just another annex of capitalism's consumer-society, he has given up making "art" and turns out advertising commercials to make a living.

As the so-called plot gets under way, he accompanies his wife on an assignment to visit a meat-packing plant to discuss labor problems with the plant manager. Once there, however, they find that the manager, and indeed the whole plant, are unexpectedly "occupied" at that moment by wildcatting workers unhappy with both the management and the unions.

In a very Brechtian way, however, the narrative of their encounter with life in a factory is not presented as a continuous narrative at all, but becomes a juxtaposition of confrontations—first with the manager, then with the union representative, then with the workers. Shot head-on, with the actors delivering little set-speeches directly into the camera, these confrontations are aimed at us in the audience, forcing us to confront the respective elements and alignments of power in capitalist industry.

The plant manager tries to gloss over the present difficulties and fatuously suggests that Marx's writings are passé now that, in his view, class struggle has been superceded by "the collaboration of the classes in order to find permanent material progress." The union representative admonishes the wildcatting workers to get back to work, even threatening them with disciplinary action; and he tries to convince them that the problem is more complex than they think, and that they should let the union officials handle it. But the workers themselves express their gut-level feelings of frustration and pent-up resentment at constantly being told to cool their anger while someone else—the management and the union officials—promises solutions that never solve anything.

Ultimately *Tout Va Bien* seems to make the point that it's precisely the experience of being frozen out of any power to make decisions vitally affecting one's own life that constitutes the most alienating and intolerable condition of the worker's existence. Moreover, as the film emphasizes, it's not just factory workers who are alienated in this way. The Fonda and Montand characters begin to see how they, too, are systematically alienated and exploited in their respective work situations. And they begin to see

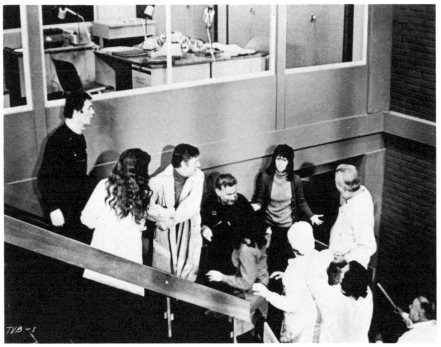

Tout Va Bien: Jane Fonda protests that she had an appointment to interview the manager.

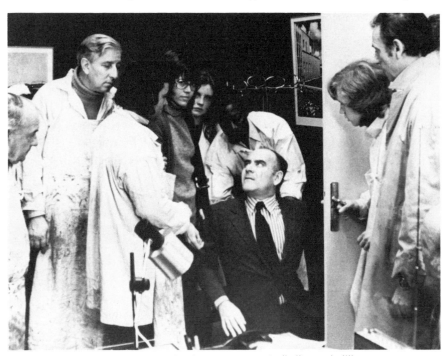

Tout Va Bien: The boss and the whole plant are unexpectedly ''occupied!''

Tout Va Bien: Yves Montand as an ex New Wave director now turning out commercials

Tout Va Bien: Jane Fonda explaining that in class society not even sex is all that simple

how their private life as a couple offers no refuge from the alienated work-relations that cast an ominous shadow over their ways of relating to each other.

Significantly *Tout Va Bien* ties up none of the loose ends of the narrative. We don't learn how the situation at the meat-packing plant develops. (We can guess, however.) Nor do we learn whether the deteriorating relationship between the Fonda and Montand characters can be saved. The film closes with the admonition to "let each individual create his own history"—a call not for individualism of the bourgeois stripe but rather for the revolutionary transfer of power to the people themselves so that history will no longer be the domain of leaders and representatives but the exercise of each individual's power over his own social practice.

And it's precisely this emphasis on "power to the people" that Godard and Gorin find blatantly missing from the news photo (and accompanying text) depicting Jane Fonda's visit to Hanoi in 1972. In *Letter to Jane*, therefore, they give what amounts to an illustrated lecture in which they analyze this photo and text, pointing out what they consider reactionary connotations within the image itself and in the combination of image and accompanying words.

They make the following specific critical observations:

(1) Jane Fonda dominates the foreground of the picture while an unidentified Vietnamese is overshadowed in the background. This composition, Godard and Gorin argue, makes the famous American actress the star of the photo while relegating the Vietnamese people to a secondary role. In reality, however, the star of the struggle in Vietnam is obviously the Vietnamese people, while a representative of the American left is obviously a secondary character.

(2) The caption states that "Jane Fonda questions the citizens of Hanoi about the American bombings" when in fact it is evident from the photo that Jane Fonda at that moment is *listening* to the Vietnamese man whose back is turned to the camera in the lower right foreground of the frame. This inaccuracy, Godard and Gorin argue, is no mere accident. Among other things, it's a question of who rightfully has the initiative in this encounter between an American movie actress and the Vietnamese people. The film-makers suggest that Jane Fonda ought to have emphasized that she was there to *listen* to the Vietnamese, that as an American her proper role was to shut up and let the Vietnamese people explain what they sought to accomplish.

(3) The camera angle is itself strongly "loaded" with reactionary connotations: it is a low-angle shot that makes the person photographed look "larger than life." It is the camera angle Orson Welles used to make Kane look imposing, and, they add, "the fascist Clint Eastwood is always shot from a low-angle" to produce this same imposing effect.

(4) Of the two persons whose faces are shown in the photo, Jane's is in focus while the face of the Vietnamese man in the background is blurred and out of focus. This, too, of course, helps make Jane the star of the photo. But Godard and Gorin point out that in terms of visual metaphors it ought to be the other way around: the anonymous representative of the Vietnamese left ought to be in sharp focus because his position is sharp and clear, whereas the famous representative of the American left ought to appear fuzzy in the photo because the position of the American left is fuzzy and unfocused.

(5) The expression on the face of the actress/militant is tragic, but it can apply to many different situations. Here Godard and Gorin show photographs of a similar expression on Jane Fonda's face in *Klute* when she asks the detective to take pity on her and stay the night, and in *Tout Va Bien* when she listens to the factory workers. They also show photos of a similar expression on actor Henry Fonda's face in *The Grapes of Wrath* and *Young Mr. Lincoln*. Then they show a photo of John Wayne with a similar expression on his face in *The Green Berets*. And one cannot fail to get the point that John Wayne's attitude toward the Vietnam War was diametrically opposed to Jane Fonda's attitude, but that

the same expression served both of them. Ultimately, Godard and Gorin argue, the expression lacks any specific content. It is devoid of sense while seeming to be heavily laden with profound sense. Like bourgeois humanist art in general, it covers up its emptiness with an appearance of fullness.

(6) If *L'Express* can characterize Jane Fonda's position on Vietnam as "pacifist," it is probably because Jane's own conception of her role as a "militant for peace" is vague and oversimplified. Simply calling for "peace in Vietnam" is not enough, they argue, since it does not deal with America's imperialist intervention in the rest of the world's affairs and therefore overlooks the reason for the fighting in Vietnam in the first place. Nor does it deal with the vital question of peace on whose terms?

On the whole, there is something very impressive about Godard's and Gorin's detailed analysis of a single photograph. In many ways their critique is a remarkable tour de force. But there is also something very disturbing about it.

Part of the problem is that Jane is singled out for criticism as if she were personally responsible for each aspect of the photograph and its accompanying text. Godard and Gorin acknowledge of course, as the text itself does, that the photo was taken by Joseph Kraft and released for circulation to the press by the North Vietnamese government-controlled news agency. Nonetheless, they argue that in going to North Vietnam Jane ought to have thought out more carefully exactly what image she should project.

Then, too, it is unfortunate that the commentary of *Letter to Jane*, spoken by Godard and Gorin themselves, hardly makes its points in the clear and concise manner outlined above but rather belabors them in a verbose and smugly condescending way. In fact, the rhetorical overkill of *Letter to Jane* smacks of an unfortunate "more radical than thou" kind of one-upmanship. Jane Fonda is thoroughly put down and Godard and Gorin appear to have all the answers. And, coming in the aftermath of Jane's professional contribution to the making of *Tout Va Bien,* their rebuke of her seems to function as a kind of parental scolding,

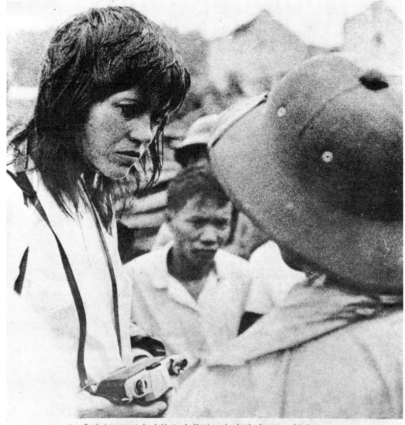

RETOUR DE HANOI

Jane Fonda interrogeant des habitants de Hanoi sur les bombardements américains.

Letter to Jane: the *L'Express* photo criticized by Godard and Gorin

as if Godard and Gorin were self-righteously demanding of Jane, "After all we've taught you, how could you possibly have gone out and made so many thoughtless mistakes?"

Moreover, if one considers *Letter to Jane* in terms of sexual politics, there is something even more disturbing about the film that goes beyond its mere condescension to and patronization of Jane. In fact, when Gorin showed a print of *Letter to Jane* to Yugoslav film-maker Dusan Makavejev (who directed *WR: The Mysteries of the Organism;* see Chapter 13), Makavejev's response to Jean-Pierre was that the film amounted to "a double rape—two men taking turns assaulting one woman."

There is indeed some of the character of a rape involved, for in *Letter to Jane* the woman, in effect, is pinned down on the screen, held there (in front of thousands of onlookers), and forced to submit to two men wielding the phallic power of *langue,* of language, of the Word. And the old sexist dualisms seem to be invoked: the male annexes mind as his domain (Freud called attention to the identification mind/phallus) and asserts the active power of his logic over the passive body (and mere *intuition*) of the woman. Significantly, Godard and Gorin depict Jane as having her *heart* in the right place (she shows pity) but as being too frail of *mind* to think things through very well.

Are they really right in *Letter to Jane,* and is Jane really guilty of making thoughtless mistakes? In terms of revolutionary struggle, both in Vietnam *and* in America, stopping the American bombing of North Vietnam was a vital objective. For the North Vietnamese it was a matter of survival. For Americans it was a question of whether the people were going to let their political and military leaders exercise unchecked and brutal force to annihilate a whole country. In going to Hanoi at the invitation of the North Vietnamese government, Jane Fonda had a very important and very politically delicate role to play. American opinion back home would certainly not be favorable toward her or the plight of the Vietnamese if she were to spout pro-Communist slogans and vilify American imperialism while in Hanoi. But American opinion could be moved by a woman's plea for an end to the horrible destruction of human life that was resulting from the American bombings of the hospitals and schools and dikes of North Vietnam.

Jane Fonda could—and did—accomplish far more by presenting herself as a "militant for peace" than she could by taking a more explicitly revolutionary stance. And the "tragic" expression on her face in the widely circulated news photo succeeds in "bringing the war home" in a way that is both genuinely moving and ideologically "correct." For in Jane's grave expression we see the heavy weight of responsibility we as a people bear for the atrocities committed in our name against the Vietnamese people. And it is we, through Jane, who become the star of that photo; only, like Jane at that moment, we find that confronted with reality our role in Vietnam isn't very glamorous. The tragedy in Vietnam is ours, and that's precisely the realization that was necessary for the American people to use their will and strength to force their leaders to stop both the bombing and the American intervention in that country.

The main problem with Godard's and Gorin's revolutionary line in *Letter to Jane* is that it is divorced from any concrete situation. It is an abstract line, all the more dangerous for its impressive militancy. Godard and Gorin may argue that they are taking the long-range view, that one must never lose sight of the long-range objectives, but they seem so caught up in the revolutionary purity of their overall view that they themselves lose sight of events taking place in the immediacy of the here and now.

Throughout their collective work, there is something disturbingly fastidious about Godard's and Gorin's systematic rejection of immediacy. They may justify it in terms of Lenin's rejection of the "spontaneous" approach to revolution; but it seems to go way beyond that. And, in any case, Lenin knew how to keep sight of the long-range goals while never losing his perspective on the immediate situation.

Perhaps control is the issue. Godard and Gorin, unlike Lenin, seem afraid to put themselves in situations they can't control. Thus, art becomes the one refuge where they can exercise maximum control. Life, however, is too elusive, too much in constant flux, too messy to permit the kind of control that they are accustomed to exercising in their art. And in some ways they appear to acknowledge as much in *Tout Va Bien*, where control is not exercised in the same way that it is in their other films.

Not that *Tout Va Bien* is exactly brimming with you-are-there immediacy; quite the contrary, it is an extremely stylized and schematized film. Even the meat-packing plant that has been momentarily occupied by wildcatting workers is not a real meat-packing plant but a specially designed studio set enabling Godard and Gorin to emphasize the schematization of their presentation. Thus, the absence of a fourth wall makes it possible for the film-makers to back off and shoot tracking and panning shots across a cutout view of the two-storied plant as a whole. And these shots are used as long, reflective "breaks" in the narrative, distancing us from the story just as they physically distance us from the scene of the action.

Moreover, symbolically the two-storied plant evokes the classical Marxist description of society being built on the economic foundations of the working class's labor while the ruling-exploiting class occupies the upper level of the superstructure. Except that in *Tout Va Bien* the workers have rebelled against this state of affairs (as Marx said they would) and have occupied, at least for a time, the whole works.

However, one striking difference between *Tout Va Bien* and the other films of Godard and Gorin is that here, for a change, their schematization is not so drastically concentrated in the Word. In fact, *Tout Va Bien* is not *logocentric* at all. The *tyranny* of the Word that marks their other films here gives way to a *materialist mise-en-scène* solidly rooted in *things*. And this change of emphasis from words to things is marked not only by the absence in *Tout Va Bien* of Godard's and Gorin's habitual reliance on a heavily rhetorical voice-over commentary; it is marked also by a change in the way words are tested against the concrete reality of things.

In a way it seems that Godard and Gorin have remembered

the lesson taught by Godard's Emily Brönte character in *Week-end:* words often come between us and things, and it's important for us to get back to things themselves. Moreover, it's as if Godard and Gorin have begun to realize that the more formally rhetorical language becomes, the more it also becomes abstract.

With this in mind, it is interesting to compare the little set-speeches delivered in *Tout Va Bien* by the factory manager, the union representative, and the young red-haired working girl who tells Jane Fonda what it's like to be doubly exploited as a worker and as a woman. The manager's speech is by far the most abstract, full of glib generalities that cover things up rather than reveal things as they are. (Incidentally, Godard and Gorin didn't write this text themselves but simply lifted it from a tract entitled *Long Live the Consumer Society* by M. Saint-Geours.)

Likewise, the speech of the union delegate (this text lifted from the Communist Party's CGT union magazine, *La vie ouvrière*) is also highly abstract in spite of his display of facts and figures, or maybe precisely because of it. As one of the wild-catting workers comments later in the film, the union officials deal with a problem by trotting out a whole bunch of statistics, and pretty soon you lose sight of the problem; except that you know it hasn't been solved because the same things keep cropping up again and again. In any case, to the film-makers, as to many leftists in France, it is clear that the Communist Party and its huge CGT union are reformist rather than revolutionary, and that they function more to keep the workers in line *within* the system than to challenge and change that system.

By contrast, the set-speech delivered by the young working girl is for the most part very concrete. And although it, too, is a text lifted from a published article (in *La Cause du Peuple*, a Maoist journal that advocates wildcat strikes and other spontaneous acts of revolt), it is less formally articulated than the other texts. In fact, it is more like an outcry, or a sudden bursting into song. (And Godard and Gorin purposely call our attention to this quality of her speech by identifying it—in a repeated voice-over phrase—as "revolutionary song.")

As she talks, she sticks to material concerns like the fatigue the working girl experiences and the factory smells that permeate her clothing and her skin (and thereby make her an object of ridicule in a sexist and classist society that forces her to spend money for costly perfumes to make herself presentable). Her words may not seem all that revolutionary. Her outpouring of words is, like the action of momentarily occupying the factory, spontaneous. And Godard and Gorin have been telling us over and over that the spontaneous approach will never bring about the revolution. But at least in *Tout Va Bien* the film-makers seem to acknowledge that the revolution has to be rooted in strong feelings, and that sometimes these feelings lie too deep for words.

One of the tasks of the intellectual, however, might be to find the right words to express these feelings, to bring people together and unite them in a revolutionary movement to change things. And this, of course, is a task Godard and Gorin have devoted themselves to carrying out, not just in *Tout Va Bien* but in all their films.

In *Letter to Jane*, however, they seem to get carried away in the tide of their own rhetoric. And in doing so they throw up a screen of words between themselves and things, between themselves and Jane, between themselves and all the rest of us. Instead of uniting us and spurring us to take a direction, their words divide us and inhibit us from taking action. Perhaps Godard and Gorin need to be reminded that in revolution, as in life itself, actions speak louder than words.

part two

Film and Revolution
on Many Fronts

10

La Hora de los Hornos: *"Let Them See Nothing but Flames!"*

When the first explorers from Europe sailed along the southeastern coast of South America, they reported seeing fires by the hundreds blazing out from the dark silhouette of the land. To one particular stretch of coast at the southern tip of what is now Argentina, the Spanish explorers gave the name Tierra del Fuego—the land of fire.

What they saw from their ships were the *hornos,* or cooking fires, of the Indians who inhabited the region; and the sight of those fires blinking on, one by one, in the evening darkness, until they blanketed the horizon like a strange new constellation, struck the imaginations of those first explorers, curious and apprehensive as they undoubtedly were about the inhabitants of this new continent. Throughout the centuries, the expression *"la hora de los hornos"* (the hour of the cooking fires) has been used by the historians and poets of Latin America, and it has recently become an anti-imperialist rallying cry taken up by Che Guevara; in calling for a socialist revolution to sweep Latin America, he proclaimed "now is 'la hora de los hornos'; let them see nothing but the light of the flames." (Guevara was, of course, an Argentine.)

Under the title *La Hora de los Hornos (Hour of the Furnaces),* Argentines Fernando Solanas and Ottavio Getino have put together a remarkable film on the revolutionary struggle that they see as imminent and urgently needed in contemporary Argentina. Traveling all over the country, Solanas and Getino made contact with, discussed with, and eventually filmed most of those who are actively involved (clandestinely as well as openly, outside as well as within the "legal" institutions of Argentina) in the struggle for a revolutionary transformation of Argentine society.

At various stages in the film's growth, Solanas and Getino showed some of the footage to the different militant groups with whom they were working. On some occasions this brought about an invaluable exchange of information and discussion between far-flung and very diverse groups that had never gotten together before—or sometimes had not even known of each other's existence. Thus, the film inserted itself in the revolutionary praxis, and the revolutionary praxis inserted itself in the film, causing the film-makers to rethink again and again their conception of the film and their conception of the revolution. The making of the film and the making of the revolution became inseparable.

For those of us who are striving to come up with a working definition of revolutionary cinema, *La Hora de los Hornos* (along with Godard's latest films) may be the most fruitful subject we could focus our attention on at this moment. I say this not only because the very existence and structure of *La Hora de los Hornos* are rooted in the day-to-day practice of making the revolution, but also because such a tremendous variety of cinematic styles and materials have gone into this film. Solanas and Getino have, in effect, created a remarkable film-mosaic, in which each individual piece, as they conceived it,

> demanded its own particular expression that would transmit the intended ideological sense. That is to say, each sequence, each individual cell has a different style of photography or a different form. There are small cells which are little stories or narratives of their own; there are others which are· free documentaries; there are some which are made up entirely of montage and counterpoint; others are absolutely descriptive scenes; others are direct cinema; still others are something like a cinematographic carnival-song. The only way to unite all this material without it all falling apart, without falling into complete chaos, was to give each individual part its own form. So, from the camera work to the montage, it was necessary to find that form.[30]

Whether they succeeded in finding the proper form for each individual cell—or even for each major section—is debatable. But it is already a major step forward that Solanas and Getino had the courage to pose themselves such a difficult problem and had the courage to disregard normal distribution requirements (of length, among other things) in order to give a presentation of the political situation in Argentina that faithfully renders its complexity.

Four hours and twenty minutes long in the original version shown at Pesaro in June 1968, *La Hora de los Hornos* is divided into three major parts: the first (95 minutes) is titled "Violence and Liberation"; the second, "Act for the Revolution," is subdivided into two segments—a 20-minute "Chronicle of Peronism" on the ten-year reign (1945-1955) of Juan Perón, and a 100-minute sequel on the post-Perón period (1955 to the present) titled "The Resistance"; and, finally, a third section, shorter than the others (only 45 minutes), titled, like the first, "Violence and Liberation."

The first section of the film consists of thirteen "Notes on Neocolonialism" in which are presented various aspects (historical, geographical, social, economic, political, cultural, etc.) of Argentina and the way the world looks to an Argentine. Blessed with a relative abundance of natural resources, Argentina, we are reminded, has always attracted a great many immigrants from Europe, and has often been called "the great melting pot" of South America. With indigenous Indians numbering only 60,000, and *mestizos* (people of mixed Spanish and Indian descent) accounting for only 10 percent of the population, Argentina, more than any other Latin American country, is overwhelmingly composed of white European immigrants. In addition to the Spanish, Argentina also has an enormous population of people of Italian and German descent, as well as significant numbers of immigrants from other European countries and Great Britain.

Moreover, far from it's being the case that political independence from Spain (in 1816) brought any real economic independence to Argentina, on the contrary, this merely threw the country into the waiting arms of the British imperialists, who gobbled up huge chunks of Argentine land (as well as huge chunks of Argentine beef—the supply of which they monopolized); they built, owned, and operated Argentina's entire railway system; and they quickly assumed indirect control of Argentina's national economy. Finally, add to this already complicated "melting pot" phenomenon the leaden weight of American economic imperialism in the twentieth century, and one can begin to understand why, as the film emphasizes, the ordinary Argentine has little sense of national identity and has a way of looking at the world that is not really his own, but rather is—and always has been—a world view imposed on him by whichever colonial or neocolonial power happened to have Argentina in its clutches. And for the Argentine masses of workers and peasants, it hasn't really mattered who was calling the shots in Argentina, for the shots—live bullets—have always been aimed at their heads, as one ruling class after another resorted to violence and repression to keep the masses in their place and protect the power and privilege of the exploiting class. In short, as the French say, "*plus ça change, plus c'est la même chose*": whether the ruling class in Argentina was Spanish colonialist, British or American neocolonialist, or simply local bourgeois oligarchy, the experience of the Argentine masses has always been the experience of violence and repression.

The film gives a rundown of the myriad forms in which violence manifests itself in Argentina—the omnipresent police; the brutal repression of strikes; the innumerable military coups; the feudalism of the great *latifundia*; the oligarchies in industry and commerce (5 percent of Argentina's population "earns" 42 percent of the national revenue); the neocolonialism that perpetuates economic dependence (America owns 50 percent of Argentina's giant meat-packing industry, England owns 20 percent); the neoracism that goes hand-in-hand with neocolonialism; the Pentagon-trained and -financed "anti-insurrectionist force" which literally occupies certain parts of the country; and, last but not least, the cultural violence carried out systematically by the communications media, controlled by the local bourgeoisie, which impose

La Hora de los Hornos: ''Let them see nothing but flames'' Che

the consumer ideology of the advanced capitalist countries of Europe and North America on the illiterate and impoverished masses of Latin America.

Again and again in the film examples are given of the way in which aesthetic attitudes are geared to mirror the capitalist ideology of the imperialist ruling classes. European styles in painting, in literature, in film, in fashions; British and American styles in popular music and creature comfort: the only models of behavior held up to the Argentine masses are the models offered "for sale" by the neocolonialists. Ideologically, the masses are inculcated with the cultural values that lead them to desire the very things which serve to perpetuate their state of dependence, neocolonization, and exploitation.

But while showing Argentine neocolonialism for what it is, Solanas also presents an alternative—*revolutionary struggle*. And precisely because neocolonialism—unlike direct colonial rule by a single mother country—is such an amorphous, many-headed monster, the revolutionary struggle has to be waged *not* against a foreign aggressor, but rather *on class terms* against the Argentine bourgeois ruling class and the capitalist system and ideology[31] which, regardless of what particular national or ethnic group is in control at a given moment, perpetuate the exploitation and repression of the proletarian masses of Argentina. The struggle, then, is a *class struggle* for a socialist revolution in Argentina.

Intensely lyrical in its presentation, this first section of *La Hora de los Hornos* is a rather flamboyant but impressive exercise in montage, in which the viewer's emotions are manipulated quite sophisticatedly by the rhythmic cutting. Again and again, serving as a counterpoint to the neocolonialist reality in Argentina, short powerful quotations from Frantz Fanon force their way onto the screen as if hammered out, letter by letter, by some invisible typewriter, literally chasing from the screen the images of imperialism and proclaiming the urgent need for revolutionary struggle. Other quotations from various Third World sources (Fidel, Mao, the North Vietnamese, and numerous Latin American revolutionaries) serve to punctuate the various "notes on neocolonialism" and to

call for liberation movements to spring up everywhere that imperialism rears its ugly head.

In one sequence Solanas's slick montage juxtaposes flashy
zooms on a long-haired Argentine hippie playing a rock song on his
guitar and singing in American slang (an image which, in this context, demonstrates that even the models of "protest" and "dissent"
in Argentina are models provided by the imperialists) with austere,
grainy documentary footage (shot by Joris Ivens) depicting the
day-to-day struggle, determination, and dignity of the North
Vietnamese people, whose response to Western imperialism has
been the courageous taking-up of arms. And, finally, the revolutionary example closest to home and closest to the hearts of the
Latin American people—Castro's Cuba—makes its entry on the
screen of history and jolts the viewer with an emotionally stirring
and at the same time reflection-provoking shot—held for a full five
minutes—of the body of Che Guevara, whose electrifying presence, even when dead, is the clearest and strongest reminder that
"the task of the revolutionary is to make the revolution."

The second part of *La Hora de los Hornos* begins with an
attempt at confrontation between the film-makers and the audience. Solanas and Getino are seen opening up a dialogue with the
audience at a screening of *La Hora de los Hornos,* and Solanas's
voice—booming out from the amplifiers of the theater where we
ourselves are sitting—invites us to consider ourselves *not* as spectators of this film act, but rather as protagonists in an action that
must be perpetually renewed. And on the screen, in huge letters,
we read these words from Fanon:

EVERY SPECTATOR IS A COWARD OR A TRAITOR.

Then the screen goes dark and there is a moment of silence "in
homage to Che Guevara and to all the patriots who have fallen in
the struggle for Latin American liberation"; after which the film
opens up a new dimension of the social and political reality of
Argentina—a "Chronicle of Peronism" which, utilizing for the most
part actual documentary footage of the important events in the
ten-year reign of the controversial Juan Perón, not only serves to
inform the viewer (especially the badly misinformed or uninformed

European or North American viewer) about this extremely important epoch of Argentina's recent history, but also invites the viewer (Argentine or foreigner) to join the authors of the film in a critical reevaluation of the politics of Perón and of the significance of Peronism to politics in Argentina today.

And here (perhaps surprisingly, depending on one's familiarity with Argentine attitudes toward Perón) is where *La Hora de los Hornos* has really stirred up a confrontation with its audience and has detonated an explosive debate on a subject that most Argentines—whether on the right or the left—have invariably preferred to bury in embarrassed silence. It is interesting to note, however, that the violence of the reactions of many Latin American (and some European) viewers to this film seems to be in an inverse ratio to the degree of audience manipulation which the film's authors have built into their handling of the material. No one seems to have objected to the first and third sections of the film, which are constructed on a principle of rhythmic montage which is strongly manipulative of the viewer's emotions, playing on them with an ever-increasing rhythmic urgency, which at the end of the film culminates in the ecstatic "climax" of the singing of the incendiary song entitled "Violencia y Liberación" (composed by Solanas expressly for this film), while in the image we see the flaming torches waved by the impassioned Argentine masses (who, whether they have been "staged" or not in this particular shot—and it seems to me that they have—nevertheless have already been established as "authentic" by their presence in the clearly documentary footage we have seen earlier).

In the presentation of the Perón material, the voice of the commentary seeks only to raise questions, not to answer them, and asks only that the viewer face the reality of a period of Argentine history that the powers-that-be have tried to efface and to discredit. And when Solanas and Getino show the extraordinary footage of the Perón charisma—of his, and particularly of his wife Evita's, electric "touch" with the masses—it is not that they use this footage to glorify Perón or to stir up anew the incredible personality cult that surrounded him, but rather it is an effort to get the viewer to face the evidence, as they express it in the film, of "the first appearance on the stage of history of the Argentine masses as *masses!*"

In other words, the film's authors are simply saying "look . . . those are masses, Argentine masses . . . rallied together as a political force. Anyone who wishes to understand the political reality of Argentina—and especially anyone who seeks to formulate a political program in accord with the needs and will of the Argentine proletariat—must necessarily confront the existence of this phenomenon, analyze its constituent parts, and see which, if any, are usable in the political situation in Argentina today."

And the authors find that the phenomenon is much more complex than we have been led to believe by the people who have a vested interest in the reflex identification of Peronism with Nazism or fascism. What, in fact, were the policies of Peronism? The film delineates them. From its beginning in 1945, the Peronist movement set forth a program aimed at putting an end to Argentina's traditional economic dependence on colonialist and neocolonialist powers. Peron, of all people, was one of the first to speak of the "Third World" and to seek to raise Argentina to a position where it could stand on its own feet. Breaking Argentina loose from the British neocolonialism (which dated from 1823, when Argentina signed the first accords granting management of their national economy to the Baring Brothers British Bank), Perón in ten years nationalized Argentina's banks, introduced foreign currency exchange controls, nationalized all public services, established government direction of the national economy, developed Argentina's infant industry, rendered Argentina competitive on the world market, built up Argentina's woefully inadequate educational system, gave women the right to vote, and passed Argentina's first social legislation protecting the rights of workers and peasants. Moreover, as an internal political phenomenon, Peronism rallied the Argentine proletariat, which found in Peronism the expression of their needs and will which they had never been able to find in the various political parties tied to the liberal wing of the bourgeois oligarchy or in the moribund Argentine Communist Party headed by Victor Godovila.

In short, as the authors of the film explain, the ten years of Peronism, whatever their faults, marked the highest point achieved by the Argentine masses in their attempt to bring about a class-based transformation of the country. And if Peronism ultimately failed, it is not because the movement was headed in the wrong direction, but because it simply did not go far enough, and *could not* go far enough, given the movement's own internal contradictions: given, for example, that it was a movement with mass popular appeal, yet entirely directed by the bourgeoisie; and that precisely because the movement had a bourgeois leadership, it failed to identify clearly the class nature of its struggle, and therefore failed to recognize, until it was too late, just how dangerous an enemy was the local bourgeois oligarchy. The latter, seeing itself held in check by Peronism but not directly attacked, simply took the offensive itself and, with the help of the army, toppled the Perón government, which, although it had broad appeal among the masses, had failed to build—in, of, and for the masses—an organization capable of consolidating political power.

The fundamental class nature of the struggle is dramatically revealed in the images of the documentary footage: when the army bombs the presidential palace, it bombs as well the central thoroughfares of Buenos Aires where the proletarian masses are spontaneously demonstrating their support of Perón. Then, once Perón is deposed, the same streets are filled by the jubilant bourgeoisie, dressed up in their Sunday best (and accompanied by a conspicuously large contingent of the clergy), whose first act is to burn books in an attempt to efface all trace of Peronism from Argentine history.

But although Perón himself was forced into European exile, Peronism was by no means forgotten among the Argentine masses —as we see in the "notes and testimonies" on the post-Perón period in the next part of the film, entitled "The Resistance." Forced into clandestine activities and labor union struggles, the members of the Peronist movement—a movement now without a leader—begin to develop their political consciousness and to speak with a voice of their own. One by one, in front of Solanas's camera, unionists, workers, peasants, students, and intellectuals all testify to the need to continue the struggle for liberation begun by the Peronist movement, and to utilize the positive aspects of Peronism as the groundwork for that ongoing struggle.

In presenting this panorama of the evolution of Peronism from the time of the fall of Perón in September 1955 up to the moment of the making of this film in 1966, Solanas and Getino emphasize the intensification of the struggle in the last few years, which have seen numerous general strikes and massive occupation of factories and the holding of "bosses" as hostages, as well as increased revolutionary terrorism and sabotage (1,400 acts of political terrorism and sabotage in 1964 alone). Finally, denouncing strikes that remain at the level of opportunistic self-aggrandizement, and denouncing as well the myths of "legality" and "nonviolence" which the bourgeoisie promulgate as a way of repressing the proletariat on the level of ideology, an activist in the Tucuman uprisings—Andina Lizarraga, the leader of the Peronist Youth Movement of Tucuman—sums up the new revolutionary consciousness of the Argentine masses: in spite of their spontaneity and their spirit of opposition, if the Argentine masses do not systematically take up the arm of *violence* in their struggle for liberation, the initiative will inevitably remain on the side of the enemy. What is needed is positive action leading to the seizing of political power by armed force—and this action must be organized and led by the avant-garde of the proletariat.

On this powerful note, the middle and longest section of *La Hora de los Hornos* comes to a close, inviting the audience to pause for a few minutes and to discuss the issues that have just been presented. Then the lights dim once again and the third and shortest section of the film begins. Functioning as a finale in the musical sense—but taking care to emphasize that there is and can be no end to this film act until and unless it is the making of the revolution itself—the third section of the film presents two long interviews and the reading of a number of letters which Solanas and Getino received in the course of gathering material for the film. (One of the letters, proclaiming that "the only path . . . is armed struggle," comes from Camillo Torres, the Colombian priest who shed his collar to join the Colombian *guerilleros*, and who was subsequently killed by government troops.)

The first of the interviews is with a marvelously optimistic and determined octogenarian, who, stepping out of his shantytown cabin, begins by excusing himself for his poor education and then recounts all of the horrors of repression he has witnessed in his lifetime—repression first by the British, then by the Argentine oligarchy. He recounts the killings in Patagonia, the massacres of peasants, the brutal repression of strikes; but, spirit undaunted, he clenches his fist and affirms his conviction that the hour of victory for a socialist liberation of Argentina is drawing ever closer, and that the fight for that victory must be carried on against all odds.

The second interview, quite a bit longer than the first, is with Peronist labor organizer Julio Troxler, a soft-spoken and intelligent man in his late forties, who, revisiting the spot where he was captured by the Argentine military shortly after the fall of Perón, tells us of the tortures enacted on him, one after another, by some of Argentina's top-ranking military figures, and of the mass execution from which he miraculously escaped. Still pursued by the military, forced to move clandestinely from place to place, Troxler implacably vows that the struggle shall go on until the socialist liberation of Argentina is won.

Solanas and Getino then remind us again that this film act is open-ended, that it remains to be completed by the revolutionary praxis of every one of us, that new material will be added to the film as new chapters of the revolutionary liberation of Argentina make their entry into history. For the time being, projection comes to a stop with the dithyrambic song, "Violencia y Liberación," as flaming torches fill the screen.

Confronted with a film of such scope, such thoroughness, such courage, and such conviction, the viewer finds it difficult to hazard an appraisal of its aesthetic merits—especially when the film's aesthetic and political merits are so inextricably intertwined. Suffice it to say that if Solanas and Getino, in seeking the proper form for each individual cell of the film, intended each of the major divisions (and major subdivisions) to be capable of standing alone, then they did not fully succeed, for it is doubtful if any of the film's basic parts could be considered wholly satisfactory on their own. (And, in fact, when for one reason or another only the first section has been shown, critics in Europe have acknowledged that in spite of its insights this section is a bit too flashy to be considered anything more than a brilliant but inconclusive *tour de force*.) But this is not a major flaw, for *La Hora de los Hornos* is not made to be seen in separate pieces. In fact, the greatest strength of the film is precisely in the juxtaposition of so many different styles and so many different types of material. Placed side by side, they give us an idea and a feeling of the complexity of the situation in contemporary Argentina. And this is an excellent starting-point—both for making the revolution and for making revolutionary cinema.

//

The Ice-man Cometh No More (He Gave His Balls to the Revolution)

Robert Kramer's *Ice* is a "political film" that is not the least bit political. It is an emotionless film that is not the least bit rational. It is a documentary of an imaginary revolution—or, to put it another way, a fictionalized account of what people like the Weathermen have actually been doing—and yet despite its seemingly objective, emotionless, documentary tone, *Ice* is really a film of very personal (Kramer's?) fantasies and fears about revolution.

But *Ice* is also a forward-looking film that will undoubtedly be one of the most important American films of the coming decade. (To call it one of the most important American films of the *past* decade would, in my opinion, be damning it with faint praise.) *Ice* is light years ahead of the recent rash of Hollywood garbage on revolution. Whatever blind spots there may be in *Ice*—and there are deep ones—they are, for better or worse, the blind spots of the revolutionary movement itself—or at least that part of the movement which is actively engaged in terrorist activity and likes to think of itself as the "armed vanguard" of the revolution. (Incidentally, if we hadn't realized it before, *Ice* ought to make us realize—although this is perhaps not at all Kramer's intention—that Lenin's notion of the armed vanguard urgently needs to be reconsidered, criticized, and placed in a new and hopefully more genuinely liberating revolutionary perspective than has been the case thus far in history.)

196

In many ways *Ice* is a film made with and for this would-be "vanguard." Using nonactors recruited from the ranks of student activists and urban militant groups around New York, Kramer made *Ice* independently, with some financial support from the American Film Institute, shooting it with a small crew of friends and *Newsreel* associates. (*Newsreel's* organization, however, apparently disowns the film—or at least disowns any official association with it.)

Although, cinematically, there is much of the *Newsreel*-style, "direct," documentary approach in *Ice,* nonetheless, the film has an eclectic array of antecedents. The film which *Ice* resembles most is perhaps Louis Feuillade's 1913 *Fantomas,* a legendary serial-thriller in which—as in *Ice*—the straightforward camera technique and the natural decor of the city are in dramatic contrast to the fragmented narrative and its fantastic aura of conspiracy. Likewise, Fritz Lang's Mabuse films, particularly the early *Mabuse der Spieler,* would also seem to be antecedents of *Ice,* although not for their expressionist sensibility, but for the nonlinear narrative and fantastic web of sinister adventures. Then, too, *Ice* recalls Godard's *Alphaville* for its eerie projection of the dehumanized future already at work in the urban metropolises of the present; and there are overt borrowings from Godard's recent militant films in Kramer's use of placards, slogans, intercut footage, and agitprop theater. Finally, *Ice* betrays its debts to the American cinema (particularly Fuller, Walsh, and Hawks) in its fascination with violence and in its typically American brand of "social criticism" (characteristic of the films of Frank Capra, as well as the three named above) that rests on the surface phenomenon of behavior while neglecting entirely the analysis of underlying socioeconomic causes.

Ice was well received in France in the *Semaine de la Critique* portion of the 1970 Cannes Festival, then in Paris (where I first saw it) a few weeks later. Now the film is being shown on various university campuses around the U.S., usually under the sponsorship of one or another radical organization, and it is often given an in-person "political introduction" either by Kramer himself or by someone connected with the radical movement. (Jennifer Dohrn,

Bernardine's sister, was scheduled to introduce the film at the Stanford screening I attended; but she didn't show.) Local militant groups seem to make a point of coming out in full force to see *Ice* and to rap over what's usable in the film and what's not—often during the projection itself, which, at Stanford, was regularly punctuated with shouts of "Right on!" "Off the pig!" and "Bullshit!"—with the reaction seemingly determined less by what was said or done in the film than by whether or not the militants in the audience could identify with the militants on the screen. (Yes, Virginia, even militants go to the movies to identify.)

Nominally set in some indeterminate near future when *Amerika* is carrying on its latest chapter of imperialist war (this time in Mexico), *Ice* focuses on the urban-guerrilla activities of an under-ground network of youthful revolutonaries who are youthful in years only. If there is anything "documented" in *Ice*, it is the freezing-up of the personality among militant youth. But even this chilling phenomenon is not presented as a process: we see only the frozen surface of a *fait accompli*. So thorough is the depersonalization in *Ice* that we never really know who is who in the film, for the people look alike (middle-class American softness), talk alike (tonelessly), and carry out the Central Command's orders with a like mechanical flatness. Moreover, Kramer's mosaic-like construction of the narrative prevents us from following any one militant and turning the film into *his* story. *Ice* remains, from beginning to end, the coldly impersonal story of militancy itself.

And, paradoxically, Kramer both dwells on the depersonalization of his militants and, at the same time, steadfastly refuses any attempt at analyzing either the causes or effects of this emotional freeze. In the end, one gets the feeling that Kramer wants you to know that he's aware of the existence of certain psychological problems in the militant movement; but that, as far as he's concerned, an individual's personal hang-ups matter only if they get in the way of his functioning as a revolutionary. Emotions—in this view—are blown up all out of proportion by bourgeois society and its cult of individualism. So far, so good, it seems to me. But carried to its extreme—and *Ice* carries it this far, at least implicitly—this

argument leads one to the position that most if not all of our so-
called "human emotions" are actually degenerate behavior patterns
of a degenerate social order. And, as such, they are not only
expendable; they are obstacles that must be eliminated if we are
to build a more enlightened society.

But the loss on the emotional side in *Ice*, quite apart from any
consideration of the psychological damage that might accompany
this loss, is not compensated for by any gain—or even any holding
of one's own—on the rational side. Kramer doesn't seem the slightest bit interested in any rational, analytical considerations other
than pragmatic ones. Even tactical questions are treated in a
truncated shorthand which lops off all but the pragmatic questions
of who will handle this and who will handle that, and that's that.
And even here, the point is made in the film that it doesn't matter
who does what. When emotions have been "offed" and individual
differences are blurred, you no longer have to match the right
man for the right job: when everyone is alike, each is equally qualified—at least to go out and kill.

Completely lacking in *Ice* is the patient, down-to-earth wisdom
of a Mao or a Ho Chi Minh or a Fidel, who take great pains (actually great joy) in explaining to the masses the political considerations that go not only into every policy-making decision, but also
into every *method* of arriving at a decision—whether in economics,
military strategy and tactics, art and culture, or whatever. In *Ice*,
Kramer pays lip service to increasing the consciousness of the
masses—placards at the beginning of the film announce that originally terrorist activity was aimed at provoking the state into ever
greater and more overt repression; while now, it is asserted, the
purpose of terrorist activity is to convince the entire population of
the need for armed struggle against the state. But implicit in this
argument itself—as well as in the film as a whole—is the predilection for *intimidation* rather than rational persuasion as the way to
deal with the consciousness of the people. And when Kramer's
militants "occupy" a high-rise (home of the masses?) for a few
hours in order to show and discuss with the occupants a political
film, this potentially educational maneuver is really only a show of

strength to intimidate them. Speaking to the hastily assembled occupants, one militant says: "We took this place over today, and we'll be back to take it over again any time we want. The SECPO [Security Police] isn't anywhere near as strong as they want you to fear."

In short, when it comes to intimidation tactics to keep people in line, the militants and the police talk the same language. And ultimately, the high-rise sequence—like so much in the film—is really only another pretext for Kramer to force the viewer into dealing with the most controversial, indeed most explosive aspect of revolution—the actual detonation of violence.

Something goes wrong in the high-rise occupation—exactly what we don't know. The militants take it on the lam, guns in hand. Somebody starts shooting at them—who we don't know. They shoot back. Somebody gets killed and somebody gets wounded. The rest of the militants manage to get away and carry their wounded with them. They will live to fight another day. And that's *all* they will live for—and all they *want* to live for. Perhaps they could tell us why. After all, there are plenty of reasons for revolution in America. But Kramer isn't interested in explanations.

The notion of *force* is central to this film, not just because *Ice* deals with terrorist force, but also because the film forces the viewer to deal with terrorist force on the terrorist's own terms. Kramer has indicated that he views his film-making activity as "a way of getting at people, not by making concessions to where they are, but by showing them where you are and then forcing them to deal with that, bringing out all their assumptions, their prejudices, their imperfect perceptions.[32] And the way to force the viewer to deal with his "reality," Kramer believes, is to "make films that . . . explode like grenades in people's faces, or open minds like a good can-opener"—in short, "convert our audience or neutralize them, threaten."

It is unlikely, however, that many people are going to be converted to revolutionary terrorism by seeing *Ice;* and it is safe to assume, I think, that in making this film, Kramer was aiming not so much at converting the audience as at neutralizing—or, to be precise, at *neuterizing*—them. And in doing so, Kramer went to the point of neuterizing himself, right there on screen, in a grisly sequence of torture applied to the genitals of one of the militants— played by Kramer himself.

As violent scenes go, this one is particularly gruesome. Castration—if *Ice* is any indication—may be the most hard-to-watch violence imaginable. And Kramer springs it on us so suddenly we don't even know who is doing what to whom. (Even in castration, *Ice* remains coldly impersonal.) All we see is someone kicked into an alleyway, men scuffling, somebody knocked down, pants loosened, a surgical instrument resembling a long fishhook thrust under the opened fly, and a sudden, spasmodic arching of the back as the victim lets out a horrible, semiconscious moan of pain.

Whether the torture is inflicted by police informers, a right-wing vigilante group, or dissident co-conspirators is never made clear. Nor are the motives. There is only the brute fact of violence, the horrifying experience of it, and the need to somehow go on functioning as a revolutionary even if you can no longer function as a man.

What is really horrifying about *Ice*, however, is that Kramer seems to seek out the most self-destructive and dehumanizing forms of violence—both physical and psychological violence—and to dwell on them until they seem to be necessary (and sufficient?) elements in the making of good revolutionaries. For Kramer, you don't function as a good revolutionary in spite of no longer functioning as a man, but *because* of it. The chilling message of *Ice* is that you've got to give up everything to the revolution—including your balls.

One could argue, however—and maybe this is one of Kramer's points—that giving up their balls is no great loss for the militants, since—as several frozen "sex" scenes indicate—they are too emotionally blocked to get much use out of them. Or even if they do manage to bring it off now and then, they seem too devoid of feeling to get much pleasure out of it. (One young militant—not the castration-victim—fails to make it with his huge-breasted bed-partner because, as he tells her, he's hung-up over the various forms of sexual torture that await him if he's captured.)

As for the female militants of *Ice*, while they at least seem un-hung-up enough to take care of their sex needs, there doesn't seem to be any indication that sex, for them either, is anything more than a matter of personal hygiene—a momentary relaxing exercise in a hard revolutionary day. And whether they are in bed or in battle, the people in the film are not so much individuals as mere cogs—interchangeable parts in the wheel of revolution—or, as Brecht put it (in *The Measures Taken*), "blank pages on which the revolution writes its instructions."

Superficially at least, there are some interesting parallels between *Ice* and *The Measures Taken*. Both deal with the problems of prerevolutionary agitation and the role of the militant cell. Both reflect (although in different degrees—and perhaps with different attitudes toward it) on the necessary submersion of the individual in the collective. Brecht's 1930 *Lehrstück* contains a song "In Praise of Clandestine Work," which extols the virtues of anonymity, and the Brechtian militants undergo a ritual "blotting out" of their own identity by putting on masks.

In *Ice*, however, Kramer doesn't need to use masks, for his militants seem to have no real identity to blot out. Nor do Kramer's militants—unlike Brecht's—have to deal with anyone who is not just like them, so what would be the need for masks anyway? (The one near exception in *Ice*—aside from a slick cyberneticist who simply outplays the militants in their own game of power politics, as well as outplaying them in pool—is a slightly mad bookseller who, although he hangs around with the would-be revolutionaries, is really more of a leftover beatnik who hasn't quite been assimilated yet into revolutionary culture. Incidentally, he is just about the only individualized character in the film—and, significantly enough, the militants' way of dealing with him is either to bully him or to ignore him.)

It is important to note, however, that Kramer's and Brecht's conceptions of prerevolutionary agitation are very different. The point is made sharply and repeatedly in *The Measures Taken* that the Marxist militants do not fruitfully nurture the seeds of revolution by blustering in out-of-season with guns and tanks or even with trains and plowshares, but rather by addressing themselves to the political consciousness of the masses. "To the ignorant, instruction about their condition; to the oppressed, class consciousness; and to the class-conscious, the experience of revolution"—this is the program carried out by Brecht's agitators. In *Ice*, however, Kramer is obviously interested only in the latter—and even there he doesn't seem interested in the experience of revolution as a whole, but only in the experience of violence.

But the most important difference between Brecht's and Kramer's treatment of prerevolutionary militancy is that what Brecht sees as a *dialectical* tension between the individual and the collective, between spontaneity and organization, between emotions that border on sentimentality and rationality that borders on inhumanness, Kramer doesn't see dialectically at all. In fact, Kramer simply does away with one whole side of the dialectic by choking off any hint of the individual, the spontaneous, and the emotional. Moreover, for Kramer, the collective and the principle of organization are not even conceived as correlatives of rationality—they are mere vehicles for violence. Bombing, shooting, and burning is all you need, baby! And if you get your balls cut off in the action, well, *tant pis*, you might be a better revolutionary without all those distracting sexual needs!

Clearly, Kramer's preoccupation with violence has very strong overtones of the obsessive. The relation he sets up between the practice of revolutionary violence and castration is a particularly revealing indication of the deep-seated psychosexual tensions involved in the terrorist's life-style—and Kramer's decision to play the role of the castrated militant himself is all the more revealing.

Granted, Kramer might argue that playing this role himself simply seemed the best way of making the point that the revolutionary has got to be prepared to give up everything for the revolution. The castration scene—combined with its victim's subsequent ability to carry on as a revolutionary—would thus function as a cinematic exposition of the militant slogan "Forget your life: serve the people." Certainly the film as a whole seems aimed at convincing us that although the terrorist's lot is a hard and de-personalizing one, nonetheless he manages to live on and advance the revolution. But what Kramer may fail to consider is the possi-bility that the freezing-up of the personality, the blocked affec-tivity, and the psychosexual tensions of the militants may not merely be necessary but surmountable consequences of militant activity, but rather, at least in part, the internal causes of it.

The psychological dynamics of emotional deprivation among young middle-class militants have recently been explored by psy-choanalyst Herbert Hendin, who utilized psychoanalytical inter-viewing techniques (free association, dreams, and fantasies) to conduct a battery of interviews with militant students from Columbia and Barnard. The emotional detachment of these mili-tants toward one another and especially toward their parents, Hendin argued, "usually conceals pain too difficult for the students to face. Their acute ability to see and feel the flaws of society is in striking contrast to their need not to see and know the often devas-tating effects their family life has had on them."[33] In case after case Hendin found that the militants he interviewed reported experiencing early in life—and often very profoundly—a with-drawal of affection or complete emotional abandonment by their parents.

Significantly, the militants now felt that they, too, were unlikely or unable to experience any sustained or profound emotional in-volvement with other people; but this fact was invariably rational-ized in such a way as to pass this weakness off as a strength—either a rejection of bourgeois individualism or, paradoxically, self-suffi-ciency—or by projecting the pent-up resentment and hostility they felt at having been emotionally abandoned onto the outside world. "If you show your feelings, you get your legs cut off," was one young militant's way of putting it.

The parallels between what Hendin discovered in his depth interviews and what one can sense underlying the frozen surface of *Ice* are really quite striking. In both cases, the world of others—

whether undifferentiated or concentrated in the concept of "the repressive state"—is feared as a menacing, castrating monster—a vampire which, in the words of one of the militants in *Ice,* "wants to suck all our energy out of us and destroy us sexually." And in both cases there seems to be a strong need to see only the smooth surface of the emotional freeze—and to see it as politically positive —while the other nine-tenths of the psychic iceberg remains something one prefers not to see.

Hendin reports, for example, that his radical subjects often recounted dreams or actual childhood anecdotes which they enjoyed talking about in political terms—rationalizing out any personal emotional content and replacing it with a more or less political interpretation. Thus, one young man's dream of being caught in a barbed-wire fence while fleeing the scene of some terrorist maneuver, of being badly cut and bleeding, of being captured and placed in a detention camp, did not lead him to acknowledge any fears or ambivalence about his violent activities; but simply brought forth the assertion that society's only way to stop the radical movement was the use of widespread repression. That the latter may very well be true, however, does not really go far toward helping the individual come to terms with his own repressed tensions.* Likewise, it seems to me, in Kramer's case: he may offer a political rationalization for castration; but the very fact that he even formulates his thoughts and fantasies about revolution in terms of castration would seem to indicate deep psychological tensions that are not likely to be resolved by tough talk about how a revolutionary has got to be able to take it.

Admittedly, however, the militant's life-style offers him certain psychological advantages which he perhaps cannot find elsewhere. As Hendin observes, when a violent action by the militants arouses a violent reaction from the authorities, at least the militants

---

* In the above case, for example, Hendin (drawing on further case material) concluded that the young man who dreamed of being put in a camp actually had an unacknowledged wish that some sort of authority would step in and prevent him from continuing the potentially destructive and self-destructive activities in which he was engaged.

can feel for once that they are eliciting some adequate response to themselves as persons. And the intoxication of violent confrontation—in an otherwise mechanical and emotionless existence—can rapidly become addictive, especially in a "revolutionary culture" which rewards violent behavior and exerts great pressure on the individual to prove himself through violence. In short, as Hendin points out, "many individuals have found in the revolutionary culture a 'family' which understands their emotional needs better than their real families ever did."

Likewise, the militants' readiness to resort to violence may be traceable, at least in part, to the pent-up resentment and hostility they feel over their childhood experience of rejection or emotional abandonment. In *Ice,* for example, Kramer tosses in offhandedly a terse parent-child confrontation that would be hilarious if it weren't so crudely evocative of what is really at issue. A callow, post-adolescent (Jewish) boy argues with his "liberal," uptight parents over the harboring of a seriously wounded girl comrade, whom the parents want removed from the house—supposedly for "her own good." The son, however, demands that she stay put. The sequence hardly gets under way when it immediately boils over—with the son lunging at the father and screaming "You'll do what I say or I'll kill you!"

Typically, Kramer cuts away at this point, and the film moves on to some other fragment of the revolutionary mosaic—never to return to the Oedipal struggle, and never really giving us much of an idea of the general outline of the revolutionary picture as a whole. As for the psychological problems in the revolutionary movement, it's hard to say what position Kramer takes. Ultimately, it's as if Kramer started out to deliver a hard-fisted, tough-talking eulogy of the militant movement, then found himself repeatedly coming out with Freudian slips that threw the movement into question; and finally decided "to hell with Freud, the revolution will advance in spite of all these hang-ups—or maybe even *because* of them!"

It's the latter position, however, that seems to fascinate Kramer

the most. In the father-son confrontation—as in the film as a whole
—one has the impression that it's mainly the psychological hang-
ups of the individuals that push them to violence. And there's almost a smug sort of implicit acceptance of this fact—as if Kramer
were saying "So what? The quicker we get to real gut-level violence, the quicker we'll bring about our revolution."

As a revolutionary strategy, however, this attitude is full of
grave inconsistencies that are harmful—and perhaps even *suicidal*
—to the cause of revolution. While this is not the place to analyze
this problem in detail,[34] there are certain observations which—by
way of conclusion—should serve to situate Kramer's *Ice* within the
terrorist context. First, on the all-important question of timing,
Kramer is particularly irresponsible. He sets his film in a vague
future that is an all too transparent veil for the present—but, in
doing so, he indulges in dreamlike projections of a future he invites us to believe is already here. (In many ways *Ice* seems to
function largely as a form of wish-fulfillment—an insidious attempt to actualize the impossible through dreaming it.) And in
revolutionary terrorism—where the dangers of miscalculating the
situation and moving prematurely are so great—Kramer's con-
fusionism can be disastrous. (Marcuse has recently reminded us
that, historically, terrorism has never been effective except when
used as a mopping-up operation *after* taking power.)

Second, *Ice* itself—like terrorism—errs in *omission* as well as in
what it does do. And *Ice*'s omissions are particularly deplorable,
for if there is anything the revolutionary movement in America
needs in order to effect meaningful change, it's rigorous Marxian
analysis of the economic foundations and ideological superstructure of American capitalism. (Huey Newton didn't lecture to
Oakland High School kids on how to make molotov cocktails; he
lectured on Marxism—getting the students to understand the
need to arm themselves theoretically as well as practically.)

Finally—and most important of all—*Ice* illustrates almost in
spite of itself the way in which the cause of revolutionary liberation
can be betrayed from within, betrayed by paramilitary structures

that mirror the hated structures of the militaristic society we seek to destroy. And the loss of the truly *liberating* qualities of revolution amounts to the loss of the revolution itself.

By equivocating—by not clearly taking a stand and unveiling this betrayal for what it is—Kramer is an accomplice to it. In the end, and in spite of its revolutionary aspirations, *Ice* is really more of a science-fiction horror film than a political film. But see it; criticize it; and prove it wrong.

12

Rossellini's Materialist Mise-en-Scène *of* La Prise de Pouvoir par Louis XIV

> The history of all human society, past and present, has been the history of class struggle.
>
> —KARL MARX

> The basis of historical materialism is the concrete analysis of a concrete situation.
>
> —V. I. LENIN

> Marx insisted on the prime importance of economic factors, of the social forces of production, and of applications of science as factors in historical change. His realist conception of history is gaining acceptance in academic circles remote from the party passions inflamed by other aspects of Marxism.
>
> —V. GORDON CHILDE

The last quotation (from Childe's *Man Makes Himself*) seems to me to describe a position very similar to the one Rossellini has developed in his recent investigations into history. *The Iron Age, Socrates, La Prise de Pouvoir par Louis XIV,* and *Man's Struggle for Survival,* like the writings of historian Childe, evidence a very down-to-earth, commonsense materialist approach which focuses on economic conditions, the organizing of society in terms of economic functions, and the importance of technology in social change—all of which, as Childe points out, are keystones of Marx's analysis of history. But Rossellini is obviously no Marx or Lenin; and although I will contend that *La Prise de Pouvoir par Louis XIV* is exemplary in providing "a concrete analysis of a concrete situation" and in bringing to the movie screen, for once, the depiction of class struggle as the motor of history, nonetheless I am well aware that Rossellini's public stance is to reject all labels and to refuse to draw any "political" consequences from his analysis of history. However, this public stance—and, in particular, Rossellini's tendency to take refuge in the lame and discredited notion of "pure research"—strikes me as possibly disingenuous. In denying any political intentions, he speaks of the need to "demystify history" and to "get at simple facts";[35] but it hardly seems possible that he is unaware of the essentially political nature of the act of demystifying history.

Rossellini's *La Prise de Pouvoir par Louis XIV* is not a film *about* Louis XIV. Rather, as the title (in the original French) clearly indicates, it is a film which examines the *taking of power* by Louis XIV. The film's principal focus, then, is not Louis himself, but the mechanism of power as understood and manipulated by Louis XIV.

The distinction is crucial, I think, for depending on the focus of investigation, one raises very different types of questions. Rossellini himself has revealed that each of his films is an attempt to answer a specific question; and he acknowledges that the question at the base of *La Prise de Pouvoir par Louis XIV* was not "What was Louis like as a person?" but rather "Why did people at the court of Louis XIV dress the way they did?" An interesting question—and one which the film answers very clearly. But perhaps intelligence consists not so much in coming up with the right answers as in asking the right questions, that is questions which open up some fruitful lines of investigation by raising further questions. In the case of *La Prise de Pouvoir par Louis XIV*, for example, Rossellini's question about fashion styles may have

LA PRISE DE POUVOIR PAR LOUIS XIV

served him as a point of departure; but the film as a whole is by
no means limited to a dramatization of the answer that "fashion
styles were deliberately set and cultivated by Louis XIV as part
of an overall political strategy." On the contrary, perhaps the
greatest of this film's many merits is that Rossellini places the
answer to his original question within the larger context of a clear
materialist examination of the basic socioeconomic situation of
seventeenth-century France, and implicitly places the whole
epoch within the ultimate context of the *process* of history itself.

To accomplish this, Rossellini resolutely avoids the crudely
psychologizing interpretations and melodramatic structures of
Hollywood's historical epics; and he rejects as well the lyrical
excesses of Eisenstein's emotionalized reconstructions of historical
events. Utilizing simple camera setups with very little movement
of the camera, long takes, and a discreet but very effective use of
the zoom lens, Rossellini maintains a cautious, alert distance from
his historical material—thereby enabling us to experience, for
once, the *strangeness* of a historical period that is not our own.
This strangeness, however, is not to be confused with exoticism—
especially the Cecil B. DeMille brand of exoticism where postcard
images of "local color" (often Hollywood plastic) are shamelessly
exploited, and every historical utterance is delivered with heavy-
handed flailing by ham actors who dream of an Oscar.

Wisely, Rossellini relies primarily on nonactors in this film
(Jean-Marie Patte, who plays Louis XIV, is a French post office
functionary); and, preferring understatements to histrionics, Rossellini eschews the big scenes of emotional intensity that are the
stock in trade of most historical films and lets us experience instead the subtle tensions of the daily, mundane deeds of history.
And even when dramatizing the high points of Louis's *prise de
pouvoir*—like the arrest of Fouquet—Rossellini evokes from Jean-
Marie Patte a curious and penetrating sense of the dogged determination and single-minded effort involved in being (or playing)
Louis XIV. Moreover, in close collaboration with historian Philippe Erlanger (who is credited with the script of this film),
Rossellini brilliantly develops what I would call a *materialist*

mise-en-scène in which *things*—the material objects of seventeenth-century France—are not mere props and backdrops for the drama, but share equal billing, as it were, with the human figures.

Rarely, if ever, has a work of art been so solidly rooted in *things;* and rarely, if ever, has an artist explored so vividly and yet so profoundly the role of *things* in the making of history. Significantly, the closest artistic antecedent I can think of for this film is Bertolt Brecht's *Galileo*, a play in which the dynamics of history are also explored from a resolutely materialist point of view.

Rossellini's eye for detail in this film is masterful. But the details are not mere flourishes added on to the major dynamics of the film; on the contrary, it is largely through the details—the cardinal's bedpan, the bloodletting, the king's morning toilet, the pastimes of the court, the preparing and serving of the king's dinner, and, of course, the all-important articles of clothing—that we begin to understand the way in which man's social existence is intimately tied to and strongly determined by his relationship to things.

But Rossellini examines as well the way in which man, starting with a concern for things, takes a detour—in his dealings with other men—into the world of *appearances*. "One rules more by appearances," declares Louis XIV, "than by the way things really are" *(la nature profonde des choses)*. True enough, in one sense—and certainly the film documents the masterful manipulation of appearances that characterizes Louis XIV's reign. Nonetheless, that sophisticated web of appearances which Louis weaves around himself is by no means unrelated to "the way things really are." Quite the contrary, it is part of an overall strategy to *change* "the way things really are" while diverting people's attentions from this material reality.

Along this detour from things to appearances, however, individual men and even whole classes may wander so far astray in the realm of appearances that they lose touch with the real world of things. But here we are anticipating: let us begin where the film begins.

In the shadow of an elegant château, the common people take a momentary pause in the morning's chores. There is news of relatives who have well-paying jobs in the service of the king. A cousin is off to Bordeaux to purchase the king's wine. The news is greeted with laughter and that characteristically Gallic mélange of envy and sarcasm. "The king can't do without his wine, eh! So our cousin is the king's number-one winetaster; what a life!"

"The king, the king," interjects another, "in the end, he's just a master like any other. In England, they cut the head off a king, and there were no earthquakes or eclipses . . . ."

"Don't complain," another interrupts, "if there were no kings, there'd be no palaces; and if there were no palaces, there'd be no work for us."

"Okay," chimes in another, "let's get back to work."

The point is worth emphasizing: *the film begins with the common people.* Not for reasons of plot, however. Granted, certain information is introduced—when the men comment on the doctors who pass by on horseback—about the illness of Cardinal Mazarin and the extended stay of the court at Vincennes. And this information then serves as a transition between the first sequence and the second, which shows the arrival of the doctors at Vincennes. But the information that Cardinal Mazarin is ill would be conveyed just as well if the film simply began at the second sequence; this news is clearly incidental to the real function of the opening sequence, which is to examine the economic foundations and ideological overtones which enlist the common masses within the socioeconomic system of the French monarchy.

One can even recognize, in this seemingly offhand beginning, the basic elements of the ideology on which the aristocracy bases its rule: Divine Right (by this juncture in history, it is taken with a grain of salt—as evidenced by the "no earthquakes or eclipses" remark); and, more important, acceptance as a *given* of the notion that there could be no *work* other than within the existing economic system. The "no kings, no palaces, no palaces, no work" remark clearly demonstrates the strong carry-over into the sev-

enteenth century of the feudal ideology in which economic relations are only thinkable in terms of control of the land (with the
feudal manor—and, by extension, the royal palace—as the locus
of control from which all work opportunities emanate). This feudal ideology, we realize, is especially deep-rooted in an agricul-
tural economy like that of France, where, in the seventeenth
century, the working class per se is still hardly distinct from the
peasantry.

It surely is no mere coincidence in a film which examines the
mechanism of power that the opening sequence should provide
us with some indication of what factors enlisted the common
masses within a given social system—particularly a system geared
to provide such ridiculous extravagances for the aristocracy as is
here the case. The "underprivileged classes" are talked about
occasionally in the film (as objects to be manipulated and won
over), and we often see them at work serving the nobility; but
nowhere, except in the opening sequence, do we get any idea of
their attitudes toward the existing social system and why they
accept their menial status.

Finally, it is worth remarking that the opening sequence has
a very distinctive nature: unlike all the other sequences of the
film, it does not have its roots in actual deeds or words of historical figures. It does not reconstruct an event which, docu-
mentably, ever took place. The people are nameless; and their
words—although they are of the sort that might have been spoken
a hundred times a day—are purely the invention of Rossellini
and scenarist Erlanger. Those words, however, perform an important analytical function. They may even be an answer to a
question Rossellini might have posed: "How developed was the
class-consciousness of the common masses?" In any case, this is
a logical way to begin a materialist examination of a given historical situation.

Throughout the film each successive sequence has a twofold
function in which information is presented to advance the chron-
ological story-line and, at the same time, to analyze different
aspects of the historical period. That the former is often less

important than the latter is illustrated best, I think, by the doctors' examination of the ailing Mazarin. In terms of story-line, this sequence is disproportionately long: all we really need to know is who Mazarin is (and the film doesn't really supply this information until the following sequences) and not *how* he died but simply *that* he died. But Rossellini is interested in aspects of history other than merely "who did what."

So the doctors' examination of Mazarin becomes Rossellini's examination of the state of man's scientific knowledge in seventeenth-century France. And what more telling index could there be of man's knowledge than his knowledge of his own *materiality?* The doctors take the patient's pulse . . . or roughly ten seconds worth. (In 1661—the year of Mazarin's death—the fact that blood circulates through our bodies was still a very recent discovery, the ramifications of which were only beginning to be understood.) They run their hands along the patient's nightshirt and bedding, then sniff their fingertips—presumably to evaluate the odor of the patient's sweat. Then they examine the . . . . The word is not spoken, out of *délicatesse;* but the request is immediately understood, and the cardinal's bedpan is quickly fetched from beneath the bed and handed to the chief consultant, who holds it up to his nose, shaking it gently to stir up the contents, sniffing it in short, businesslike inhalations.

After several moments, he passes the bedpan to a colleague, accompanying this move with a telling arching of the eyebrows; and, turning to the cardinal's resident physician, he concludes: "He must be bled." The other consultants quickly voice their agreement. Informed that the patient has already been bled several times that day and may be too weak to be bled again, they reply that "the human body contains 24 liters of blood and can lose 21 liters and still live." And to reassure the resident physician, they support their argument with analogies in the form of aphorisms: "The deeper you have to go to get water from a well, the better the water" and "The more milk a mother gives, the more milk she has to give."

The cardinal is lifted from bed, placed in a chair, and bled from the ankle. As he faints, the blood is collected in a small pot. Repeating the same procedure as with the cardinal's urine, the chief consultant grimaces resignedly: "Unless there's a miracle . . . ."

Finally, the renowned physicians withdraw. Outside the cardinal's chamber they discuss several treatments that might be tried in desperation. "Perhaps His Eminence needs to be purged of his 'bad humeurs,'" suggests one doctor. "But I already gave him rhubarb," counters the resident physician. "Precious stones," suggests one; "A mother's milk," suggests another. But they admit they have never tried these measures and don't really have any faith in them. The scene ends.

Quite tangential to the film's story-line, this sequence is absolutely central to the film's basic preoccupations. The dialectic between objective and subjective factors, between things and man's perception of their appearances, is *mise en scène* in the cardinal's death chamber. The doctors recognize the importance of the material things of this life—like our bodies. But at this stage of history they can only examine what is externalized—like urine, sweat, blood, and the general outward appearance of the patient—and their basic tools are their senses of sight, smell, and touch. Their information is limited to sense data. They can smell the urine, but they cannot yet perform a chemical analysis of the urine. Sense data is a prerequisite and an important part of analysis, but alone it often does not accomplish very much. And while we concentrate on the outward appearances of things, things go their own way—they degenerate, decompose, and are transformed into something else. And when *we* are the things that degenerate, decompose, and are transformed into something else, all the other *things* that we accumulated in our lifetime are then passed on to someone else. We make out a will to determine who gets what.

Enter the Church. Mazarin—himself a cardinal—is dying. He must be confessed and prepare himself for death. In the eyes of the Church this means settling his accounts in the material world in order to enter the realm of the spirit. "Settling accounts" is a business term. Entering the realm of the spirit is a business deal. There is an entrance fee. The Church sends a business representative to hammer out the terms of the bargain.

Things and our perception of their appearances . . . matter and spirit . . . which is more important? Louis XIV might claim that "one rules more by appearances than by the way things really are"; but how true is this? The Church—any church—might claim that the spiritual realm is infinitely more important than the material realm; but how can this be reconciled with the Church's well-documented appetite for the material things of this world? Who is fooling whom? If material things are really so unimportant and insignificant, why do rulers and priests throughout history resort to such devious and complicated appearances to accumulate and control things? And since this film is an examination of the mechanism of power, what role does the Church play in the struggle for power? Isn't this, too, a question Rossellini is likely to have asked himself?

Enter Colbert. Briefly, the ailing Mazarin discusses with his assistant the affairs of government. Colbert tells of the state's depleting financial reserves and the flagrant corruption which permits ambitious individuals like Fouquet to fill their pockets at the state's expense. Colbert concludes with a warning that if Fouquet were to become prime minister, anything could happen.

Finally, enter Louis—or rather Louis *se lève.* Our first glimpse of Louis XIV is in bed. We, like the assembled nobles of the court, witness the opening of the bed-curtains and the morning ritual of a seventeenth-century monarch. It is quite a spectacle— complete with *esprit de vin* for the king to wash his hands and face with, prayers that are mumbled (for appearances' sake) to sound like Latin, an announcement by the young queen to the effect that the king performed his conjugal duty during the night, and, finally, the dressing of the king by his servants while the nobles of the court look on admiringly.

By introducing the figure of Louis XIV in this manner, Rossellini very skillfully suggests the purely *ceremonial* function of

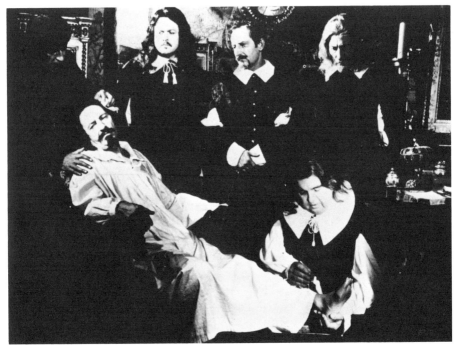

The Rise to Power of Louis XIV: things and appearances in seventeenth-century medicine

The Rise to Power of Louis XIV: The queen mother asks, ''Since when has a king of France really governed?''

The Rise to Power of Louis XIV: the Sun-King and his right-hand man Colbert

The Rise to Power of Louis XIV: "Everyone should stay in his place."

the young French monarch under Mazarin's regency. Like Cardinal Richelieu before him, Mazarin as prime minister is entrusted with the actual tasks of governing, while the function of the French monarchy is now almost entirely symbolic. In the pomp and circumstance which surround His Royal Highness, the nation shall see the image of its greatness and prestige. Louis XIV, acutely sensitive to the public image, even refuses the dying Mazarin's generous bequest of his personal fortune—for "the public must never be able to say that a king received a fortune from a mere subject." (What the public doesn't know, however, doesn't hurt them—as we see later when Mazarin's fortune is *secretly* put at the disposal of Louis XIV, who, under these circumstances, has no hesitation about using it.)

But the twenty-two-year-old Louis XIV has no intention of remaining *only* a symbolic figure. In a conversation with the queen mother, Louis pours out his frustrations and very petulantly asserts his determination to change things. Power, he tells his mother, is shared by too many hands. The Parliament is getting too strong; it might get the idea of turning against its master. Louis fears the recurrence of the infamous *Fronde*—a rebellious coalition of bourgeois parliamentarians and dissident nobles who challenged the monarchy and ravaged French politics from 1648 to 1653, even forcing the royal family to flee Paris on several occasions.

The problem, Louis insists, is that the nobles of the court, living far from their lands, are in need of money and therefore turn to the bourgeoisie—putting themselves in debt at the hands of bourgeois creditors. "It's reached the point," he declares with disgust, "where *honneur* is for sale just like sugar or tobacco." "Power, today, equals *money*." Insisting that the selling of titles must cease, Louis sums up his aspirations: "What I want is that everyone should keep in his place!"

And the king's place, it is clear, is at the helm of his country, actively steering the ship of state. Everyone else—even his own mother—may be convinced that Louis is a self-indulgent, spoiled fop who will quickly tire of the responsibilities of government;

but Louis XIV intends to fool them all and govern in his own
right.

Slowly, painstakingly, with innumerable seemingly irrelevant
details, Rossellini has drawn the basic issues of Louis's rise to
power. Now, the stage having been set, thing move very quickly.
Mazarin dies. Keeping abreast of the situation minute by minute,
Louis quickly hurries to assert his power. A well-placed remark
makes a calculated impression of Louis's determination to exercise power himself. Then, to assert his will, Louis goes against
tradition and imposes full mourning—normally reserved for the
royal family—to honor Mazarin. Further, he immediately calls
an emergency meeting of the Council of Ministers and stalks in
brusquely to announce his intention of governing personally without the intermediary of a prime minister. Then, in private con-
ference with Colbert, whom he appoints as his personal adviser,
Louis inquires about the ambitions of the influential Fouquet,
his minister of finance; and he carefully excludes from the council
meetings several individuals known to be closely associated with
Fouquet—including his own mother and brother.

When the queen mother subsequently reproaches Louis for
his ingratitude toward her and scolds him for his none too delicate flaunting of his affair with Louise de La Vallière, Louis
dutifully implores her forgiveness and quickly hastens from the
room as if overcome with remorse. As always, Rossellini's handling of this scene raises questions without imposing any heavy-
handed answers. When Louis falls to his knees and buries his
face in his mother's breast, the gesture seems quite natural. But
the perfunctoriness of this gesture is highlighted by the quick
exit that immediately follows; and, in any case, with Louis's face
buried, we—like his mother—cannot see what emotions may or
may not be expressed in his features and we thus have only the
gesture itself and the seemingly fervent request for forgiveness
to judge by. Is it just the appearance of remorse or the real thing?
Perhaps we'll never know; or perhaps we should look elsewhere
for clues. In any case, immediately following this encounter between Louis and the queen mother, Rossellini carefully inserts a

brief but telling exchange between Colbert and Louis in which the king reiterates his insistence that neither his mother nor his brother shall take part in council meetings.

Brief glimpses of the court at play (at the country retreat at Chantilly) then reveal that far from reforming his promiscuity, Louis indulges ever more openly, in spite of his mother's disapproval and the increasing humiliation this brings to his wife Marie-Thérèse. And the love intrigues, it is clearly demonstrated, often become enmeshed in the political intrigues of ambitious nobles like Fouquet who try to buy over the confidence of the king's favorites.

Fouquet himself, this most dashing and ambitious figure whose prestige and flair rivaled that of the young monarch, is abruptly arrested by the captain of Louis's guard, D'Artagnan, in a move of calculated audacity. Planning the move with an eye to public opinion, Louis stages the arrest of his most powerful rival right in the man's own stronghold at Nantes—thereby accentuating the boldness of his action and the confidence he has in his own omnipotence. Rossellini subtly underscores the strategy of Louis XIV by having Louis tersely order that the arrest be shrouded in secrecy beforehand and announced with "as much stir as possible" afterward. Even the queen mother—a close associate of Fouquet—can only respond to Louis's unexpected audacity with an awestruck "*Louis, vous me faites peur!*"

Having thus eliminated his chief potential rival, Louis sets about consolidating the power he has so assiduously acquired. And, as Rossellini suggests, it is the king's personal adviser, Colbert, who plays the pivotal role in devising and implementing Louis's long-range political program. Granted, the king himself dictates certain basic principles. "Each person must derive everything from the king, just as all of Nature derives everything from the sun . . . and the nobility must be kept separate from the bourgeoisie . . . these are the general goals of my policy." But Louis turns immediately to his confidential adviser and asks, "What are the practical means of implementing them?"

Colbert, a bourgeois technocrat with a genius for organization, responds to the challenge with a zealous, far-reaching program of economic reform and development that will reshape France from top to bottom. "Industries must be developed to enable us to produce for ourselves what we now must import from abroad; roads and canals must be built and maintained to facilitate commerce; we must build a fleet of ships to compete with Holland in trade with the New World; the lower classes must be taken off the 'dole,' it is dangerous for them to be idle, and we must provide public works to keep them busy; we must also reduce the tax burden of the most underprivileged classes, this way we'll win their allegiance and remove a source of discontent; on the other hand, we shall increase the indirect taxes which hit all classes of society—taxes on tobacco, alcohol, salt, etc.; and we should reduce interest rates on loans to cut the profits of the bourgeois money-lenders. . . ."

As Colbert systematically elaborates his proposals for reorganization, we cannot help but admire the foresight and thoroughness of this "bourgeois from Reims" (as Fouquet had contemptuously called him); and we may remark how fortunate it was for Louis XIV to have such a practical-minded man as Colbert for his chief adviser. But we begin to be aware, too, of a curious paradox involved in the collaboration of Louis XIV and Colbert—a paradox which becomes more evident in the session with Louis's tailor that follows, but which is already implicit here in the juxtaposition of Louis's ends with Colbert's means.

Louis's goals have an anachronistic, backward-looking quality about them. In desiring that "each person must derive all from the king," Louis seeks nothing other than a return to the central institution of the early feudal age, where the basic social contract was the sacred pact of personal indebtedness and devotion that bound each subject to the king. And just as the planets revolve around the sun in fixed orbits, Louis would have his subjects revolve around him in a clearly defined hierarchy where "everyone would keep his place." In short, Louis's ideals are the ideals of a feudal age long past. Even his attempt to restore the monarchy to active rule is an attempt to stem the tide of history—as his mother has earlier in the film pointed out to him.

How strange it is, then, that the resolutely forward-looking proposals of Colbert should seem to fit in so well with the anachronistic ideals of Louis XIV. As the saying goes, politics makes strange bedfellows. But then so does history—and it is often only through the light of history that we can see how strange certain political alliances really were.

The brilliance of Rossellini's artistry, however, is that he knows how to visualize not just historical events themselves, but also the *internal contradictions* of a given historical situation. And here, in the meeting of the minds between Louis XIV and Colbert, one of the primary internal contradictions of class struggle in seventeenth-century France is subtly brought to the fore. The bourgeois, practical-minded outlook (here personified by Colbert) is concerned with *things;* while the aristocratic spirit (here personified by Louis XIV) is excessively preoccupied with *appearances.* And although, as the session with the tailor indicates, Louis XIV is a masterful manipulator of appearances for political effect, nonetheless he seems very limited in his ability to comprehend the economic (and ultimately political) consequences of the scheme he elaborates.

As Louis carefully specifies the number and placement of ruffles and feathers on the outlandish costume he intends to impose on the court, he explains to Colbert that these extravagant costumes will cost the nobles roughly one year's income apiece—thus bringing in a substantial income for the state treasury at the same time that the financial power of the potentially dissident nobles will be drained. Then, to placate the nobility and to keep them out of the hands of ambitious bourgeois creditors, Louis reveals that he will personally undertake—with funds from the state treasury—the housing and feeding of the court at the newly planned palace of Versailles.

Throughout this session with the tailor, Colbert keeps silent and lets Louis do all the talking. Louis's plan is so bold and Machiavellian in design that even its excesses are fascinating.

But the look on Colbert's face, so evidently cautious and skeptical, tends to highlight, by contrast, the inconsistencies and excesses of a scheme which financially entails giving back with one hand more money than the other hand just took in, and which requires that enormous sums of money be pumped continuously into an almost totally nonproductive sector of the economy. Through the stolid presence of Colbert we begin to sense that while in the short run Louis's concern with appearances may seem to complement and reinforce Colbert's concern with things, in the long run the forces of history have them headed in two very different and conflicting directions.

And, in fact, it is perfectly clear from the perspective of history that Colbert's practical development of French industry and commerce served to accelerate the very patterns of social change —particularly the rise of the bourgeoisie— that Louis deplored and sought to reverse. Moreover, Louis's own policy of hosting the nobility at Versailles while ruining them financially eventually ruined the state's finances as well; and life at Louis's extravagant court, with its single-minded concern with appearances, so distracted the nobility from the material world of things (except as luxury items for conspicuous consumption) that by the end of Louis's reign this once mighty economic class no longer played a vital role in the system of production and was, as Marx put it, reduced to a mere "parasite" in the new industrial and commercial economy dominated by the bourgeoisie.

All of this is simply implicit, however, as far as the film is concerned, for Rossellini traces only the ascendancy of Louis XIV from 1661 to the mid-1680's. Nevertheless, the film as a whole, and particularly the later sequences dealing with Versailles, suggests quite clearly that despite the flamboyance of Louis's court, his reign is by no means a healthy, fruitful flowering of the French monarchy. Rather, it is simply the last flowering— dazzling in its sickly hues—of a dying plant artificially kept alive in a hothouse.

And what a hothouse! Louis instructs his chief architect, Le Vau, to build Versailles large enough to accommodate 15,000 guests. Versailles is to be the showcase of his reign—and, after his death, the temple of his glory. And at this moment, in a magnificent long shot of the construction in progress, Rossellini reveals the simultaneous *splendeur* and *misère* of Louis's grandiose conception. Seen from a distance, countless laborers scurry about like so many ants, their backs glistening with sweat as they strain under the enormous stone blocks which are cut, measured, and endlessly fitted into place. And for what? The way the shot is framed, it is hard to tell just what they are building. We know, of course, that it is the palace of Versailles; but, aside from a small arch in the foreground, it might just as well be the pyramids at Giza or the temples of Babylon. There are historical variations, to be sure; but it's the same old story: the privileged few live in lavish luxury, while the impoverished masses are forced to bear the burden, giving their lives to build the tombs and palaces of the rich. The shot is held only a few seconds, but it seems like an eternity, so powerful is the moral impact of this image of man's injustice.

Finally, the scene shifts and we jump ahead to the completed palace of Versailles, where Louis imposes his will unabashedly, gradually transforming the ceremonial functions of the court into a quasi-religious cult over which he presides as the living incarnation of the divine. Louis XIV becomes the "Sun-King"; all eyes are focused on him, and every glance or word which he deigns to address to one or another of his subjects is a life-giving ray of sunlight.

Absolutely faithful in each detail, Rossellini depicts the daily ritual of the king's *grand couvert*—the evening meal at which Louis, seated alone at a raised daïs, eats a dinner consisting of several dozen courses prepared and served by a legion of domestic servants, while the entire court stands respectfully and engages in courtly gossip. And when Louis XIV majestically demands some musical accompaniment, Rossellini's camera obediently follows a court functionary as he makes his way amid the gathered nobles to communicate the king's orders to the musicians, who are seated in a tiny balcony at the rear of the long, narrow hall. At the appointed signal, the musicians pop up like so many choirboys; and the camera's perspective from behind the king clearly emphasizes the churchlike atmosphere—with Louis seated at the raised altar, the focus of everyone's devotion.

Then, in a brief concluding sequence, Louis XIV is seen taking a short stroll, followed by his sycophantic retinue, in the ordered gardens of Versailles. Entering the palace, Louis momentarily withdraws to a private salon. In a scene that somewhat paradoxically recalls Brecht's famous dressing of the pope in *Galileo*, Louis XIV removes, one by one, the numerous articles of clothing that are the outward symbols of his power. But as the gloves, sword, wig, medallion, vest, and various collars and sleevelets are removed, it is questionable whether Louis—although perhaps a tiny bit more "human"—is any the less majestic. So painstakingly has he woven the web of appearances around his person that he has now almost completely identified himself with the fabulous demigod of his public image.

The private, intimate Louis XIV—we suddenly realize—has never existed! Eating, sleeping, participating in the hunt, presiding at court, even lovemaking, have all been political functions: for the sake of his public image, every act of Louis's daily life —no matter how trivial—has been carefully executed with a calculated aura of serene omnipotence. Only now—when we see him *alone for the first time in the film*—can Louis allow himself a brief moment of privacy: and even here, the private Louis and the public Louis XIV are barely distinguishable.

Almost totally absorbed now in the artificial rituals of the court at Versailles, Louis XIV is also almost totally isolated from his fellow men and the real world of things. In his lofty solitude, he can take comfort only in the spiritual ruminations of La Rochefoucauld, whose book of maxims Rossellini depicts Louis as meditating over endlessly—presumably finding in their Delphic ambiguity an inspirational pastime for his godlike aloofness.

The case has here been argued that the analysis of history in *La Prise de Pouvoir par Louis XIV* is a materialist analysis and that the dramatic presentation of that analysis—its *mise-en-scène* —is a materialist *mise-en-scène*. By way of conclusion, however, it is worthwhile to examine the limitations of Rossellini's achievement and to ask why such a resolutely materialist work of art (assuming that we are justified in identifying *La Prise de Pouvoir par Louis XIV* as such) should have, as it were, so little political *bite*. (One objective indication of this film's political innocuousness is the simple fact that the French national television network —for whom the film was made—went ahead and showed the film, a precedent they have certainly not followed in their dealings with other film-makers (like Godard and Marcel Ophuls, to name only two) from whom they commissioned films which were subsequently suppressed by the government and refused TV exposure.

Why is it, then, that in spite of its subtle artistry, the depth and scope of its materialist analysis, and its uncompromisingly unemotional, antimelodramatic structure, *La Prise de Pouvoir par Louis XIV* is a film so easily digestible by the general bourgeois "art-film" audience? Part of the answer, of course, is simply that the opportunity to take a peek at the life of a king (and this is not just any old king) is one of the great dreams of the social-climbing bourgeoisie; this is a constant theme of bourgeois art (as well as of tabloid journalism, which bourgeois art often resembles). Consequently, the magnetic pull of the anecdotal aspect of this film is so strong that it is very easy for the bourgeois spectator to shift the film off its basic axis, which, as I indicated at the outset, is not the person of Louis XIV but rather the mechanism of power as understood and manipulated by Louis XIV— and to deal with the film on his own self-indulgent terms rather than on Rossellini's more austere and intellectually demanding terms. Moreover, *La Prise de Pouvoir par Louis XIV* admittedly has a great deal of sumptuous spectacle to divert the spectator, and there is enough that is bizarre and extravagant (after all, Louis XIV did reach a certain zenith of the bizarre and extravagant) to titillate even the jaded bourgeois audiences who are wallowing these days in the self-indulgent decadence of Visconti and Fellini.

Nonetheless, it is the task of the serious critic to penetrate beneath the surface of spectacle and to recognize—in this film and on each of the few occasions the cinema offers him—that even spectacle can serve as a practical tool to focus our attention in directions which will produce some *useful knowledge of our objective condition* instead of merely mystifying us once again with more sugar-coated dreams that are useful only to the privileged few, who, like Louis XIV, would forever "keep us in our place."

13

Sex and Politics: Wilhelm Reich, World Revolution, and Makavejev's WR: The Mysteries of the Organism

> More than any other figure of our
> times, Reich has had things to say—
> and do—essential for the chief
> revolutionary actions of the young,
> whether in their politics or their
> hippie life style: indeed he is the
> connecting link between these
> tendencies.
>
> —PAUL GOODMAN

In the past few years there has been a renewed surge of interest in Reich, evidenced by new American editions of several pioneering works from the early part of Reich's lifelong research into human sexuality, the human psyche, and the psychosexual foundations of political behavior. (The original American editions of many of Reich's books were mostly burned by the Federal Food and Drug Administration after Reich's death in 1957.) A new translation of Reich's very important *Die Massenpsychologie des Faschismus (The Mass Psychology of Fascism)* is available in paperback, as well as the first English translation of Reich's companion-piece to his study of fascism, *Der Einbruch der Sexualmoral (The Invasion of Compulsory Sex-Morality).*[36] In addition, the October 1971 issue of *Liberation* is devoted entirely to Reich and includes the first English translation of Reich's 1934 essay "What Is Class-Consciousness?"—an essay Reich wrote in response to certain criticisms from the left of his study of fascism.

Another related manifestation of a burgeoning Reich renaissance is the Cambridge, Massachusetts-based publication *The Radical Therapist,* which serves as a mobilizing broadsheet for a group of young psychologists and psychological social workers who are committed to the notion that "therapy is change . . . not adjustment." Included in their December 1971 issue (which pictures Reich on the cover) is an article devoted to Reich's correlation of sexual and political repression, and a translation of the concluding chapter from Reich's *The Sexual Struggle of Youth.*

In addition—and this is what mainly concerns us here—a number of widely discussed feature films have been released in the last few years or so which, with widely varying degrees of insight and artfulness, have directed the film-goer's attention to issues of sex and politics which Wilhelm Reich was one of the first to explore. Of these films—among which the most prominent are Visconti's *The Damned,* Petri's *Investigation of a Citizen Above Suspicion, Z* by Costa-Gavras, and Bertolucci's *The Conformist*—far and away the most original and most probing film, in my opinion, is Yugoslav film-maker Dusan Makavejev's *WR: The Mysteries of the Organism.* And not incidentally, I would argue, of all the films just mentioned Makavejev's is the only one explicitly inspired by the film-maker's desire to come to grips with the life and work of Wilhelm Reich.

Reich, Freud, and Marx

However, before undertaking an analysis of this complex film, I think it will be useful to summarize briefly the main points of Wilhelm Reich's pioneering work in the field of sex and politics. As a young protegé of Freud in the 1920's and early 1930's, Reich directed his attention to the overwhelming importance of infantile and adolescent sexuality in the development of personality. What seems to have been the catalyst for Reich's examination of the relations between sex and politics was the recognition that parental suppression of naturally developing sexuality in their children has the effect of anchoring, in the character structure of the individual, the authoritarian and repressive principle on which class society is based. In other words, Reich saw that the patriarchal family's authoritarian structure and its taboos on childhood sexuality were tremendously effective *ideological* weapons that served to perpetuate and reinforce, on the *unconscious* level, the authoritarian political structures of class society.

Unlike Freud, however, who believed that the Oedipal conflict—and therefore sexual repression—were biologically rooted, Reich argued that sexual repression was unknown in matriarchal societies and therefore could not be biologically rooted, but was rather the historical product of the rise of patriarchal, authoritarian class society. For Reich, in other words, *suppression* of sexuality by society preceded and produced the individual's internalized *repression* of sexuality. In answer to the troublesome question of *why* society suppressed sexuality (Freud's answer was "for the sake of culture"), Reich took the boldly materialist position that it was for the sake of class interest: he traced sexual suppression to the interests of the ruling class in protecting its inheritance lines and property; he pointed out that, historically, chastity was first imposed upon members of the ruling class alone, particularly the patrician women. Sexual repression then becomes the rule in all classes of society simply because, as Marx pointed out, "the dominant ideology in any society is always the ideology of the dominant class." And, of course, the exploited classes are by no means immune to envying the ruling class and either consciously emulating "their betters" or unconsciously internalizing the ruling-class values.

It was this "mass-psychological" vulnerability of the exploited classes that intrigued Reich as he began to study the burgeoning fascist movement in Germany in the early thirties. In his brilliantly prophetic *The Mass Psychology of Fascism* Reich analyzed the powerful emotional content of fascism, pointing out that the German masses were attracted to the Nazi movement not so much

by its political platform (which was purposely vague) as by the
emotional appeal of mystical notions of "blood," "racial purity,"
"fatherland," "master race," etc. Through close readings of innumerable Nazi pamphlets and texts, as well as of the Nazi
propaganda distributed through the German churches and religious organizations, Reich brought to light the underlying sexual
content of these mystical notions; and he argued that religious
mysticism—indeed all mysticism—was a symptom of unfulfilled,
repressed, or distorted sexuality. The "mystical longing," he maintained, was really an "unconscious orgastic longing."

Because mysticism was such an important element of fascism,
Reich argued that combating fascism on the strictly rational level
of political analysis would be futile, and that since, in his view,
both mysticism and authoritarianism could be traced to repressed
sexuality, the way to combat fascism was to combat sexual repression. As a therapist, Reich's way of combating sexual repression, however, was very different, theoretically and practically,
from Freud's "depth psychology" approach, for Reich concentrated on the *physiological* manifestations of repression—on the
rigid, tense, unyielding muscular "armor" that the individual uses
to shield his emotional vulnerability. And instead of using therapy to help sublimate libidinal energy away from direct sexual
expression into what Freud considered more socially constructive
channels, Reich boldly rejected the value of sublimation, which
he saw as still another way in which the ruling class inculcated in
the working masses "civic virtues" which were against their individual and class interests. He proclaimed that only free and
unmitigated satisfaction of mature genital sexuality could be
genuinely healthful and liberating for the individual. And only by
liberating individual sexuality, Reich argued, could the authoritarian behavior structures of class society be eliminated. Toward
this end, Reich, who at this period in his career conceived of his
"sex-economy" approach as filling a long-ignored gap *within* Marxism, founded a Communist youth group known as *Sexpol* and organized informal dances and open forums for Communist youth

where problems of sex rather than politics were the topic of discussion and where the avowed goals were to encourage and assist young people to attain a full and healthy sexual expression.

As one might expect, such a heretical approach got Reich in trouble with the "vulgar Marxists" who controlled the Communist Party; but it also got him in trouble with Freud and the politically conservative psychoanalysts—with the result that by 1933 Reich was excluded from both the German Psychoanalytic Society and the German Communist Party. And by 1934 he went into hasty exile from Hilter's rapidly burgeoning fascist state.

Reich settled briefly in Norway, where he developed his body-oriented therapy, then came to the U.S. in 1939. Extremely bitter and resentful over the German Communist Party's refusal to heed his warnings regarding Hitler's mass appeal, and particularly rankled by the Party's hostility toward his attempts to redirect the energies of the Marxist movement to the neglected "cultural front," Reich gradually but strikingly changed his mind about Marxism, eventually railing against the Communists—whom he called "red fascists"—and heralding the average bourgeois American as the world's greatest hope for genuine liberation. Thumbing his nose at all politics, Reich devoted his later years in America to esoteric research on something he called "Cosmic Orgone Energy," to which he attributed marvelous powers, including fuller orgasms and the cure of cancer.

Sex and Politics in Some Recent Films

Turning now to look at the way the relations between sex and politics are examined in some recent films, it seems to me that with this brief introduction to Reich's thought fresh in our mind we will be better equipped to appreciate the complexity of Makavejev's *WR: The Mysteries of the Organism* and to understand more clearly just how simplistic is the superficial "Reichianism" heralded in films like *The Damned, Investigation of a Citizen Above Suspicion, Z,* and *The Conformist.* Let us deal with this latter issue first.

The claim has been made—somewhat misleadingly, I think, by Joan Mellen[37]—that the portrait of the fascist mentality that emerges from these films corresponds to Wilhelm Reich's theory of the psychosexual foundations of political behavior. However, more than merely establishing certain similarities in approach, Mellen encourages us to take the picture of fascism presented in these films as Reich's picture of fascism, and she deals with all details of character portrayal in each of these films as if they were individual instances conceived by the film-makers to exemplify Reich's general theory.

Attempting to defend these films against the charge that their relating homosexuality to fascism is simplistic, Mellen invokes Reich—carefully adding, however, that "the implication is not that homosexuals all display such a pattern. Too many homosexuals are artists, rebels, and gentle people for that." Here I think Mellen misses an important point: the implication which needs guarding against is not the obvious oversimplification that all homosexuals are fascists, but rather the more insidious oversimplification that all fascists are homosexuals or have latent homosexual tendencies.

Moreover, the *singling out* of homosexuality as *the* fascist character structure (a point emphasized by each of these films) does not at all correspond to Reich's views, which were that the roots of fascism are in the "normal" family, particularly in parental suppression of the naturally developing sexuality of the child. It is this normal inhibition of sexuality which, according to Reich, "makes the child apprehensive, shy, obedient, afraid of authority, 'good' and 'adjusted' in the authoritarian sense; it paralyzes the rebellious forces because any rebellion is laden with anxiety. . . . At first the child has to adjust to the authoritarian miniature state, the family; this makes it capable of later subordination to the general authoritarian system."

In short, there is a vast difference between Reich's position and that reflected in *The Damned, Investigation of a Citizen Above Suspicion, The Conformist,* and *Z:* while Reich offers a process-oriented approach that sees both homosexuality and fascism as *effects* of sexual repression, these films either invite a terribly simplistic notion of cause and effect ("They were fascists because they were homosexuals") or they simply equate the two, omitting any consideration of their underlying causes. In addition—and this is especially deplorable—these films all too often make the correlation between homosexuality and fascism in a snickering, elbow-nudging way that merely invites the spectator to add a self-righteous condemnation of the fascists' sexual behavor to a self-righteous condemnation of their political behavior. Far from inviting us to consider—as Reich did—the ways in which our "normal" sexual mores might contribute to the development of fascism, these films offer us a scapegoat—the homosexual—which absolves us of responsibility for fascism and allows us to gloat in smug complacency over the evil decadence of these fascist "perverts."

WR: The Mysteries of the Organism

Fortunately, however, a film has come along which confronts Reich's ideas directly and, unlike the work of Visconti, Petri, or Bertolucci, succeeds admirably in suggesting the complexity of Reich's notions on the psychosexual foundations of political behavior. Makavejev describes his film as "in part, a personal response to the life and work of Wilhelm Reich."

WR—the initials, by the way, stand not only for "Wilhelm Reich" but also for "World Revolution"—actually seems to start out as a free-wheeling documentary on Reich; then not quite a quarter of the way into the film it takes a sudden lurch into fiction with the introduction of a parallel plot set in contemporary Yugoslavia (Makavejev's homeland); and from then on the film jumps back and forth from America (Reich's adopted home) to Yugoslavia, from more or less documentary material to more or less fictional material, and from sex to politics as well as from politics to sex.

Makavejev edits all this diverse material with a great deal of virtuosity and brio; he is an immensely talented film-maker whose experiments with montage and collage are among the most stimulating and original to come along in recent years.[38] While sharing

WR: Milena exercising before stepping into her Orgone box

WR: Reich being hauled off to jail by the FBI

WR: "Workers of the world . . . your attitudes toward sex are revolting!"

WR: "Socialism without fucking is dull and lifeless."

WR: Vladimir Ilyich is not easily distracted from the lofty ideals of the revolution.

WR: Milena's worker boyfriend barges in to protect her from bourgeois intellectuals.

WR: Makavejev arranging the severed head of Milena

certain characteristics in common with Godard's experiments with montage and collage, Makavejev's films have a greater emotional density than Godard's most recent films (although not more than, say, *Vivre sa vie, Une Femme Mariée,* and *Masculin-Féminin*), and Makavejev's work probably shares more affinities with the early Surrealist experiments of Buñuel (*Un Chien Andalou, L'Age d'Or,* and *Las Hurdes*) than with anything else. And although Makavejev acknowledges the fundamental importance of Eisenstein's theoretical elaboration of montage, his own use of montage differs radically from Eisenstein's: whereas the author of *Potemkin* used montage primarily to reinforce an idea or an emotion, Makavejev uses it to build a highly complex network of cross-references, associations, and above all, of contradictions—with the result that one montage-cell does not reinforce another but rather calls it into question.

In *WR: The Mysteries of the Organism,* however, the complexity of the collage construction is almost undermined and neutralized by the insistent and, to some, irritating tone of lighthearted humor that sometimes smacks of the crowd-pleasing ploy aimed at young audiences who couldn't help but respond favorably to the film's bouncy appeal for sexual freedom. While I personally do not find this to be a major problem, I am aware that there is a danger that the film's flippant tone will make Makavejev's treatment of sex and politics seem deceptively facile and frivolous.*

This is a particularly strong danger in a film dealing with Wilhelm Reich, for even many of Reich's admirers will admit that there is a great difference between Reich's early illuminating work in Europe and his later, seemingly facile and far-fetched work in America. Opting for a tone of irreverence and *insouciance* throughout his film, Makavejev seems to have focused primarily, if not exclusively, on later Reich—and in doing this he has perhaps compounded the weaknesses and contradictions embodied in Reich himself.

---

* In San Francisco, the exhibitors advertised *WR* in the sex-house section and it closed in a week. In Boston, newspapers refused to run ads for the film. Its "real" run, on university campuses, has only begun.

In any case, where the man himself is concerned, the film tells us very little, for the documentary material on Reich is, by necessity I am sure, rather thin. Even scouring archives in Germany and America, Makavejev was able to come up with very little documentation on film of the young Reich's activities with the German *Sexpol* organization he helped found in the early 1930's; nor, for that matter, could he find much film footage of Reich's activities during his later years of exile in America. So, aside from a snapshot glimpse or two of Reich himself, what we see in *WR* is footage shot by Makavejev's small 16mm crew during their 1968 visit to the little town in Maine where Reich had lived and worked in his later years.

There are brief, amusing interviews with local people who knew Reich—including one with the pokerfaced deputy sheriff who doubles as town barber stepping out of his barber shop in his police uniform to tell us that, yes, he cut Dr. Reich's hair many times, and that "Dr. Reich was a little eccentric; he didn't wear his hair like normal people"—pointing, as he says this, to his own butch crewcut. (This fortuitous little anecdote has very rich associations and connotations, evoking as it does the politically as well as sexually repressive notions of "normality" that dominate society —and which Reich devoted his life to combating.)

Then, too, there are brief interviews with Reich's widow (who accuses the socialist countries of stifling and suppressing the "creative individual") and with Reich's son, who recalls the time his father grabbed a gun and went to confront a bunch of Maine citizens who had marched up to Reich's research center shouting "Down with the Commies, down with the Orggies"—the latter being their term for Reich and his Orgone Research colleagues. A tape recording of Reich's own voice then recounts this event, with Reich explaining that he simply told the angry mob he was no more a Communist than they were; that he, too—"like everybody else"— had just voted for Eisenhower, and that, in fact, if they wanted to fight the Commies, he was glad, adding "I've been fighting the Commies longer than you have."

Finally, there is a long tracking shot of the forbidding outer walls of Lewisburg Penitentiary in Pennsylvania, where Reich died in 1957 while serving a two-year sentence for contempt of court arising out of his refusal to appear to answer charges alleging that he violated interstate commerce laws in selling his Orgone Accumulator Boxes, which the U.S. government argued "could have deleterious effects on one's health." Prison authorities at Lewisburg, by the way, refused Makavejev's request to do any filming inside the prison.

In addition to the material on Reich himself, there is some brief footage devoted to Reich's disciples and their ongoing practice of Reichian therapy. This footage is of two basic types: there are interview-statements by several Reichian therapists who explain one or another aspect of their practice of therapy, and there is some brief footage of therapy in process. In the first category Dr. Alexander Lowen (author of *Love and Orgasm*) does a slightly hammy demonstration of the way a person's inner tensions are expressed in body language—what Reich called "character armor." Another protegé of Reich's gives us a humorous explanation and demonstration of how the Orgone Accumulator Box supposedly works. In general, the Reichian therapists come off as rather nice, gregarious people, but there is just enough of a touch of glibness about them to evoke the kind of skepticism we muster when we suspect we're somehow being taken.

Footage of actual therapy in progress, however, reveals a more serious—although not necessarily more reassuring—aspect of the Reichians' approach to psychological problems. When we see patients being encouraged to scream and sob and shake, we may recognize the therapeutic potential of their giving physical vent to their emotional tensions, but the actual experience of therapy itself seems so traumatic we may wonder if the cure isn't likely to be as psychologically disturbing as whatever was bothering them in the first place. And since Makavejev gives us only very brief glimpses of isolated aspects of Reichian therapy but does not provide us enough information to place these within the context of an overall program, whatever we do see is very likely to appear gratuitous and merely exotic. This is particularly true of the footage where we see a huge roomful of men and women lying in rows on the floor, stripped down to underwear or bathing suits, taking turns standing on each other's stomachs or jumping up and down on each other's buttocks. (Moreover, the poor lighting of this footage, producing a fuzzy image, combined with the prominence in the foreground of several very fat individuals in their underwear, unfortunately evokes a rather dingy, sleazy atmosphere that would not even be flattering to a reducing salon—which is what the scene resembles.)

All in all, then, Makavejev's presentation of Reich and Reichian therapy raises a great many questions in our minds, not just about Reich but also about Makavejev's attitude toward Reich. Obviously he is sympathetic to Reich, and the film is in some ways a tribute to Reich, but it is also clear, I think, that Makavejev's attitude toward Reich is by no means uncritical. And this is a very healthy sign. For one thing, it enables us to begin to appreciate the complexity of the relations between sex and politics that Reich was one of the first to examine.

To further complicate matters, Makavejev suddenly introduces in rapid succession two new blocs of material whose relation to Reichian therapy or to Reich's ideas in general is very ambiguous. The first, introduced in the guise of a "Sexpol film, Yugoslavia, 1971," is a humorous allegorical fiction about a cute Yugoslav girl (Milena Dravic) who, much to the chagrin of her jealous worker boyfriend, advocates free love. Significantly, this allegorical fiction (which will dominate the latter half of the film) begins with an argument between Milena and her boyfriend, who yells angrily that she is betraying her working-class origins by hanging around with the Party crowd, whom he contemptuously accuses of indulging in the same kind of consumer-product fetishism as the capitalists. In a pun on "Max Factor," he shouts that Yugoslavians are urged to buy "Marx Factor"—and at this instant Makavejev cuts to a shot of New York's 42nd St. and a heavily made-up drag queen sharing an ice-cream cone with his/her homosexual boyfriend. Since this traveling shot, which follows the "couple" as they walk, is obviously not a part of the Yugoslav material, and since it brings us back to America, we associate it with the Reichian documentary material and suspect that it somehow refers to still another aspect of the Reichian movement in America—an association that is strengthened when Makavejev cuts from this shot to more documentary footage of Reichian therapy in action.

However, although certain associations with the Reichian movement are intentionally set up by it, this shot itself belongs to a third bloc of material that is neither documentary footage on Reich nor part of the allegorical fiction set in Yugoslavia, its function being to mediate between these other two types of material and to raise questions about both of them. Also included in this third bloc of intercut material are a brief visit to the office of *Screw* magazine (whose editorial staff walks around nude), an interview with a woman artist who specializes in painting portraits of people in the act of masturbating, and a long sequence which examines an enterprising young sculptress's process of making a plaster cast of an erect penis in order to turn out "individualized" penis-shaped sculptures for display on your own or your girlfriend's coffee table. Aside from its shock value and its humorous quality, this material seems intended primarily to illustrate what Makavejev considers certain characteristically American *aberrations* of sexual identity. Makavejev has said that the case of the drag queen—who later in the film recounts his first homosexual experience and reveals that, turned on to homosexuality, he went transvestite, only to be spurned by his original homosexual partner, who, "being used to boys, just couldn't make it with 'girls' "—seems to him perfectly symbolic of contemporary America's deep confusion over sexual identity.[39]

The intercut material also has the effect, however, of calling into question Reich's ideas—particularly the directions his later work in America was leading him. Although Makavejev is careful to respect the integrity of the documentary material on Reich and Reichian therapy, nonetheless his montage construction of the film as a whole suggests certain associations and affinities between Reichian sexology and the attitudes toward sex of the individuals in the intercut material. And as bizarre as these attitudes may seem, there is, after all, almost a family resemblance between them and the Reichian pitch on the Orgone Accumulator Box. In fact, the penis sculptures, the masturbation portraits, and the Orgone Box might all be considered fertility or potency *fetishes*. (My own guess is that Reich intended the Orgone Box to function as just such a fetish and thereby to open up a *mythic* dimension that he hoped would enable people to relate more freely and fully to their own sexuality.)

The problem with fetishes, however, as Marx brilliantly observed, is that in capitalist society all consumer products are fetishes (and today nearly all have sexual overtones, as scrutiny of any advertising pitch will reveal). For contemporary Americans, then, the mythic dimension is plugged directly into the consumer economy of advanced capitalism, which tries to sell us ever greater quantities of fetishes. Instead of liberating our natural sexuality, we get bogged down at the level of what Marcuse calls repressive desublimation, where, deluded by the new aura of permissiveness and hedonism cultivated by advertising, we throw ourselves— without any more guilt pangs, but *compulsively* nonetheless—into the consumption of sex, which becomes another commodity. The old Puritan morality which was necessary to a society dominated by scarcity has given way to a new, more permissive but equally repressive morality geared to serve the needs of the consumer society.

But Makavejev's use of the intercut material not only points out the fetishistic aspect of American society, it also comments on the fetishistic aspect of Russian Communism, particularly under Stalin. There the mythic dimension is plugged directly into politically cultivated hero-worship. Stalin becomes a fetish. And a cut from a shot of Stalin (as played by the actor Guelovani) to a shot of the finished penis sculpture, then back to Stalin, clearly suggests the affinities between these two fetishes—both of them representing, at the psychic level, sexual energy that has become rigid and lifeless while enshrined as an object of veneration.

But in order to understand clearly the rich implications of Makavejev's montage of the Stalin footage, we need to establish, as closely as possible, the shot-by-shot progression of this important sequence. As Milena finishes her impromptu speech advocating free love, she joins arms with the Yugoslav workers whom she has been haranguing and leads them in a triumphal march around the inner balcony of the low-cost apartment house where they all live (recalling incidentally both the workers' housing in Eisenstein's *Strike* and the central courtyard which, more than just functioning as a décor, was almost the central protagonist in Renoir and Prévert's examination of a worker's community in *Le Crime de Monsieur Lange*). At this point, as they move from left to right across the screen, Makavejev cuts to a shot of Mao, also moving left to right across the screen as he walks along a reviewing stand waving triumphantly to a huge throng of admirers, who, red book in hand, jubilantly wave back. The last words of Milena, just before the cut, are that "socialism without fucking is dull and lifeless." The first impression created by this statement and the sudden cut to Mao is that Mao's brand of socialism is not exempt from Milena's criticism. However, as the camera moves from Mao himself to the wildly cheering sea of humanity in the huge public square, we are reminded that, numerically at least, the world's most populous nation must necessarily do a healthy amount of fucking; and that in this literal sense, "lifeless" is hardly a word that applies to China.

To add to the ambiguity, however, Makavejev then cuts to a shot of Stalin, who is also parading triumphantly from left to right across the screen. Moreover, superimposed on the shot of Stalin (again, it is the actor Guelovani) are images of Nazi flags unfurled beneath Stalin's feet as he walks. Not having seen Tchiaorelli's *The Pledge* (1946), which is the film Makavejev has borrowed his Stalin footage from, I can't say whether the superimposed flags are part of the original or whether Makavejev has added them; but more likely they are in the original and were used to suggest that to Stalin goes the credit for trampling underfoot the infamous Nazi banner. Here, however, in the context of Makavejev's *WR*, the Nazi flags suggest a certain affinity between Stalin and Nazism and seem to indicate that the path down which Stalin was leading socialism was in reality the path of fascism.

This latter interpretation clearly becomes the dominant if not the exclusive one when immediately following Stalin's ceremonious declaration that the Russian Revolution not only destroyed the old bourgeois order but also succeeded in building a new socialist order, Makavejev intercuts a gruesome shot of a hospital patient being force-fed by having a tube jammed up his nose while uniformed attendants hold him down (an image that recalls an almost identical shot in Frederick Wiseman's *Titicut Follies*). Then there is a cut back to Stalin, who declares that Russian Communism continues to advance on the path marked out by Lenin—"with the present leaders carrying out each directive he passed on to us." And at this instant Makavejev cuts to another hospital patient (or perhaps the same one?) being given electric shock treatment which induces uncontrollable body spasms.

The implication is obvious here, and although one could argue that Makavejev intends the reference to Lenin ironically in order to point out how Stalin invoked Lenin's name to justify policies of ruthless self-aggrandizement, nonetheless in light of the thinly veiled indictment of Lenin which later follows, this particular sequence must be seen as the film's first attempt to trace the authoritarian and repressive trends in Soviet Communism to Lenin himself. Finally, the sequence closes with a return to Stalin, then a cut to the young American sculptress removing the finished penis sculpture from the plaster cast and placing it for display on a table, followed by a cut back to Stalin again as he proudly announces that "the first stage of Communism has been achieved"—at which point Makavejev intercuts one final shot of a mental patient repeatedly banging his head against the wall of his locked cell.

At the close of this important sequence, then, a certain "false climax" has been reached, and Makavejev has skillfully and humorously associated the betrayal of the genuinely liberating potential of the Russian Revolution with the channeling of sexual energy into rigid and lifeless fetishes. Now the scene returns to Yugoslavia and there ensues a gradual development of the fictional plot of Milena's love life.

The Russian Ice Follies comes to Belgrade. Milena and her

roommate attend a performance, where a pair of Yugoslav soldiers on leave try to pick them up. Milena, however, is fascinated by the handsome star of the ice show, the Russian figure-skating champion named Vladimir Ilyich. She goes backstage to meet him, flirts with him, and invites him to accompany her back to her apartment. Once there, Milena and Vladimir carry on a conversation that is quite funny because of Vladimir's persistence in avoiding Milena's questions about his personal life—which he dismisses by saying that personal accomplishments don't matter much when, as in Russia, everyone is "happy to be a servant of the state." Moreover, Vladimir remains so caught up in his pronouncements of lofty idealism that he is completely oblivious to the antics of Milena's comely roommate, who has casually taken off all her clothes and nearly sat in his lap in an unsuccessful attempt to get his attention. Meanwhile, Milena's working-class boyfriend—who has been locked out by Milena—uses his pickaxe to break through the wall from the nextdoor apartment, barging in triumphantly and shouting that he will "protect Milena from bourgeois intellectuals," as he throws Vladimir Ilyich into a closet which he nails shut.

After some brief (rather gratuitous) intercut material depicting the antics of a street-theater "guerilla-fighter" who clowns around the financial district of New York City with a toy machine-gun, the film returns to Milena and Vladimir as they go for a walk in the snow—apparently the morning following the scene in Milena's apartment. Vladimir's incarceration in the closet seems to have been in fun and presumably brief, for he laughs over the incident and speaks admiringly of Milena's boyfriend's having broken right through a wall to protect her. He also speaks of having enjoyed listening to music the night before—particularly, he says, the "Appassionata Sonata" by Beethoven. "The trouble is," he adds, "I can't listen to music too often. It's bad for my nerves; it makes me want to say stupid, nice things and stroke people gently on the head; but you stroke people on the head today and you might get your hand bitten off. What we need to do today . . ." he adds with sudden anger, "is hit people over the head, without mercy . . . although in principle of course we are opposed to all violence."

These words—which Makavejev puts in the mouth of his Russian figure-skating champion—are, of course, the actual words of none other than "Vladimir Ilyich" Lenin himself, as recounted by Maxim Gorky in his *Days with Lenin*. Makavejev has simply tacked on to the end of Lenin's remark the qualification that "in principle we are opposed to all violence." (Makavejev has also framed the shot after a famous photograph of Lenin vigorously driving a point home to the masses.)

As Vladimir says this, Milena, who has been waiting in vain for him to make a pass at her, makes one herself; but he turns suddenly and slaps her brutally in the face, knocking her down in the snow. Shaken, she looks up at him, and here Makavejev cuts to a shot of Stalin standing in the snow presiding over a public rally while a huge banner is unfurled behind him bearing the image of Lenin. Stalin declares proudly that Russian Communism need fear no would-be enemies, for the life and work of Lenin are "an arrow thrust boldly and with true aim toward the enemy camp."

Stalin's metaphor is then taken up by Milena, as Makavejev cuts back to her. Sobbing, she throws herself at Vladimir, pounding him on the chest repeatedly with her fists, slapping his face, and telling him what a phony he is—"a petty human lie dressed up as a great historical truth." "You profess to love all humanity, but you are incapable of loving one human individual. Have you ever loved anyone as a man should? Have you ever been able to fulfill a woman, thrusting your arrow boldly and with true aim?" Finally, overcome at last by Milena's emotional goading, Vladimir passionately draws her to him and kisses her on the lips, eyes, face, then full-mouthed as Milena acquiesces in spite of her anger.

What happens next in the drama of Milena and Vladimir, however, is only pieced together in retrospect by what transpires in the next sequence—following more brief intercut material—in which two police inspectors discuss clues relating to a savage murder of a young woman whose body and severed head were found along a riverbank. The severed head is brought to a police laboratory and placed on an examining table. We recognize it immediately, of course, as Milena's. One officer remarks that the presumed murder weapon was found nearby—pulling out of a sack an ice-skate which he admiringly identifies as of professional championship quality. The other officer remarks in passing that an autopsy revealed that the victim's vagina contained four to five times the normal amount of sperm. Since there didn't seem to be any marks on her body, however, or signs of a scuffle at the scene of the crime, he concludes that it is unlikely that she was the victim of a gangbang or repeated rape. "It seems," he adds, "that she had sex willingly, perhaps at some orgy." Nonetheless, he decides it wise to check with local insane asylums to see if any sex-starved maniacs have escaped.

This attention to seemingly incidental detail is characteristic of Makavejev's method—and this sequence recalls the very similar autopsy sequence in *Love Affair*. And, as usual, the detail is by no means incidental. The police, of course, are trying to gather information that will help them solve the crime—and the evidence leads them to consider the possibility of a sex crime. Moreover, Makavejev subtly evokes the connection between an individual's repressed or distorted sexuality and society's repressive structures by having the police officer suggest that they call the local insane asylums to see if any sex-starved maniacs have escaped; and this reference to insane asylums ties in nicely with the earlier shots of mental patients intercut with footage of Stalin—thus reinforcing the earlier suggestion that under Stalinist domination all of the Soviet bloc is turned into an enormous network of insane asylums.

Dramatically dominating this entire discussion by the two police inspectors, however, is our own awareness that we know something they don't know: namely that the skate presumed to be the murder weapon very likely belongs to Vladimir Ilyich, and that when Milena was last seen (by us, of course) she was locked in a volatile embrace with Vladimir at the very spot where later her dead body was discovered. Consequently, where the vicious decapitation and the sperm in Milena's vagina are concerned, we have reason to believe that that was no sex-starved maniac who put it to her, that was Lenin!

Ah, but there's the rub. With this seemingly incidental set of details, Makavejev has suggested a possible affinity between Lenin and a sex-starved maniac. And Lenin's readiness to resort to violence (even though against it in principle) is here associated by Makavejev with a sex crime in the sense that the violent behavior arises out of the individual's insecurity and tension in relating to his own repressed sexuality. (In conversation Makavejev voiced the opinion that in fact Lenin's relations with women were not well resolved and were a source of serious tensions in his life.) The fictional plot concerning Milena's love life has thus enabled Makavejev to examine and dramatize Wilhelm Reich's insight and to apply these Reichian notions to a friendly but critical reevaluation of Lenin's role in shaping the Communist movement.

The verdict on Lenin is harsh—and it is pronounced by Milena herself, as her severed head suddenly comes to life and she declares that "Vladimir Ilyich was a genuine red fascist"—adding, however, that "even now I am not ashamed or regretful of my Communist past." The film does not close here, however, as Makavejev cuts from the severed head of Milena to a long, poignant panning shot of the Russian figure-skating champion, Vladimir Ilyich, walking aimlessly in the snow while on the sound track we hear Bulat Okoudjava's plaintive Russian song dedicated to François Villon. Phrased in the form of a prayer addressed to a god who doesn't exist (a touch Makavejev particularly liked), the song is a plea to "grant to each person some little thing, but remember I'm here too"—words which touchingly evoke the Communist commitment to a just distribution among all citizens, but which also touchingly evoke the personal plight of the individual, who, no matter how great his ideals may be, remains as frail and emotionally vulnerable to life's troubles as the rest of us . . . even if his name happens to be Vladimir Ilyich.

Ending on this poignant note, WR, like all of Makavejev's films, leaves us with an acute sense of sympathy for the solitary individual whose private, personal turmoil and struggle are dialectically set against the public aspirations to grand humanitarian ideals. But precisely because Makavejev's method is so profoundly dialectical, we sense that the contradiction between the individual and the social aspirations need not necessarily be an antagonistic one: the plea in Okoudjava's song is a plea for the individual, but for the individual who himself subscribes to the Communist commitment to create a society which provides to each according to his need.

The film, then, while critical of the authoritarian and repressive elements within the Communist movement—some of which are traced to Lenin himself—seems clearly to be an honest and sincere attempt to bring out the revolutionary potential for genuine liberation which has so often been betrayed and distorted by our neglect of the all-important psychosexual foundations of political behavior. And the tribute offered to Wilhelm Reich by *WR: The Mysteries of the Organism* is all the more meaningful because Makavejev no more adopts an uncritical attitude toward Reich than he does toward Lenin, but instead chooses to respect the complexity of our human predicament—caught up as we are, and as they were, in a sound and fury of sex and politics.

14

The Sorrow and the Pity:
France and Her Political Myths

Every country has its political myths. In *Le Chagrin et la Pitié (The Sorrow and the Pity)*, however, film-makers Marcel Ophuls and André Harris have prepared a mild but surprisingly effective antidote to one of the most highly cherished political myths of Gaullist France—the myth of *la résistance*. To a young, postwar generation of Frenchmen nourished on the edifying storybook image of occupied France as a network of *maquisards* rallying unanimously to the famous Appeal from London of General DeGaulle, it may come as a surprise to learn from *Le Chagrin et la Pitié* that this was not exactly the way it all happened; that in actual fact very few people heard DeGaulle's broadcast; that De Gaulle himself had very little popular following at that time; that *collaboration* with the Nazis was far more characteristic of the French nation as a whole than *résistance;* and, finally, that by far the greatest percentage of active *résistants* came from the ranks of the French Communist Party.

This is hardly the image the Gaullist regimes in postwar France have tried to cultivate. Consequently, although *Le Chagrin et la Pitié* was coproduced by the state-owned French television (along with the state-owned West German and Swiss networks), the film has been denied a television screening in France. (It has been shown on West German and Swiss TV.) According to *Le Monde*, the decision to keep the film off French TV screens was taken by none other than Jacques Chaban-Delmas, prime minister under Pompidou, who passed on his orders directly to the ORTF television administration.

Moreover, in spite of having obtained first prize at the 1970 Festival of French-Speaking Films at Dinard, *Le Chagrin et la Pitié* had trouble making its way into the commercial cinema circuit in France. Initially, it was booked only into two small Paris theaters frequented almost exclusively by students. And when left-wing newspapers began publicizing the fact that the government had stepped in to prevent the film's being shown on television, the conservative newspapers tried to pass off the film as just another wild-eyed manifestation of misguided militancy, a by-product of May 1968.

In fact, however, *Le Chagrin et la Pitié* is anything but a militant film. Rather, it is a low-keyed, even bland, "liberal" examination of the Nazi Occupation and the French collaborationist regime of Maréchal Pétain. Letting the extensive interview material and documentary footage speak pretty much for itself, film-makers Ophuls (incidentally, Marcel is the son of Max Ophuls) and Harris seem to have scrupulously avoided any hint of political editorializing. And in this they have succeeded so well that, aside from the prominence given to Pierre Mendès-France's pointed observations and personal reminiscences, the film seems remarkably devoid of any political *partis pris*.

What is ultimately most remarkable, then, about *Le Chagrin et la Pitié* is simply that such a politically vacuous film should be capable of stirring up such big political waves. (I even heard expressions of high-level concern in England that the BBC's television screening of the film in the fall of 1971 was likely to be considered such a provocative act toward France that it might jeopardize Britain's hopes of gaining entry into the European Common Market.)

As for the problem of censorship in France, the most significant aspect of the Pompidou government's suppression of this film is simply the revelation that even after DeGaulle *not even* a subdued, reflective film like *Le Chagrin et la Pitié* is allowed to be shown widely to the French people. (Incidentally, it joins a long list of films—including *La Religieuse, Le Gai Savoir, The Battle of Algiers,* and *Les Cadets de Saumur,* to name only a few—which have been kept off the television and movie screens of France, either by direct government intervention or through pressure exerted on the government and the commercial movie exhibitors by right-wing lobbyists and agitators.)

Subtitled "Chronicle of a French Town under the Occupation," *Le Chagrin et la Pitié* focuses primarily on the occupation of the medium-sized provincial city of Clermont-Ferrand in the mountainous heartland of the French Massif Centrale, a locale chosen both for its proximity to Vichy (the capital of occupied France under the regime of Pétain) and for its importance as a center of underground resistance.

The choice of Clermont-Ferrand, however, is not without serious repercussions. Many French commentators have pointed out that this region is not at all representative of France as a whole; that, in particular, Communist Party membership has always been disproportionately small in this traditionally anti-Communist region; and that, consequently, unlike most other parts of France where the resistance was organized and carried out largely by Communist Party members, Clermont-Ferrand's resistance was organized by an aristocrat, Emmanuel D'Astier de la Vigerie, and contained a much smaller Communist participation than was normally the case throughout France.

The fact that this discrepancy is acknowledged in the film, it is argued, does not in any way correct or excuse the distorted picture of the phenomenon of resistance that the choice of Clermont-Ferrand entails. Moreover, it is particularly inexcusable that with the exception of a few brief remarks by Communist Party chief Jacques Duclos, the Communist role in the resistance is simply mentioned in passing. And on one of the few occasions when it is brought up, the Communists are disparaged as *"peu recommendables"* by a former Clermont *résistant* who declares himself a *monarchist.*

If the film's perspective on the *résistance* is vague and fuzzy, its perspective on the phenomenon of collaboration is much sharper and clearer. And the portrait that emerges is especially rich since the collaboration is presented from the points of view of both the occupiers and the occupied. Throughout the film considerable attention is given to the reminiscences of the German occupiers. In fact, *Le Chagrin et la Pitié* begins with the edifying discourse of one Helmuth Tausend, former commanding officer of the occupying German forces in Clermont-Ferrand, as he delivers an extemporaneous little speech to his family on the occasion of the wedding of one of his children. And although the complacent, rationalizing "clear conscience" of the "man who simply followed orders" is transparent—and his capacity for arrogant self-righteousness downright objectionable—nonetheless, the film reveals enough striking parallels in the attitudes of the French collaborators to suggest that the two sides of the collaboration were really only two sides of the same coin . . . and that *fascism was the common currency of both the Germans and the French.*

Undoubtedly the most remarkable moment in *Le Chagrin et la Pitié* is the revelation of one Christian de la Mazière, a suave, socially prominent aristocrat, who tells why in his early twenties he enlisted in the "Charlemagne" Division of the German *Waffen* SS —a special divison made up of some 7,000 young Frenchmen who were so won over by their occupiers that they chose to join the German army and were sent to fight on the Russian front. Mazière explains that, as an aristocrat who came from a family of French military officers, he could not help but admire the iron discipline and machine-like efficiency of the German army—so different, he emphasizes, from the sloppy and poorly trained French army!

The sight of those "blond, handsome, upright, barechested conquerors," he admits, was awe-inspiring and irresistible. Moreover, for him and for many young men from the aristocratic milieu, the defeat of France seemed almost a "Judgment of God"— something the nation had deserved for turning away from the old aristocratic values. Acquiescing to God's will, Mazière explains, meant joining forces with the German conquerors, who were seen to be His terrestrial agents.

The Sorrow and the Pity: Maréchal Pétain, president of the Vichy collaborationist government

The Sorrow and the Pity: The liberation of Paris

The Sorrow and the Pity: Louis Grave, Auvergnat peasant and member of the Résistance

The Sorrow and the Pity: Charles de Gaulle, attempting to rally the French in a broadcast from London

And, as Mazière acknowledges, his political notions had been formed by the tremendous right-wing fear of the growing socialist sentiments of the *Front Populaire* movement in France and the fear of a Communist victory in the Civil War in Spain. The combination of all these factors, he concludes, made him what he was. When asked by the film-maker if the term "fascist" would be inappropriate, Mazière amiably replies, "No, not at all inappropriate. I was a fascist, a young fascist, in those days."

But if Mazière's case is the most remarkable expression of French fascism in the film, this is only because it is the most extreme and the most frankly acknowledged. However, there are also innumerable indications in *Le Chagrin et la Pitié* of a more pervasive, although more passive, brand of fascism which attracted the French bourgeoisie to the paternalistic leadership of Pétain and to the authoritarian principles of the Vichy government's prime minister, Pierre Laval. (Incidentally, one of the most pathetic moments in the film occurs when Laval's son-in-law, the Count of Chambrun, tries to restore the reputation of his father-in-law by telling the film-makers how kind Laval was to a man from the local village who had been held in a German concentration camp. Chambrun summons the ex-prisoner, who is now working for him as a laborer, and puts him on exhibition for the cameras, manipulating the old fellow like a puppet on a string, asking him to "tell these gentlemen all the kind things Monsieur Laval did for you.")

If the tone of the interview material tends to be exculpatory, the tone of several short films of Vichy propaganda that are included in *Le Chagrin et la Pitié* is strident and aggressive. Particularly revealing are the glimpses of the program organized by Georges Lamirand, Pétain's Minister of Youth and a zealous advocate of the fullest collaboration with Nazi Germany. Footage of Lamirand's racist, demagogic speeches to youth groups and of the militaristic youth camps he set up for French children would look right at home in Leni Riefenstahl's Nazi panegyric, *Triumph of the Will*.

Also disconcerting is the evidence presented in *Le Chagrin et la Pitié* of the virulent anti-Semitism that came to the fore in France under the Vichy regime. So pervasive was this "unofficial" anti-Semitism that the names of all Jewish actors and technicians were systematically blacked out on the credits of French films shown during the Occupation. And in Clermont-Ferrand, as elsewhere in France, announcements began appearing in newspapers to the effect that such and such a merchant—one Monsieur Klein, for example—although bearing a name that could be mistaken as Jewish, did hereby assure his clientele that he was both 100 percent Aryan and 100 percent French. Finally, we are reminded by a Jewish scholar that on one infamous day in 1942, the Paris police not only carried out the occupiers' orders to round up all Jews over sixteen years of age from the *Vel d'Hiv* Jewish quarter of Paris; but, in an excess of zeal (which even caused some momentary embarrassment to the German command), the French *flics* also rounded up 4,000 Jewish children, forcibly separated them from their parents, and persuaded the Germans to deport them all to Nazi concentration camps.

Still another indication of the anti-Semitism that was rampant in occupied France is provided in the interview with Pierre Mendès-France, which dominates the first half of the film as Mendès-France gives a marvelously nuanced account of the troubles he encountered as a prominent Jew under the Vichy regime. Already a political figure of some stature, Mendès-France was put on trial by the Vichy government for supposedly having been a deserter when he sailed from Marseilles to Morocco to join the fighting forces of Free France, a move taken by his entire regiment. Arrested immediately upon his return to France and put on trial under extremely prejudicial circumstances, Mendès-France opened his defense with a simple statement of defiance: "I am a Jew; I am a Freemason; I am not a deserter. Let the trial begin." Found guilty and sentenced to six years in prison, he served only a few months of the sentence before making his escape by climbing over the prison wall—an escape, he adds, which was delayed for what seemed like an eternity by the inopportune presence on the other side of the wall of an amorous soldier and his all-too-hesitant girlfriend.*

Interspersed with the interview material in the opening half of *Le Chagrin et la Pitié* is some remarkable Nazi documentary footage depicting the debacle of the French defenders of the famed Maginot Line. One Nazi film presents long tracking shots filmed from a car as it drives past mile after mile of abandoned French vehicles lining both sides of the road—eloquent testimony to the chaos and desperation of the French retreat from the on-rushing invaders. Another short propaganda film presents Hitler visiting conquered Paris at five o'clock in the morning, stepping out of his escorted jeep to climb the steps of the Church of the Madeleine, visiting the Arc de Triomphe, and receiving the Nazi salute in the early morning gloom from a contingent of Paris police.

One particularly odious piece of Nazi propaganda is a short film that depicts the conquering German army as discovering to their amazement that the great French nation, "supposedly one of the finest flowers of European civilization," was defended by an incredible potpourri of Turks, Arabs, black Africans, and Orien-tals—"a rag-tag bunch of savages in French army coats"—whose exotic physiognomies are exhibited before the camera like so many specimens of prehistoric stages in the development of the blond master race.

To further round out the picture of the sad situation in the early days following the German invasion of France, Ophuls and Harris include some interesting material with Anthony Eden, whose measured comments, delivered in more than passable French, set forth the point of view of the British government in

---

* In another humorous anecdote, Mendès-France recounts that at the close of his trial, one naïve young man wrote to the lawyer who defended him, asking for a transcript of the trial . . . "in order," so the letter stated, "that I might personally call this matter to the attention of Maréchal Pétain, who obviously must not be aware of your case, for he would certainly not allow this miscarriage of justice to occur." The naïve young man, Mendès-France reveals, was none other than Valéry Giscard d'Estaing.

those troubled times. Of particular interest is Eden's description of the dilemma confronting England when it was feared that France—which had not only ceased fighting but had also, against all previous agreements with her allies, signed an armistice with Germany—might deliver her naval fleet into the hands of the Nazis. Acting quickly to prevent any such eventuality, the British navy made a surprise attack on the fleet of its allies (who, it was subsequently reported, were at that moment sailing to place themselves at the disposal of the British), sinking many of the ships and effectively disabling the rest. All in all, a most inglorious chapter in the saga of the war, Eden acknowledges, but one that must be considered in light of the fact that France was the only country in occupied Europe whose "legal" government practiced a policy of collaboration with the Nazis.

In the second half of this four-and-a-half-hour film, the focus shifts from the big events and the actions of prominent individuals to the choice that confronted the ordinary man of the street in occupied France, particularly in the streets (and nearby fields) of Clermont-Ferrand. Many individuals, of course, preferred to turn their backs on the choice and pretend it wasn't there. One bicycle-racer-turned-bar-owner tells the interviewers that the Germans couldn't really have occupied Clermont-Ferrand or he would have seen them—and, he declares, "I never saw a single German!" Newspaper photos, however, show this bicycle-racer proudly accepting a trophy from the commanding officer of the occupying German army.

For others the choice was one of which accommodation to make and which not to make. An elderly hotel-owner in Clermont whose establishment was commandeered by the occupying forces tells us that he and his wife decided that they would consent to house and feed the German soldiers but would not allow their premises to be used for prostitution. And where this latter issue is concerned, a former occupying soldier (now a farmer in Bavaria) gives us a pathetic reminder of the choice imposed on countless young girls in occupied France.

Some people, of course, tried to have it both ways, bending

whichever way the wind was blowing. Near the beginning of *Le Chagrin et la Pitié* footage from the early years of the occupation shows Maurice Chevalier singing songs to the glory of Maréchal Pétain; then toward the end of the film we see Chevalier after the liberation, explaining (for the benefit of his English-speaking friends) that there are lots of foolish rumors floating about; that, for example, it isn't true that he made a singing tour in Germany at the invitation of the Nazis; that, in fact, he only sang "one little song" for the French prisoners of war, "just to cheer up the boys a little."

Perhaps most illuminating of all is the reunion of former *résistants* in a small rural commune just outside of Clermont-Ferrand, where the men recount the various excuses that were offered, after the liberation, by those who hadn't taken part in the resistance. "Quite a few of them said they had heard talk about a group of *résistants* and had wanted to join up, but didn't know where to go or whom to ask. Well, believe me," (the speaker pauses, making a gesture for the benefit of the camera) "this group of men right here is about the least well-educated group of men in Clermont-Ferrand, and none of *us* had any trouble finding out where to go or whom to ask!"

Eloquently indicative of the quiet courage and dignity of the lowest classes of French society is the story recounted by two Auvergnat peasants, Alexis and Louis Grave. While working for the *résistance*, Louis was denounced to the occupiers by an anonymous letter and sent off to Buchenwald. When he returned after the war, he immediately set out to discover who had denounced him. After a brief, discreet search, he determined that it was a certain neighbor. But, now that he knew who it was, Louis didn't take any revenge. As he puts it, "When one has been beyond the scope of all justice, what good would it do to take justice into one's own hands, or even to turn things over to the 'official' justice?"

That it was invariably the lowest classes of society—the peasants and, particularly, the workers—who rallied wholeheartedly to the resistance, is also the testimony offered by one Dennis Rake, a British secret agent who operated clandestinely in France during the occupation. "The workers were magnificent," Rake recalls with gratitude. "They would do anything to help our operations. They gave us our *bleus* [the blue coveralls worn by French workers]; they housed us, fed us, hid us from the Germans and the French police. Without the French workers and their organized resistance, we couldn't have accomplished anything."

When asked about the French bourgeoisie, Rake can only reply, tactfully, that they were "more or less neutral." Then, not wanting this observation to sound too damning, he adds, "I suppose it's only those who have 'nothing' who can afford to act on their convictions."

However, one of the very questions which *Le Chagrin et la Pitié* raises, at least implicitly, is whether the bourgeoisie in occupied France had any convictions at all—and, if so, which ones? For the bourgeois owner of a prosperous pharmacy in Clermont-Ferrand, for example, "the important thing was to keep the store running." He explains that he had a large family to feed and a large house to heat, and that he needed a steady income to keep everything going. To make sure the Germans didn't just take over his house or his store—as he says they often did with people they didn't like—he just "kept quiet and minded my own business."

And when asked if he found those years of occupation a period of unrelenting hardship, he replies that it wasn't all bad, that there were some good moments, like the year the Germans allowed them to reopen the hunting season, which had been canceled the preceding year. "*Alors*, here in the Auvergne, *vous savez*, we have a passion for hunting. And I can tell you, the reopening of the hunting season was an enormous consolation to us!"

In general, one of the most striking features of *Le Chagrin et la Pitié* is the pervasiveness of this capacity of the bourgeoisie to carry on business as usual while turning their backs on what was happening all around them or simply dividing their lives into a number of different segments whose interrelatedness they manage not to see. This departmentalizing attitude is reflected in the self-righteousness of the former German commander at Clermont, Helmuth Tausand, who blusters indignantly about the disgraceful behavior of the French resistance fighters. One day, he recalls, some of his men were marching down a country road near Clermont-Ferrand. They passed by a handful of peasants who were planting potatoes. Just as his men marched past them, the peasants threw down their shovels, picked up rifles that were hidden in their bundles, and shot down the German soldiers. "That's not guerrilla warfare," he insists; "that's just plain murder. Real partisans," he adds self-righteously, "should wear badges or armbands to identify themselves."

But, as *Le Chagrin et la Pitié* reveals again and again, this departmentalizing attitude was just as characteristic of the occupied French, particularly of the French bourgeoisie, as of the occupying Germans. And, as Marcel Ophuls expressed it in a statement to the newspaper *Combat*, "*the terribly bourgeois attitude of believing one can separate what is commonly called 'politics' from other human activities such as one's work, family life, love, etc., this attitude which is so prevalent constitutes the worst possible evasion from life, from the responsibilities of life, that one can imagine.*"

Ultimately, *Le Chagrin et la Pitié* is not just a film about the occupied France of World War II. Relying extensively on interviews filmed in 1969, it is also very much a film about France today and the kinds of attitudes the French have about their own recent history. And although this film collapses the past and the present in a way that might recall Alain Resnais's *Nuit et Brouillard (Night and Fog)*, the effect is very different. For where Resnais's film about concentration camps is poetic and personal, very clearly the stylized work of an *auteur*, *Le Chagrin et la Pitié* is so unstylized, so pedestrian, that it seems almost *authorless*. Or, rather, one gets the feeling that the French people themselves were the only real *auteurs* of this film.

Normally, of course, this window-on-the-world approach serves to reinforce the bourgeois myths that the ruling class seeks to pass off as reality. But what makes this film so threatening to the ruling class is precisely that through the same window-on-the-world approach that is characteristic of bourgeois films, *Le Chagrin et la*

Pitié manages to puncture some of the bourgeoisie's most cherished myths.

And where Resnais's *Nuit et Brouillard* can be "read"—and passed off—as one man's very personal appeal to our conscience, *Le Chagrin et la Pitié* reads as a *self-incriminating* revelation by the French people themselves! Moreover, Resnais's collapsing of past and present is carried out in a way that points to the future. The tone of *Nuit et Brouillard* is prophetic. It is the oracular tone of the artist-priest. As in Greek tragedy, the message is chilling but the medium is so exhilarating that the effect is cathartic. (Once again, however, the medium is the ultimate message.)

In *Le Chagrin et la Pitié,* however, the collapsing of past and present does not point prophetically to some vague but ominous future that awaits us like the *fate* of a tragic hero. The *temps* (time/tense) of *Le Chagrin et la Pitié* is neither the *mythic future* nor even simply the *de-mythified past,* but rather the *political present* that is the *temps politique par excellence*—the *continuous present* which teaches us to *think ourselves historically.* And in this respect, *La Chagrin et la Pitié* has the very considerable merit of reminding us just how pronounced the narrow-minded bourgeois departmentalizing attitude was—and still is—in France . . . and just how disastrous were—and still are—its consequences on the political life of the French nation.

15

The Working Class Goes Directly to
Heaven, Without Passing Go: Or,
The Name of the Game
Is Still Monopoly

"The factory is a prison," says a militant on the picket line in Elio Petri's *La Classe Operaia Va in Paradiso (The Working Class Goes to Heaven)*, a film whose jarringly abrasive depiction of life in a factory reminds me a bit of Jonas Mekas's harrowing presentation of life in another sort of prison, a military one—*The Brig*. While full of humor—and therefore not nearly as unrelenting in its assault on the spectator as *The Brig*—*The Working Class Goes to Heaven*, like the Mekas film, effectively uses a dissonant orchestration of jerky hand-held camera movements, aggressive close-ups, a constant barrage of noise, and a histrionic acting style (full of violent hand gestures, sudden head jerks, and abrasive voices whose habitual mode of speech is the shouted expletive) in order to give the spectator a gut-level feel of the brutalizing system —in this case, industrial capitalism—which, in a very real sense, imprisons the film's protagonists.

And, in fact, Petri's factory-prison and Mekas's military-prison have much in common, for both impose their ironclad regimentation on human beings in the name of machine-like efficiency. And neither in the military nor in the factory are you allowed to question just where that machine-like efficiency leads. A machine, after all, doesn't ask questions. And if in the process of becoming as "efficient" as a machine, you become a little less human, well, as drill sergeants and shop foremen would say, tough shit!

What is human nature anyway? Massa, the factory worker (colorfully portrayed by veteran actor Gian-Maria Volonte) who is the chief protagonist of *The Working Class Goes to Heaven*, gives a little discourse on human nature in the film's first sequence. For him, man is thought of in crudely mechanical terms: "You put in a little raw material called food; various machines in the body go to work on it; and the final product that comes out the other end is . . . shit! Man is a perfect little shit-factory. Pity there's no market for the stuff; we could all be capitalists."

That's a cynical, dehumanizing attiude, to be sure; but, as the film brings home to us constantly, working conditions in a factory *are* overwhelmingly dehumanizing. And, as Petri emphasizes, the machine patterns of factory life not only impose themselves on the worker physically—buffeting him relentlessly in the factory's frenetic rhythms and cadences of movement and noise—but also may impose themselves on him conceptually—channeling the worker's consciousness into very linear, mechanical models of thought which limit his ability to understand and transform his situation.

In many ways *The Working Class Goes to Heaven* is an extended analysis and dramatization of a situation which was only sketched, however pointedly and insightfully, by Godard in the assembly-line sequence of the Dziga Vertov Group's *British Sounds*. Exploring, like Godard, the effect of factory working conditions (particularly the constant barrage of machine noise) on the consciousness of the worker, Petri has found a way to demonstrate dramatically from the standpoint of the individual worker what Godard suggested intellectually—through a provocative juxtaposition of various elements on the sound track. Already assailed by more than enough noise on the factory floor, the worker may simply tune out or even resent any attempt to raise his political consciousness—particularly when, as in *The Working Class Goes to Heaven*, the militants' agitation (with bullhorns in front of the factory gates) may very well sound to the beleaguered worker like just more abrasive noise. In short, the alienation of the worker on the job is so pervasive that it effectively impedes the development of the Marxian political consciousness that would enable him to understand and to start changing his situation.

Bombarded with noise on all sides, the worker's resentment may even be exacerbated by the bitter recognition that the militants are right in pointing out the unnatural bleakness of a workday routine which begins before sunrise, ends after sunset, and, day after day (at least in the Northern Italian winter), imprisons the worker in a sunless world where, as Petri emphasizes, the rhythms of nature are overwhelmed by the rhythms of the machine. Moreover, as Petri subtly points out, management—adding their paternalist verbiage to the barrage of noise—actively encourages the worker's identification with his machine. As Petri's workers enter the shop each day, a taped public-address message wishes them *buon giorno* and, in a little peptalk, encourages them to treat their machines with "tender loving care," reminding them that the key to "a good productive workday"—and to the piecework bonuses that go with increased output—lies in each worker's intimate relation to his machine.

Massa may be bitter about his workday routine, but he has taken on some of the qualities of a machine and is a super-productive worker. He boasts that his name heads the factory list each month for total output; he gloats over the extra money he earns on the piecework system. Contemptuous of the other workers who cannot keep up with his productivity, Massa even lets himself be used by the shop supervisors to set extremely high, frenetic rates of output which are then imposed on everyone as "shop standards." Although he is slightly ill at ease about doing this, Massa obviously can't resist the opportunity to show off and lord it over his fellow workers—especially since, as a reward, he extracts from the overseers tacit approval to smoke a cigarette in spite of the strict "No Smoking" rules.

Asked to break in a couple of new workers, Massa explains that the secret of his productivity is concentration. "You gotta pick out something that'll hold your concentration. Me, I concentrate on

Adalgisa's ass over there," he says, pointing to a factory errand girl. Thinking of that ass and what he'd like to do with it, he explains, enables him to work up just the right rhythm with his machine, so that once this basic rhythm is established—"a piece . . . an ass . . . a piece . . . an ass"—he can gradually increase the pace to turn out the maximum number of pieces.

It is through this crude male-chauvinist sexual imagery that Petri introduces the film's underlying theme—that sexuality is the characterological ground that will tell us the most significant information about how and to what extent the machine patterns of the factory workday permeate every aspect of the worker's life. Using this scene's obviously sexual associations of the thrusting motions of the machine, Petri develops throughout the film the way even the worker's *ideas* of sex are geared to the productivity paradigm of his relation to his machine.

Sex, like everything else for the worker, is thought of in terms of output. Quantity is emphasized. Massa is always bragging emptily about how many times a night he can do it, with no concern for the quality of experience shared by two persons. (After subjecting a young virgin from the factory to a joyless quickie in the front seat of his car, Massa insensitively boasts how she ought to be grateful to be "broken in" by someone as good as he is; and he likens his "performance" to that of his car—a remark which Petri has made ironically appropriate by staging the scene in the cramped quarters of the front seat of Massa's car so that the girl's initiation into sex seems to be accomplished as much by the gearshift lever as by anything else.)

At first glance Petri's emphasis on sexuality in *The Working Class Goes to Heaven* might seem a direct extension of his treatment of sexuality in his preceding film, *Investigaton of a Citizen Above Suspicion;* but a closer look reveals, I think, some striking differences. As I have argued in Chapter 13, Petri's *Investigation* seems to me to share with several other recent films an oversimplified view in which homosexuality—or latent, unacknowledged homosexual tendencies—are suggested as the root cause of fascism. In any case, the methodology of Petri's *Investigation* is the familiar one of examining an individual's behavior in search of clues that will suggest the underlying psychological causes (invariably childhood traumas) of that behavior.

Surprisingly, however, in *The Working Class Goes to Heaven* Petri boldly changes direction: for once the "present factors" of neurosis are not glossed over as merely superficial symptoms of an older, "deeper," unresolved Oedipal complex. For once the methodology is not infinitely retroactive; and instead of invoking a rather crude psychosexual determination, Petri in this film explores the way in which even the supposedly deep-seated character structures of sexuality are not necessarily "fixed" once and for all in earliest childhood, as most Freudians would maintain, but may on the contrary be constantly in process of formation even well into maturity and perhaps all through one's life. And, significantly, what Petri concentrates on in *The Working Class Goes to Heaven* are the relations between sexuality and the machine patterns imposed on the life of the mature adult factory worker in industrial capitalism.

This approach to the relations between sex and politics is long overdue;[40] and what is especially thought-provoking in Petri's film is his thorough examination of the concrete, tangible effects of the factory work experience on the character structure of the individual worker. If the worker seems a little neurotic, Petri is clearly saying, no need to go back to his childhood relations with mama and papa; just go take a good look at your nearest factory. For a factory worker in his middle or late thirties like Massa, that work experience, day after day, year after year, all his adult life, is bound to leave its mark on his character.

And, sure enough, Massa has quite a few problems. His home life is unstable and obviously less than wholly satisfying. Separated from his wife (who has custody of their young son, and who is now living with one of Massa's coworkers), Massa is currently carrying on a listless affair with Lidia, a divorced hairdresser with a young son (about the same age as Massa's own son); they live with Massa in his apartment.

This particular family arrangement serves to point out the way

The Working Class Goes to Heaven: Massa waves his good hand and exhorts his fellow workers to stop work.

industrial capitalism tends to reduce people, even in their most
intimate relations to one another—such as marriage and parent-
hood—to interchangeable parts in the big social machine. Moreover, this family arrangement has certain financial ramifications.
While contributing to the financial support of his own son (and
Massa seems just a little resentful about handing over money to his
wife's new lover), Massa also finds himself having to support
Lidia's son. When asked why Lidia's ex-husband doesn't pay to
support his own kid, Massa can only reply—with a mixture of scorn
and resignation—that the guy is a clerk and therefore doesn't make
enough to support a kid. Thus Massa's productivity is a vicious
circle: as a particularly fast and efficient worker, Massa earns more
money than most men; but precisely because he makes so much
and the wages of so many others are barely above subsistence level,
he finds himself having to assume more financial responsibilities
than would normally be his.

Finally, Massa's productivity causes him trouble in still another
way. His fellow workers, envious of his high output and resentful
of his collusion with the overseers in the speed-up, begin to heckle
and harass Massa in the factory. When this happens, Massa's tem-
per really boils over, and contemptuously shouting that he'll show
them what "a real Stakhanovite" can do, he furiously pushes himself to work faster than ever. Sputtering with rage, Massa quickens
his already frenetic work pace—grabbing each piece with his fin-
gers well before it has stopped turning in order to move on to the
next piece a few seconds faster. Suddenly, however, in his anger,
Massa loses concentration for an instant, loses the rhythm, and,
missing his timing by a split-second . . . loses a finger in the moving
parts of the machine.

With this accident Massa's life undergoes a profound change.
The loss of most of one finger itself is not disabling: he'll be able
to go back to work after a brief layoff for the hand to heal. But
during this enforced respite, Massa has time to think. Suddenly
removed from the relentless rhythms and exhausting pace of the
factory workday, Massa can pass his time in a more relaxed but
also disoriented way—paying a visit to his son to show off the

now four-fingered hand, and also visiting a grizzled old ex-worker, Militina, who is living out his old age in a mental institution. This latter experience, however, proves most disquieting to Massa. For one thing, he recognizes in himself some of the same behavior patterns—a compulsive ordering of the silverware whenever he sits down to table—which Militina, probably echoing some psychologist's report on his own case, offers as the first hint he had that he was going crazy. (Militina also makes the excellent point, however, when asked just when he actually went crazy, that "It's others who decide that.")

Equally disturbing to Massa, however, is the disorienting ambience of the mental institution (which Petri has accentuated by staging this scene in a fenced-in compound that even seems to have a wire-mesh roof). In fact, so disorienting is this encounter with Militina that in the course of their conversation their roles somehow get reversed, with the result that Massa, who came in blustering with self-confidence to cheer up old Militina by bringing him a book he had requested *(Quotations of Chairman Mao)* and to give him news of the rising sentiment for a strike at the factory, ends up listening with awe to the supposedly crazy Militina give a very forceful and articulate critique of the workers' petty, opportunistic strike plans and point out vividly the need to overthrow the entire capitalist system. Militina's spirited monologue includes his recounting that what ultimately got him fired from the factory and put in a mental institution was stepping out of the assembly line one day, grabbing a passing boss by the neck, and shouting "For God's sake tell me what product I'm working on or I'll strangle you!" Massa is so confused that he almost forgets that it's he, and not Militina, who is supposed to leave the mental institution when the visit is over. (And to add to his surprise and confusion, Militina's parting request to him is simply "Next time, bring guns!")

In one way or another, the visit to Militina gets to Massa, for when he returns to the factory to resume work (and is greeted by an unctuous supervisor who welcomes back "such a productive worker"), Massa inexplicably takes his own sweet time, singing while he works, apparently not giving a damn any more about productivity. When asked by one of the time-study overseers if he can't work fast any more because of the missing finger, Massa contemptuously demonstrates that he *can* work as fast as ever, but bursting into anger he declares that he no longer sees any sense in busting his gut to fill the pockets of the bosses. This outburst— along with his new snail's pace—quickly gets Massa in trouble; and he is ordered to report for an interview with the factory psychologist, who asks him what a certain obviously phallic-shaped figure suggests to him.

With a vague awareness of what he's getting into, Massa acknowledges that it reminds him of a "cock," but then to cover his tracks he warns the psychologist not to think he's having any troubles with his sex life. "Any rumors you might have heard about me are false," he declares, not realizing he is giving himself away as he goes on to explain that if he can't make it with Lidia it's simply because she's such a bitch, and that, in any case, he can do it as many times a night as ever with other women.

This brief interview with the plant psychologist is a nice touch —revealing as it does both the facile application of psychoanalytic dogma (the rote ferreting out of Freudian symbolism) and the fact that a worker's psychological problems only get attention when they begin to interfere with his output on the job and thereby endanger the boss's profit margin. Moreover, it's interesting that Massa, who is now starting to see the absurdity of his old compulsive productivity as a worker, is unable to see that his attitude toward sex shares that same obsessive concern for output —and this insight into Massa's problems is not likely to be recognized by the plant psychologist, whose job is to reintegrate the problem worker back into the productivity pattern and who therefore will simply not even consider the possibility that this obsession with productivity is a large part of the problem itself.

Meanwhile, the workers have called a general meeting to hear various proposals for a strike. The large Communist union, attempting to take advantage of—and at the same time head off— the rising momentum stirred up by the Maoists who are agitating each morning at the factory gates, has formed a united front with the two small noncommunist unions who are calling for an increase in the incentive pay rate on piecework. A more militant stand is taken by the small group of workers aligned with the Maoist students: this faction calls for an end to the piecework system. Massa, arriving a few minutes late at the meeting, impulsively speaks out in favor of the more militant position, calling for abolition of piecework in spite of the bonuses he himself reaps by his extraordinary productivity. Dramatically waving his now four-fingered hand in the air, he shouts that it isn't worth it, that the system makes everybody a victim!

Despite the impressiveness of Massa's sudden turnabout, the vote is overwhelmingly in favor of the reformist proposal of the union leaders; and the workers again opt for the more moderate, union-sponsored proposal of a limited strike (two hours per day) instead of the total shutdown called for by the Maoists. Massa's disgust and disappointment at the outcome of the meeting, however, are then somewhat compensated for by his taking quick advantage of his newfound popularity—by seducing the factory virgin in the car-seat encounter referred to earlier.

As the strike begins, Massa plays a leading role in physically preventing the white-collar workers from entering the factory. First he hauls a frightened time-study overseer out of the employees' bus and extracts from him a hasty pledge to honor the picket line. Then Massa leaps on the hood of the shop supervisor's car to prevent him from entering the parking lot—an act which touches off a melee as the riot cops, who have obviously been on hand all along though hidden from view, charge the striking workers with clubs flailing. The strikers are forced to flee; Massa offers his apartment as a refuge for the Maoists. This gets him in trouble, however, with Lidia, who resents finding the apartment filled with bearded longhairs, fears that they'll steal her trinkets, and generally disapproves of their politics. Shouting "I'll never be a Communist," she indignantly exclaims, "I want nice things and I'm willing to work for them. I want a fur and I'll get one because I deserve one." Taking the TV set and her son with her, she storms out, while Massa, trying to cajole her into staying, promises "I'll get you a fur." The Maoists, fearing that Lidia's wrath might prompt her to reveal their whereabouts to the police, quickly leave —sententiously citing "revolutionary caution."

Back at the picket line the next day, the strikers are told that management wants to negotiate. However, when Massa tries to pass through the factory gates with his fellow workers to attend the negotiating session, he is prevented from entering and is handed a notice of dismissal for his role in the previous day's riot. Confused and frustrated, Massa runs along the fence that surrounds the factory, trying to find an unguarded spot where he might climb over to join his comrades. Petri expressly emphasizes Massa's sense of panic at this sudden disorienting of his life by having the camera truck giddily apace with Massa as he runs along the fence. Massa gets small consolation from a comrade who yells to him from inside the gate that his immediate reinstatement has been added to the workers' demands—adding, however, that "the negotiations are likely to be long and complicated: you'll just have to be patient."

Disconsolate at being cut off from "his" world, Massa passes seemingly endless days in this limbo state. The negotiations drag on. Earlier, when laid up with the hand injury, Massa hadn't minded having the time to reflect on his situation as a worker; but his layoff then was only temporary. He knew he would soon go back to work, even if less dedicated to productivity. Now, however, faced with the prospect of *never* being able to return to his familiar place, Massa experiences tremendous anxiety. After all, it's the only job he knows. Moreover, separated from his wife and son—and now deserted by his mistress (and her son)—Massa fears that his whole world is falling apart. And to top it off, there's his nagging awareness that his sex life wasn't really that good—and now he's even got to put up with the psychologist's transparent attempts to read a castration complex into his loss of the finger.

Desperately seeking reassurance and help, Massa even finds himself rebuffed by the Maoist students. Carrying on their struggle on several fronts simultaneously, in the local high schools as well as in the factories, the Maoists bluntly tell Massa that his case doesn't interest them "at a personal level, only at a class level"—pointing out that their own personal careers and health are being sacrificed to the cause.

Thoroughly confused and demoralized, Massa visits Militina once again at the mental institution. Now fearing for his own sanity, Massa listens numbly as Militina recounts a dream of knocking down the wall to Paradise. "Wherever there's a wall," shouts Militina, "knock it down!" Still in a funk, Massa leaves, but not before handing to Militina a big red package looking suspiciously like guns.

Back in Massa's apartment we come to the real crisis, the central moment of the film—the individual worker, isolated and powerless, reduced to stasis and despair. The unshaven, abject Massa morosely takes stock of what little remains of the threads of his life: innumerable knick-knacks, four alarm clocks, "magic" candles by Ronson (never used), a "loving couple" vase, a few worthless stock shares tucked away in a basement closet, and a huge inflatable Donald Duck belonging to Lidia's son. Suddenly overwhelmed by the absurdity of this existence geared to mindless accumulation, Massa grabs Donald Duck and tries to wring his neck—only causing the duck to emit a screeching sound. Finally, in a fit of fury, Massa presses his burning cigarette into Donald Duck's body, causing Donald slowly to deflate. (At which point the San Francisco Festival audience broke into loud applause.)

His frustration now spent, Massa wearily slumps down on the couch, and, without bothering to undress, pulls a blanket over himself and falls into a fitful sleep, only to be awakened shortly thereafter by Lidia's unexpected return. Petri moves the narrative swiftly at this point, signaling the couple's reconciliation simply by cutting from Lidia's unexpected arrival (with the abject Massa asleep on the couch) to a shot of the two of them being awakened in their double bed, an indeterminate amount of time later, by the buzzing of the doorbell.

This time it's the jubilant union delegates, who tell the dazed Massa that the strike is settled, that he's been reinstated, and that the workers have won "a great victory." "It's the first time in our

region that a worker fired for political activities has been reinstated." The irony of this is beautiful. All through the film, we,
along with Massa, have gradually achieved a gut-level awareness
of just how dehumanizing life in a factory really is; and now the
"great victory" of the reformist unions merely allows a worker who
was fired for rebelling against the intolerable system to go back to
work under that same intolerable system . . . and be thankful for
the chance. "And what's more," the union men add, "we won the
pay increases on piecework."

So the next day, life at the factory returns to normal. Once again
the workers, Massa among them, file through the factory gates
while Maoist militants with bullhorns try to stir them up: "The sun
isn't even up yet and you're going into the factory. When you come
out it will be night. You won't see the sun today."

But the film doesn't quite end yet. In a brief concluding sequence we see Massa back at work. Only now, instead of turning
out pieces on his own machine, he's at work on the assembly line.
As always, there's a lot of machine noise, but Massa manages to
shout loud enough to communicate with the man next to him,
telling him about a dream he had the previous night. As Massa recounts the dream, the man next to him repeats the story, in turn,
to the next man down the line, and so on. Massa's dream, very
similar to the one Militina recounted to Massa earlier, is about
breaking down the wall to Paradise.

When they hear it was a dream about Paradise, the workers
each ask, "How about me, was I there too?" And the word gets
passed on that all of them were together in Paradise. Another question gets passed back up the line to Massa: "What were we doing?"
But before we get a chance to hear the answer the camera suddenly picks up a worker pushing a cart and, in a panning movement, follows him as he goes down the assembly line. At the end
of the line he swings the cart into place, adjusting it to pick up the
finished product as it rolls off the assembly line.

But just as he gets ready for the pick-up, the film ends: the shot
freezes. We never see the finished product. It remains a mystery,
although a huge finger painted on the wall points down ominously

and insistently to the spot where the end product of the worker's labor should be.

Having some of the qualities of a dream itself, this conclusion seems to suggest that even workers' dreams are likely to be linear, mechanical models wherein all it would take to achieve a workers' paradise would be—as Militina in his younger days had demanded—knowledge of what product they were working on. Unfortunately, as old Militina now realizes, it isn't that easy: the task of achieving a workers' paradise requires, among other things, guns . . . and the willingness to knock down walls.

But the walls that present the biggest obstacles, as Petri's film provocatively emphasizes, may be the walls imposed on the workers' minds—barriers erected by an industrial capitalist system which insidiously perpetuates the vulnerability of the exploited worker by imprinting its machine patterns on even the deepest level of his character.

part three

Post-Bazin Aesthetics:
The Theory and Practice
of Marxist Film Criticism

16

Contra Semiology:
A Critical Reading of Metz

What I shall attempt here is a critical reading of the body
of work that has served as the foundation of the proposed semiology of the cinema—the writings of Christian Metz.[41] My reading
of Metz, like Althusser's reading of Marx, will be a "symptomatic
reading" in which I shall be interested not only in what the author
says but also in what he does *not* say; and I shall direct my attention not only to what Metz highlights but also to what he prefers
to leave in darkness.

Such a reading is said to be a symptomatic reading simply because one of its basic operations is to consider what *is* said as
"symptoms" of what is *not* said, of what is *repressed*. A symptomatic reading of Metz is particularly appropriate and particularly
revealing, for there is one vast and crucial area of conceptualization
that is conspicuous in its absence in Metz's writings. And in light
of Althusser's insistence that it is ultimately *ideology* that determines the "structuring absences" in a text, it is striking to note
that what is taboo in Metz's writings, what violently shapes and
disfigures his theoretical model by its structuring absence, is precisely any consideration of ideology itself.

This is strange, to say the least, for by 1968 the ideological
character of the cinema was so hotly debated in France that it was
very much a potentially explosive issue. A number of things con-
tributed to this: the growing radicalization of Godard; the leftward
turn of the old Bazin-oriented *Cahiers du Cinéma;* the solidarity

of French film-makers in the face of government attempts to de-
pose Henri Langlois as director of the Cinémathèque; the dis-
ruption (by Godard and, of all people, Truffaut) of the Cannes
Film Festival in the spring of 1968; and, finally, the May Events
themselves and the participation of film-makers—indeed of a large
segment of the French film community—in the rethinking from
"zero" of French cinema in *Les Etats Généraux du Cinema* as well
as in the tumultuous debates over education and culture in the
Sorbonne and the Theâtre de l'Odéon, or simply *in the streets*. All
of these phenomena (and many more, such as the debates over
television programming and government interference with news
broadcasts on the state-owned television network, the ORTF) had
catapulted the cinema (and television) into the forefront of the
debates over the function of art in society. And the debate
continues.

Old assumptions now are being challenged; and many people
are discovering for the first time the profoundly *ideological* character of art. In the cinema two notions in particular have been
challenged and largely discredited for their ideological ramifications. The primacy of the narrative, the use of the cinema to tell
stories, has been denounced for playing up to people's escapist
tendencies and for leading the passive spectator down the path
of least resistance, thereby inculcating a painless, even pleasurable
but nonetheless *authoritarian* relationship between the cinema and
the audience. And, second, the notion that the cinematic image was
a faithful reflection of reality, that the camera doesn't lie, was seen
to fit in all too well with the ruling class's need to present the status
quo in the guise of some natural, immutable *reality*.

Within this historical and political conjuncture—and with the
cinema clearly the focus of ideological struggle on the cultural
front—Christian Metz's *Essais sur la signification au cinéma* inexplicably became the latest fad in academic circles, at first in
France, then in England and America. The reasons for Metz's popularity among academics are not at all easy to understand. After
all, his *Essais* are extremely difficult and tedious reading, and his

overall argument is impenetrable to most readers and only barely discernible to a diligent few.

One has to understand the intellectual *market*, however, and the central position within that market of the latest intellectual fads from Paris. With interest in the cinema mushrooming on university campuses—especially in the U.S.A. but also in England and France—Metz's book was timely. Moreover, Metz's recourse to structural linguistics enabled the book to ride the already swelling wave of popularity of structuralism. At the same time, Metz's semiology could be—and was—touted in the intellectual press as a "new and improved structuralism." (An even better product than our previous model!)

Finally, by a strange twist in the workings of ideology, Metz's writings also benefited, in a sense, from the political debates over the cinema, and this is true in spite of the fact that Metz systematically ignores the political debates. In the arts, however, there is often a confusion (which the promoters of culture are quick to take advantage of) between the artistic avant-garde and the political avant-garde. Generally, we can expect the artistic avant-garde, no matter how commercial or decadent—in fact, the more commercial and decadent the better—to be promoted as somehow *subversive*. (We have the Dadaists and Surrealists to thank for this fetishization and commercialization of *scandal*.)

In the case of Metz's writings, however (and let us note that the first volume of *Essais sur la signification au cinéma* was published in 1968), the fact that the political turmoil had been felt in the cinema as well; and that people were talking about rethinking the cinema from "zero"; not only provided a nice market for a book which put forth a new approach to the cinema, it also endowed such a book with connotations of *political avant-gardism*. Regardless of its content (and in this sense the highly dense, impenetrable style of Metz's writings helped to mask the content), a book on the cinema, featuring a new and improved structuralism, and coming from Paris in 1968, could very easily pass for a work of the political as well as the artistic avant-garde.

But let us look at where Metz stands on the very issues which were—and still are—hotly debated by those of us who are concerned about the ideological function of art. What do we find? Well, it is hard to find where Metz stands. So dense is Metz's elaboration of his semiology that the ideological ramifications of his theoretical model almost pass unnoticed. Few readers of Metz penerate sufficiently the web of his rhetoric to recognize that at a time when the cinema's famous "reflection of reality" argument has been discredited for its ideological complicity with the status quo, Metz blithely revalorizes both the argument and the complicity. Few recognize that at a time when the narrative film has become suspect for its authoritarian pacification of the audience, Metz simply equates the cinema with narrativity, and leaves it at that. Finally, few recognize that at a time when the exploration of the relation between cinema and *ideology* has come so urgently to the forefront of our critical and theoretical debates, Metz archly refuses to confront the existence of ideology, drawing back inside his methodological shell each time he finds ideology looming in front of him.

But just what is Metz's system? What is Metz's semiology? It is very difficult to answer these questions satisfactorily, for in spite of Metz's obsessive preoccupation with the notion of "science" (what kind of science we shall see a bit later), there is regrettably little clarity either of organization or of expository style in the convoluted ruminations of Metz's two volumes of *Essais sur la signification au cinéma* or of the later *Langage et Cinéma*.

And where there is a bit of clarity in Metz's work—as in his ability to sift through possible confusion over terminology and to make distinctions between, for example, the terms "cinema" (and "cinematic") and "film" (and "filmic")—one cannot avoid the observation that Metz really doesn't tell us anything new but merely gives the academic's seal of approval, after pages and pages of explanation and qualification, to the common usage of these terms. (Metz laboriously spells out, for example, that we don't come out of the theater after seeing Renoir's *La Grande Illusion* and say to a friend we happen to meet, "I just saw a marvelous cinema";

therefore, he concludes, the terms "film" and "cinema" are not interchangeable *in both directions;* although, in some cases, for example, when speaking in English of the "art of film" or of "film history," Metz acknowledges that the term "film" in this sense is interchangeable with the term "cinema" although Metz prefers the latter.)

Moreover, one cannot avoid the additional observation that such distinctions are by no means arrived at through some special methodology of semiology. (Significantly, however, Metz will later use these distinctions as a justification for ignoring, in this particular semiology of *cinematic language,* the study of individual *films.*) Rather, Metz's clarification of the terminology is simply the product of a rhetorician's respect for words (as well as for simple logical consistency) and an academic's patience to plod tediously through the many different uses and misuses of these terms in the literature of the cinema. In short, Metz's clarification— if it is that —is really nothing more and nothing less than an example of pedantry. One can argue that it is pedantry at its very best; but it is definitely pedantry, and not semiology, unless one wants to argue that these two terms are interchangeable.

Let us concentrate, however, on the elaboration of Metz's semiology. Let us attempt to discover on what foundations it is laid. As Stephen Heath put it, "In fact, the development of Metz's semiology itself might be grasped in connection with its posing and exploration of a central issue; it is given as a systematic appeal to the methods and concepts of modern linguistic theory in order to examine rigorously the prevalent metaphor in writing on film of *cinematic language.*"[42]

Thus, in attempting to use the methods and concepts of modern linguistics in order to determine whether the term "cinematic language" has any validity, Metz is faced at the outset with the question of whether cinema ought properly to be considered what French linguists, after Saussure, call a *langue* or a *langage?* Taking Saussure's definition of *langue* as "a system of signs for the purpose of intercommunication," Metz finds cinema lacking the status of a *langue* because, in his view, (1) cinema is a one-way communication with no return channel for the response of the viewer-listener; (2) cinema is only partly a system of signs; and (3) cinema has very few true signs (*ESC*, I, p. 79).

Now in some ways all three of these reasons for denying cinema the status of a *langue* are debatable. Even within the framework of linguistic theory, as we shall see in a moment, the latter two conclusions by Metz are extremely questionable. And where the first objection is concerned, one can certainly argue, following Godard, that the real dynamics of the cinema are not on the screen (or even in the relations between images and sounds) but in the relations between the images and sounds, on one hand, and the viewer-listener in the audience.

The fact that the general practice of (bourgeois) cinema systematically deemphasizes the possibility of any active intervention by the viewer-listener—even *mental* intervention—thus indicates simply that intercommunication takes place in an *indirect* and *unequal* way in the cinema because intercommunication takes place in an *indirect* and *unequal* way in society as a whole. And the ruling class (which controls, among other things, the cinema) makes sure things stay that way.

Thus, in Godard's far-reaching view, the cinema serves to inculcate the bourgeois concept of representation, of our acquiescing in letting other people represent us, speak for us, give us images of the way we ought to be. There is intercommunication in the cinema all right, but the stage on which it takes place is not the stage (or the screen) of the movie theater itself, as if it existed in a vacuum, but rather the stage of *social practice*, of which the cinema, like everything else, is merely a part.

Even comfortably seated in the movie theater in our habitual role as passive consumers, we are vaguely aware that "behind" the film "someone is talking to us." Who is talking? Well, we occasionally say that such-and-such a film got produced because so-and-so's money was "behind" the film. Perhaps, then, in the logic of our unconscious formulations, we already know who is talking. *Money talks.*

And far too often we communicate back to the people who have the money in just the way they want us to—by our passivity, by our silence, by our compulsive consumption, by our readiness to let others represent us, both in the cinema and outside. But it doesn't have to be that way, either in the cinema or outside. We can change our ways of responding to films that seek to pacify us or to brutalize us. (We can even stop going to see them.) We can change the kinds of films that get made. (Critics can educate the public to support films other than those that pacify or brutalize us.) And we can change society. In fact, the struggle to change society is a struggle on many fronts: one of them is the cinema.

In any case, Metz's bland assertion that the cinema does not provide for intercommunication should not simply be taken as a fact and left unquestioned. Moreover, what is at stake is certainly more than merely finding out whether the cinema fits into the category *langue* or the category *langage*. In itself, the question of whether cinema is a *langue* or a *langage* is an academic question. But we should recognize that academic questions don't just fall from the sky. And we should recognize that it is precisely the function—the *ideological* function—of petit bourgeois intellectuals to defuse potentially explosive issues by transforming them into academic questions in which the masses of ordinary people can't see the issues clearly and couldn't care less because everything is worded in such an abstract and convoluted way.

But just what constitutes a methodology that has permitted Metz to define for himself such a severely—and to my mind, falsely—delimited object of research? Moreover, just what are the foundations of Metz's semiology? Even in the light of structural linguistics the issues are by no means as cut-and-dried as Metz makes them out to be.

As Stephen Heath points out,

It is the idea of the image that represents the blind spot of Metz's initial formulations, the point at which the articulation of significance collapses in the face of analogy. It is the "pure analogy" of the image (*ESC*, I, p. 51) that determines the absence of signs; where the linguistic sign is arbitrary, the image of a dog resembles a dog; the distance between *signifiant* and *signifié* is minimum, there being a "quasi-fusion" of the two. The image is envisaged as a duplication of reality; "cinema has for its basic material a set of fragments of the real world mediated by their mechanical reproductions" (*ESC*, II, p. 49). Hence cinema lacks any equivalent to the double articulation of linguistic *langue*, its very economy, the combination of systematically defined units of a lower level (phonemes) to form units of a higher level (monemes): instead of articulation, duplication; instead of economy, an infinity of analogical resemblances.[43]

In other words, Metz's semiology rests on the presupposition that the cinematic image is a "pure analogy" of the "real world"; and that, therefore, the image is not a *sign*. However, even within the realm of semiological research, this position is flatly rejected by Umberto Eco, among others, who argues that images, as well as verbal signs, are cultural rather than natural; that they are arbitrary and subject to conventions in a systematic way.[44]

Thus right at the foundational starting-point of Metz's investigations—the *langue/langage* opposition—we find that there are presuppositions that underlie Metz's thinking (here, for example, the tendency to consider the cinematic image as a duplication of reality) which, although cryptically stated or simply implicit in his writings, are generally not identified by Metz, nor recognized by the majority of his readers, for what they really are, namely, *presuppositions* which one has the obligation to question and upon whose theoretical foundations the entire edifice of Metz's semiology must ultimately stand or fall. Moreover, as we shall see shortly, these presuppositions carry with them *ideological* ramifications of the gravest consequence—ramifications which Metz feels entitled to ignore precisely because he has methodologically ruled them out, naïvely or duplicitously, right from the beginning.

On the question of the cinematic image's relation to reality, as on most questions, however, Metz is careful to cover his tracks. As Heath points out,

In fact, Metz's early statements concerning the image almost always add the condition that the image is not reality, that it

is a mediation, that it is a "deformation" (*ESC*, I, p. 111). . . .
As generally in this kind of discussion, however, the qualifying
condition tends to be overshadowed and the impression of
reality the cinema may produce is seized directly as "reality,"
foreclosing the thinking of the production of· that impression
of reality . . . ; the explication serves, in fact, less to analyse
the production of that impression than to confirm its reality; it
becoming an established and unchallengeable fact; cinema
equals impression of reality.[45]

Another of Metz's presuppositions—which does not come into
play until he has anchored cinema on the side of *langage* rather
than *langue*—is his equation of the cinema with *narrativity*.
Granted, Metz recognizes, as anyone must, that there are films
which simply cannot be characterized as narrative films. But these
Metz simply sets aside, acknowledging that such films are outside
his area of competence; while at the same time he defines his own
area of competence as "cinematic language" and unabashedly
equates the cinema with narrativity. (It is characteristic of Metz's
rhetorical style that even in reducing his claims to competence—
and seeming to make them more "precisely and scientifically
delimited"—he really makes them infinitely more vast.)
    Where Metz does address himself to the question of why he
identifies the cinema with narrativity, his arguments (as Michel
Cegarra, writing in *Cinéthique*, has pointed out) are circular,
specious, and often so naïve as to be possibly disingenuous. For
example, observing that the cinema took the path of narrativity
quite early in its history, Metz makes the following pronounce-
ment: "It was necessary that the very nature of the cinema made
this evolution if not inevitable, at least possible, perhaps even
probable" (*ESC*, I, p. 52). As Cegarra cautions in a footnote,
"This would give us a tautology to infinity: the cinema is narration
because it is cinema, therefore narration, therefore cinema,
etc. . . ."[46]
    Or, for another example, there is Metz's explanation of how
demand is to be taken into account as one of the foundations for
equating the cinema with narrativity: "There were the spectator's

needs, in short; the *demand*" (*ESC*, I, p. 52). And this pressure is, Metz acknowledges, "perfectly capable of exerting an influence . . . on the formula of the spectacle" (*ESC*, I, p. 52). Therefore, Metz tells us, "the basic formula which has never changed consists in calling a 'film' a large unit which tells us a story; and to 'go to the cinema' means to go and see that story" (*ESC*, I, p. 52). And the reason why that formula has never changed, Metz informs us, is because "it has been accepted . . . it is a rather pleasing one." As Cegarra, justifiably taken aback by such reasoning, points out, "The naïvety of such an analysis is astounding. One wonders whether Metz has ever heard of *ideology*, or whether he knows that film is also a commodity which can be sold and makes *profits*."[47]

Having laid such shaky foundations (that, as we have seen, ultimately rest on implicit presuppositions which themselves are extremely shaky), Metz then proceeds to use another set of concepts and methods borrowed from linguistic theory. What he does, however, is to use the breakdown of linguistic units into those which sustain *paradigmatic* relations and those which sustain *syntagmatic* relations, in such a way as to appear to justify "systematically" what in fact he has simply built into the "system" right from the start, namely, the apparent primacy of *narrativity*.

Because Metz has already denied the cinematic image the linguistic status of a *sign* (the validity of which would entail its being systematic along linguistically formal lines), he can now argue that since, in his view, the image is "pure analogy" (the validity of which is mere "duplication of reality"), it is thus extremely difficult if not downright impossible to speak of the cinematic image sustaining anything but *syntagmatic* relations. In other words, images can be *combined*, but they cannot in any linguistically systematic way, he argues, be *substituted* for one another.

(Incidentally, denying the image the status of a *sign*, of course, also denies it the status of a *word*. This forms another of Metz's original justifications for denying cinema the status of a *langue*. And, consequently, Metz can now assert that the cinema could not a priori possess significative paradigmatic oppositions—between words—and distinctive paradigmatic oppositions—between phonemes.)

Thus, applying the linguists' commutation test to the cinematic image (in order to determine which relations are paradigmatic and which are syntagmatic), Metz "finds"—because he has stacked the deck—that where paradigmatic relations would be expected to appear there is in fact no commutation, merely an infinite set of possible images. "In the cinema . . . the number of realisable images is indefinite. Indefinite many times over. . . . For profilmic scenes are themselves unlimited in number" (*ESC*, I, pp. 102-103).

Drawing from this commutation test the following conclusion, "It seems thus that the paradigmatic of film is condemned to remain partial and fragmentary, at least if one looks for it at the level of the *image* [Metz's italics]" (*ESC*, I, p. 103), Metz then attempts (at a later date and chiefly through additional notes and corrections to the second version of the text) to reintroduce the paradigmatic—but primarily as *a paradigmatics of the syntagmatic order*. Recognizing that "the syntagmatic and the paradigmatic are by definition correlatives of each other" (*ESC*, I, p. 73, note), and acknowledging that "this is precisely why I am less sceptical today on the question of the paradigmatic of the film than I was when I wrote that article" (*ESC*, I, p. 75, note), Metz nonetheless persists in privileging the syntagmatic and conceives of the paradigmatic in the only way his particular bias—for the cinema as *narrative*—can account for, namely, as a choice between ways of *combining* images, as *paradigms of syntagms*.

Once again, however, Metz attempts to cover himself on all sides, acknowledging that "the existence of different kinds of paradigmatic associations between *the images themselves* is not excluded, since different social groups all have cultural 'symbolisms' which also relate to iconography. The point is simply that these paradigms are not specifically linked to cinematic language" (*ESC*, I, p. 73, note).

But in this seemingly offhand disclaimer there is still another Metzian presupposition, or, more precisely, another bias ensuing from his initial presuppositions regarding the nature of the image and his equating the cinema with narrativity. In casting out the paradigmatic relations between images themselves from the sacred realm of cinematic language, Metz happens to be conveniently ridding himself of something that could cause him trouble. (For one thing, these "cultural symbolisms" he alludes to might force him to deal with *ideology*.) In any case, he betrays here not only his bias for the syntagmatic relations at the expense of the paradigmatic relations, but also his bias for *denotation* at the expense of *connotation*.

While, characteristically, Metz is careful to acknowledge that "the semiology of the cinema may be conceived either as a semiology of connotation, or as a semiology of denotation" (*ESC*, I, p. 99), his own exclusive bias toward the latter and his inability to conceive of connotation as anything but an *ornament* to denotation, that is, to *narrative*, have been exposed quite clearly by Cegarra.[48] Moreover, at the point where Metz denies the paradigmatic associations between the images themselves the right to enter the kingdom of cinematic language—conveniently pushing them somewhere "out there" in the mundane world of the cultural —Metz seems to prefer not to consider that, as Cegarra insists, "the paradigm of the image never exists *in itself* for it is also (and above all) a paradigm of *connotation*."[49]

It is clear, however, that the object of study awaiting Metz's longwinded and circuitous foundational justifications has all along been nothing other than *the denotation of the narrative*. Thus, his "discovery" of the "surprising poverty of the cinema's paradigmatic resources" (*ESC*, I, p. 72) hardly comes as a surprise. On the contrary, he now has exactly what he has been looking for—sufficient excuse for turning his attentions exclusively to the syntagmatic relations, to the combination of images into sequences, to, in fact, narrative.

Defining his own practice of semiology ever more narrowly— but at the same time imputing ever grander significance to its findings—Metz now focuses his attention on what he calls the

Grande Syntagmatique of the narrative film—or, still more "modestly"—of cinema. (For Metz, of course, the two are synonomous.)

The *Grande Syntagmatique*, as it is worked out in two different versions, is developed as a model for analyzing a film into the possible sets of narrative "figures" or "autonomous segments." In its later—but, as Metz cautions, not necessarily definitive—version, the model consists of eight types of combinations of images into autonomous segments of the narrative. And the model is then applied descriptively to Jacques Rozier's film *Adieu Philippine*, which is laboriously broken down into a total of eighty-three autonomous segments of the narrative, each of which is classified as one or another of the eight basic types.

Much has been made of this *Grande Syntagmatique*, and particularly of its application to an individual film. If one was hoping —and it is a legitimate expectation—that theory, when finally applied, even if descriptively, would enrich our understanding of the film by providing us with some food for thought, one comes away malnourished. The table set for us by *maître* Metz is spare indeed. Metz's "Table of the 'Autonomous Segments' of Jacques Rozier's film *Adieu Philippine*" (*ESC*, I, pp. 151–75) turns out to be a desiccated and ossified *taxonomy of the banal*. All it can offer us as food for thought are the bare bones of the story—picked clean, of course, with scientific rigor.

Having persevered in following Metz's laborious and circuitous wanderings in linguistic theory to arrive at this frugal repast is too heavy a price to pay for too little—a price one pays in those most precious of commodities, time (lost) and energies (misdirected). Moreover, aside from the meager pickings at the end of the journey, there is also the risk of having swallowed along the way some of those half-baked presuppositions that Metz has tried to slip in unnoticed right from the start. And to swallow these, we have insisted, is to swallow a dose of ideological poison.

Granted, Metz (unlike all the journalistic reviewers whose film criticism consists of retelling the story) concentrates less on what the story is about than on *how* it is told in images. (Incidentally, Metz's *Grande Syntagmatique* is unable to explore any relations between images and sounds. It is designed to apply only to the images.) Nonetheless, the story is still preeminent, even if Metz, unlike the journalistic reviewers, approaches the story from a certain (false) notion of science rather than shooting from the hip with his subjective impressions. (But, as Ernest Callenbach insists, those journalistic reviewers are able to tell us just as much, if not more, about *how* a film is told as Christian Metz does . . . and in an infinitely more interesting way!)

In any case, as the editors of *Cinéthique* point out in their critique of Metz's *Langage et Cinéma*,[50] this shift from the impressionistic to the scientific merely marks the passage from one form of idealism (subjective) to another (objective). And the latter is perhaps more dangerous precisely because its practitioners, unlike the subjective idealists, can't be accused of simply ignoring the realm of ideology; instead they rule it off limits "methodologically."

Thus, "the idealist discourses of the new type find an accomplice in semiology: like them, semiology leaves the class struggle at the door of its laboratory, never for a moment examining what it is that always gives signification (its object) a class character, namely, the inscription of films into the ideological struggle."[51]

Moving from Metz's two volumes of *Essais sur la signification au cinéma* to his later *Langage et Cinéma*, one becomes gradually aware of three things. First, in the later work there is less single-minded concentration on *narrative*, and in its place a rather belabored development of the notion of cinematic language conceived as a schema of codes and sub-codes (about which more in a moment). Second, far from bringing about any radical rethinking of his earlier positions, *plus ça change plus c'est la même chose*. And, finally, Metz's shift of emphasis in the later book seems motivated by an attempt to buttress his earlier positions by arriving at them from a slightly different, although equally circuitous, path. Interestingly enough, in the course of *Langage et Cinéma* this defensiveness on Metz's part becomes increasingly focused on warding off criticisms from the *left,* particularly the kind advanced by Cegarra in *Cinéthique.*

Let us examine, however, Metz's development in *Langage et Cinéma* of the schema of codes and sub-codes that in his view constitute cinematic language. Drawing further on structural linguistics, Metz defines "code" as follows: "What is called a code is a logical entity constructed in order to explain and elucidate the functioning of paradigmatic relations in the texts and to explain and elucidate the functioning of syntagmatic relations in these same texts. The code carries in it the intelligibility of the syntagm as well as that of the paradigm, without itself being either paradigm or syntagm" (*LC,* p. 122).

We'll leave Metz the responsibility for *demonstrating,* and not merely asserting, the intelligibility of the syntagm as well as the paradigm; but where intelligibility is concerned we can't help but point out that such a definition of "code" does not go beyond the original elaboration—without the term "code"—of the paradigmatic and the syntagmatic in his earlier *Essais.* In short, Metz is introducing, or constructing, a logical entity that will be used to justify, and thereby salvage, his earlier positions.

And, in fact, it quickly becomes clear that what is at stake, ultimately, in Metz's formulation of the schema of codes and sub-codes is the original *langue/langage* problem and all of its ramifications. Speaking of Metz's *Langage et Cinéma,* Stephen Heath observes,

> Cinematic language is now defined as the totality of cinematic codes and sub-codes in so far as the differences separating them are provisionally set aside so that the various codes may be treated as one unitary system (*LC,* pp. 51 and 98). . . . The advantages of the term "cinematic language" lies simply in the possibility it allows at certain levels of the analysis of thinking of the various cinematic codes in one block together . . . in order to arrive at propositions of the type, "There is nothing in cinematic language that corresponds to the word in linguistic language."[52]

The reader interested in *films* will most likely greet this type of proposition with a resounding "so what?"—and he is hardly likely to find much of an advantage in such terminology. But, of course, Metz is not methodologically interested in *films* but in *cinema;* and, in this respect, the notion of the code provides Metz with material for defending his definition of cinema as a *langage* without a *langue.* (Incidentally, it is not my intention, in criticizing Metz, to reverse his position on the *langue/langage* question and to assert that cinema is indeed a *langue.* Whether it is one or the other or neither is, as I stated earlier, an academic question. The ramifications of asking such a question about the cinema are of far greater consequence than the answers Metz, or anyone else, may come up with. But even in terms of Metz's answers, the ramifications need to be pointed out, for Metz carefully avoids doing so.)

Contrary to *langue* (which in Saussurean terms is constituted by a single code—*le code de la langue*), language is not a single code but a combination of several codes. And Metz now lays stress on what he calls the "pluricodic character of cinema," or the "heterogeneity of cinematic language" (*LC*, p. 143). In the face of this "pluricodic character of cinema," then, it will become Metz's central focus in *Langage et Cinéma* to disengage those codes which are "specific" to cinema—the "cinematic codes."

In Metz's terminology the codes qualified as "specific" are distinguished from those qualified as "nonspecific" in that the nonspecific codes (for example, the code of dress or the code of speech), although they may be present in films, are present elsewhere as well; thus, they are not specific to cinema. Whereas the cinematic codes appear only in films and are thus specific to cinema.

We'll come back in a moment to the relations between the specific and the nonspecific codes; but within the specific codes themselves, Metz makes a further distinction between what he calls at one point *general* and *particular* cinematic codes, or, as he later chooses to call them, between *cinematic codes* and *cinematic sub-codes.* General cinematic codes (or "codes") are those that

are not simply specific to films but are effectively or potentially
common to all films—for example (Metz's), the general code of
cinematic punctuation. On the other hand, particular cinematic
codes (or "sub-codes") are those which, while specific to films,
are only found in certain particular classes of films—for example
(Metz's), the particular codes of cinematic punctuation peculiar
to certain schools or genres of films.

So far so good, although it is difficult to say where all this
terminology leads. And once we get some idea of where it leads,
there is still the question one always has to ask with Metz of
whether the journey is *productive*. For example, let's pursue the
elaboration of the schema of codes and sub-codes a bit further.

Stephen Heath, echoing Metz, tells us that

> it is important . . . not to confuse codes and sub-codes. Codes
> are not in competition with one another in the sense that they
> do not intervene at the same point of filmic process; there
> is no choice between, say, lighting and montage. Choice arises
> between the various sub-codes of a code, they being in a rela-
> tion of mutual exclusion; there is no possibility of choosing at
> one and the same time the montage developed in Russian films
> of the twenties and that associated with the theories of Bazin.
> Codes and sub-codes of different codes are in a (syntagmatic)
> relation of addition and combination; sub-codes of the same
> code are in a (paradigmatic) relation of substitution.[53]

If we stop and reflect on this summary of Metz's position for a
moment, it is rather revealing. Not that it tells us anything new
about cinema, but it does reveal something we might not have seen
clearly before about Metz. Heath's paraphrase of Metz is not only
accurate (Heath is a very diligent exegete), it also has the advantage (believe it or not) of being more concise and coherent
than the original. And yet Heath, absorbed as he is in the unen-
viable task of faithfully explicating Metz, seems not to realize that
in rendering Metz's exposition somewhat clearer he is also making
it easier for the discerning reader to grasp the ludicrously pedantic
and superfluous character of so much of Metz's work.

Who needs to be told—much less in such a convoluted way—
that "there is no choice between lighting and montage"? Can

anyone imagine a film-maker laboring under the delusion that lighting and montage represent an either/or proposition? And certainly no critic or theorist who wasn't wearing the methodological blinders of the semiologist would deem it necessary or the slightest bit enlightening to work out a structural linguistic "proof" of such a self-evident fact. Once again, it is clear, Metz's semiology boils down to little more than a tedious taxonomy of the banal.

Moreover, precisely because it restates in a pedantic and uninteresting and *unproductive* way the commonplaces of cinematic practice, Metz's semiology ignores or is admittedly unable to deal with films that challenge and break down these commonplaces. (Metz acknowledges, for example, that even within his chosen area of competence, narrativity, there is a sequence in Godard's *Pierrot le fou*—the escape down the side of the building from the Paris apartment—which, although clearly belonging to the narrative, could not be fitted into any of the eight combinations of shots that comprise his *Grande Syntagmatique*.)

When Metz (and, following him, Heath) pedantically spell out that "there is no possibility of choosing at one and the same time the montage developed in Russian films of the twenties and that associated with the theories of Bazin," they seem to ignore the fact that in several of his films Godard has explored these seeming oppositions *dialectically;* and that in *One Plus One* Godard has demonstrated the possibility of *dialectically* employing, "at one and the same time," Eisenstein's principles of montage and Bazin's principles of *mise-en-scène*. Moreover, it is also worth pointing out here that Godard's dialectical explorations in *One Plus One* go against the grain of another of Metz's basic assumptions, for contrary to Metz's emphasis on the primacy of denotation and his relegating connotation to a mere ornament of the narrative; Godard demonstrates in *One Plus One* the richness and primacy of connotation in contrast to the crudeness and poverty of denotation —while narrative itself, in this film, is revealed as a perfect vehicle (perhaps *the* perfect linguistic vehicle) for fascism. (See Chapter 5, which is devoted to Godard's dialectical explorations in *One Plus One*.)

Nonetheless, there is one way in which Metz's elaboration in *Langage et Cinéma* of the schema of specific and nonspecific codes might have a limited use—although, characteristically, Metz himself does not do so, for if he did he would finally be obliged to deal with ideology. On the question of the relations between specific and nonspecific codes, Metz, whose preoccupation is largely, almost exclusively, the specific codes, nonetheless acknowledges that "a code which is more specific than another is not necessarily more important; it is merely a code which the language under consideration shares with fewer others (and which therefore characterises that language to a greater degree)" (*LC*, p. 183). But the whole thrust of Metz's work, emphasizing as it does the narrative properties of cinematic language, persistently privileges the codes that are specific to cinema's ways of *telling stories*.

But, as the editors of *Cinéthique* point out, "If the analysis takes into account not just the primary object of semiology (the study of cinematic language), but its secondary object as well (the study of films as systems), it is possible to argue that the specific codes are not necessarily the most important codes of a film system. The nonspecific codes also play a role in the establishment of that system, and the question then is whether this role is not perhaps always the primary one."[54]

For *Cinéthique* even to pose such a question amounts, as they are the first to acknowledge, to a rigorous rethinking and autocritique of their own earlier dogmatic position emphasizing cinematic *specificity*. (Of course, *Cinéthique* emphasized specificity for very different reasons than Metz.) Moreover, so thorough is *Cinéthique*'s self-criticism that they are now willing to characterize as a "fanaticism" their own (past) and Metz's (continued) "fetishism" of specificity.

In the past *Cinéthique*'s own fanaticism regarding specificity manifested itself in their dogmatic refusal to consider any film that did not operate *self-reflexively in an explicitly political self-questioning of its own cinematic elements*. Of course, such a self-reflexively political "meta-film" is still highly valued; but it is hoped that *Cinéthique*'s insistence on this kind of specificity will no longer be invoked so dogmatically. (In the past, even such a film as *La Hora de los Hornos* was dismissed by *Cinéthique* because it was found to lean a little too heavily on the cinema's notorious "impression of reality.")

In any case, where my friends and comrades at *Cinéthique* are concerned, it is my hope that once having relaxed their rigidity on the matter of specificity—one of the few points on which they and I ever disagreed during our many discussions (and even on this issue the disagreements were only on degree of emphasis)— the editors of *Cinéthique* may now open up the magazine to some of the productive work that urgently is needed in examining just how ideology is inscribed (within what Metz would call the combination of heterogeneous codes) in various types of films with varying degrees of self-reflexiveness about their specificity.

On the question Metz poses (but does not resolve) of the relations between the specific and nonspecific codes within one filmic system, *Cinéthique* quotes with qualified approval Metz's assertion that "the system of the text is the instance which *displaces* the codes, deforming each of them through the presence of the others, contaminating the ones by the others . . . and *placing* each code in a determined position in the overall structure. The process of displacement thus results in a putting into place, which is itself destined to be displaced by another text" (Metz, *LC*, p. 78 . . . as quoted by *Cinéthique*, p. 199).

But the qualification advanced by *Cinéthique* makes far more sense than Metz's original statement—and in my opinion can simply supersede the former, since it poses an *anterior* question, indeed, the fundamental question that Metz has so systematically avoided. In any case, *Cinéthique*'s qualification is of crucial importance: "We could agree with this structural view of roles if the question of *what* produces this structure and its systems were posed with equal explicitness. In a sense, Metz does pose the question, but fails to follow it through to the end, invoking reasons of a methodological order, whereas we see the evasion as a concrete result of the limits within which semiology is enclosed by its ideological presupposition" (*Cinéthique*, p. 199).

Here, finally, is the real crux of Metz's elaboration of the code systems in films. And, as we have seen again and again, what is methodologically ruled off-limits by semiology's ideological presuppositions is precisely any consideration of ideology itself. Moreover, to pose the question of the relations between the nonspecific and specific codes in a filmic text without considering them *individually and in combination in terms of ideology* is simply to leave out the only conceptual element that can bring clarity out of confusion and make the theoretical model at all useful. (Its use, however, even *with* ideology taken into consideration, would be very limited, for all the really productive work would have to be accomplished outside of the framework of semiology, that is, within the framework of the Marxist analysis of class struggle and its censorship in ideology. In other words, *all semiology offers is an uninteresting and unproductive way of mapping, after the fact, the productive explorations carried out by another methodology, in this case Marxist methodology.*)

Cinéthique spells it out quite clearly in the following passage, in which they pick up, and transform, Metz's terms:

> Translating this into Marxist terms, a film is therefore a set of *contradictions* between two types of heterogeneous elements— the specific and the nonspecific codes—and of contradictions within the specific and within the nonspecific codes. These are the contradictions which can be distinguished from the standpoint of ideology. The contradictions which traverse the non-specific codes are in fact those which principally characterise the conflict between the proletarian and bourgeois ideologies. . . . The contradictions which structure the specific codes are those which assign a greater or lesser role to some element from the standpoint of its ability to conserve or reproduce a particular ideology. In this context, the codes of iconic analogy are certainly among the most ideologically loaded. (Metz says that analogy is itself coded, which is of course true, but it should also be said that it is coded by the conflict of ideologies [what some would call "culture"].) (*Cinéthique*, pp. 198–99.)

For his part, Metz may lay out a topographic map of codes classified according to their varying degrees of specificity; and he may even call for an exploration of the relations between specific and nonspecific codes—whose relations, however, he can only characterize in terms of a vague "balance of forces." But Metz himself draws back timorously from such exploration, and he can only repeat in summary "that the 'balance of forces' between the cinematic contributions and the external contributions is extremely variable from one filmic system to another. But these considerations engage the psycho-sociology of cineastic 'creations' (and of the spectatorial receptivities), as well as diverse problems of general epistemology, rather than the structural analysis of films themselves" (*LC*, pp. 83–84).

Once again Metz seeks refuge in cinematic specificity, conveniently thrusting everything else "out there" into "the psycho-sociology of cineastic 'creations,'" whatever *that* may be. Moreover, Metz may argue that his theory is *descriptive* and not *normative;* but that is actually a false issue. The fact is that Metz's description is incomplete; and it leaves off at precisely the point where, because ideology would finally have to be confronted, the theory would inescapably become *normative,* i.e., for one class's ideology or another, *against* one class's ideology or another. (Actually, of course, Metz's theory, like all theory, has been normative all along, only without seeming to be. And that camouflaging of its normative character is eminently *ideological in itself,* and is what has made Metz's semiology such an attractive ideological tool for the bourgeois intellectuals of our academic institutions.)

Significantly, it is precisely at this point in *Langage et Cinéma* where, having set out—but not having followed through—on the exploration of the balance of forces, Metz makes a backhanded allusion to the overtly *normative* character of *Cinéthique*'s theoretical positions. Metz acknowledges the existence of what he calls "a new type of 'political' film—such as those that *Cinéthique* would like to see the multiplication of." But Metz brings up the subject in a way that implies that ideology is only the determinant factor in a few aberrant cases, in the overtly political films that appeal to the lunatic fringe of the far left. And this transparent maneuver makes it all too easy for Metz to invoke the familiar defense mechanisms by which he attempts to preserve his peaceful sanctum of specificity and to dismiss the unruly children with a stern admonition to "go play elsewhere"—in those realms of "the psycho-sociology of cineastic 'creations' "—if they insist on saying that bad word *ideology.*

It has not clearly enough been recognized just how much Metz's semiology has developed not just *alongside* of but *in opposition* to the simultaneous development in the 1960's and 1970's of the Marxist theory of ideology and its application to film theory and criticism. But Metz's work, which goes through the most excruciatingly painful methodological contortions to avoid having to deal with ideology, is literally haunted by a specter, the specter of Marxism and the Marxist conception of ideology; and this specter hovers constantly over the pages of Metz's circuitous detours and semiological deadends. Moreover, like all taboos, the Marxist concept of ideology is constantly present in its repressed state in Metz's writings—a presence-as-absence, or, in Althusser's terms, a "structuring absence" whose very repression must violently shape and form/deform the text *in* which it is "absent."

One reason, of course, why this fact has not been widely recognized is simply that it is so difficult to pin down just what Metz *does* say, much less what he represses, covers up, and does *not* say. But, to utilize the currently popular metaphor of an author's *strategies,* one might say that Metz's density and abstruseness almost seem part of an overall diversionary strategy. And if this were the case, it ought to be clear from our foregoing analysis of the lengths Metz will go in order to avoid ideology, just what it is that Metz's diversionary strategy would divert us from. (Incidentally, one does not even have to impute such a conscious strategy to Metz personally, it being one of the curious properties of ideology to work its strategies *through* individuals whether they are conscious of its workings or not. And in this sense one does not have to say that "Metz speaks bourgeois ideology" but rather that "bourgeois ideology speaks Metz.")

In any case, on the few occasions where Metz cannot avoid at least some allusion to Marxism, he is capable of being extremely coy and even downright duplicitous. One case in point is Metz's treatment, in *Essais sur la signification au cinéma,* of Eisenstein, whose "genius" he is careful to acknowledge at the same time that he repeatedly rebukes this "great artist" for his refusal to avoid the cinematic "heresy" of *manipulation.* At times Metz sounds just as caught up in the transcendentalist position of idealist metaphysics as was André Bazin, who, of course, was also highly critical of Eisenstein's "manipulation." And in a confusing and ultimately self-contradictory argument, Metz ultimately winds up reproaching Eisenstein for not acknowledging "the 'natural' sense of beings and things" (*ESC,* I, p. 45), whatever that might be; and he laments Eisenstein's refusal to show us "the course of the world, but always, as he himself says, the course of the world refracted through 'an ideological viewpoint' . . ." (*ESC,* I, p. 44).

Ultimately, of course, it's the same old argument left over from Bazin's realist aesthetics. While protesting that "it's not a matter of politics," Metz, like Bazin (whom he praises, significantly, for being "more subtle than those who reproach Eisenstein for being a Communist"), seeks to cast aspersions on any film-maker who openly acknowledges the ideological character of a film's discourse. (And is it mere coincidence that Metz, like Bazin, singles out as the main example of such an ideological discourse the work of a Communist?)

Here it is clear that Metz has learned absolutely nothing from all the critiques that have been leveled at Bazin. Metz here betrays a belief in the cinema's ontological realism just as naïve as the one Bazin once championed. And, like Bazin, Metz thinks that the only films which function *ideologically* are the films which do so openly and consciously, like the films of the Soviet silent masters, or the "new type of 'political' film . . . that *Cinéthique* would like to see the multiplication of."

Needless to say, there couldn't be a grosser distortion of ideology and how it works. Is Metz really unable to see that a filmic discourse which purports to show us "the course of the world" in its so-called "natural" state (we'll leave it to Metz, and God, to define that one for us) really performs an immensely more effective and an immensely more manipulative ideological function than the openly ideological discourse of an Eisenstein, precisely because this bourgeois filmic discourse covers up its own signifying practice and seeks to pass off the status quo—"the course of the world" under the thumb of the capitalist mode of production—as *reality* . . . as "the 'natural' state of beings and things"?!?

And this brings us to another instance of Metz's disingenuous mistreatment of Marxist notions. As the editors of *Cinéthique* have pointed out in their critique of *Langage et Cinéma*, the word "ideology" (used as little as possible by Metz) nonetheless "never appears without pejorative connotations . . . and is often associated as a synonym or equivalent with: 'stereotype' . . . 'propaganda' . . . 'phantasm' . . . 'banality' . . . 'constraint' . . . 'fanaticism'. . . ."

As if this weren't bad enough, however, Metz twists the opposition ideology/science (first elaborated by Althusser) to his own uses, distorting and devaluing the concept of ideology while at the same time valorizing his own very narrow and idealist notion of science.

In fact, nothing could be farther apart than the positions of Althusser and Metz, for where Althusser elaborates the foundations (which he finds in Marx's *Capital*) of a new science that will, among other things, enable us to understand and account for ideology, Metz merely discredits and devalues ideology in order not to have to deal with it. Moreover, in his very notion of science, as *Cinéthique* pointedly observes,

> Metz remains true to the general project of the "human sciences." These "sciences" segregate their objects in order to make them autonomous and to cut them off from one another and from what links them, namely, the class struggle. For the basic exclusion on which these sciences are established is clearly that of historical materialism. Metzian semiology is no exception in this respect. . . . The multiplication of the human sciences is in fact very convenient for those who want to stay locked up in their laboratories—they can always tell a caller to try next door, look in another drawer or a different cup-

board. Thus Metz can say: "These considerations involve the
psycho-sociology of cineastic 'creations' (and of the spectatorial
receptivities) as well as diverse problems of general epistemology, rather than the structural analysis of films themselves."
. . . In this way, the problem which expresses the ideological
struggle in a condensed form is no sooner posed than it is
thrust somewhere "prior to" film or beyond it, as if the ideological struggle did not intervene decisively in the formation of
every filmic system. (Cinéthique, p. 205.)

However, Metz's avoidance of ideology and his cloak of scien-
tificity are bound to be attractive to academics who are threatened
by the intrusion of politics into their sanctuaries. With Metz,
though, they have nothing to fear. No unruly disturbances by
proletarian and Third World youths here . . . just the reverential
murmurings of the mumbo-jumbo of semiological jargon. The
academics of film studies, uptight about their intellectual respecta-
bility, get a whiff of salvation when they encounter semiology.
They rediscover the religious vocation of the pedagogue. At last
they have some densely obscure mysteries to impart to the uninitiated.

The distressingly egalitarian, even plebeian, aspect of the study
of films gives way to a hierarchically structured ritual presided
over by a glib priestly elite, which, in the name of Metz, excuses
itself from the need to bother with the critical analysis of individual films. The path to salvation lies in the semiology of the
cinema. But like all paths to salvation this one is poorly marked,
obscure, and difficult to follow. Quite a lot must be taken on faith.
Meanwhile, the uninitiated are asked to await The Word. An
article on Metz in the American review *Cinema* announced the
publication in English, at that time still forthcoming, of Metz's
Essais sur la signification au cinéma in terms that unabashedly
equated this event with the Second Coming.

One would hope, however, the fact that Metz's writings are
now available in English will have the effect of deflating rather
than expanding the cult of semiology. In fact, the bubble of the
semiology fad may very quickly burst as readers of the English

translation of *Essais sur la signification au cinéma* discover for themselves how much hot air is contained in Metz's rhetoric.

In any case, where intellectual fads imported from abroad are concerned, there is generally an inverse ratio between availability of the works in English and their position on the ladder of intellectual snobbery. As long as Metz's writings had not yet been translated into English, there was a certain mystique about them. And the mystique, of course, was played up by the academic impresarios who can be counted on to hop on the bandwagon in a rush to import the latest intellectual acts from Paris. Now that Metz's work is available to English readers, however, the mystique is fading quickly as the obscurantist mystification that went into the mystique is more clearly discernible.

17

The Ideological Situation
of Post-Bazin Film Criticism

There is a specter haunting current thinking and writing about the cinema and its relation to society—the specter of Marxism. Given capitalism's ideological prejudices, however, it is hardly surprising that Marxism should appear in spectral form. For bourgeois capitalist society there are two traditional responses to the specter of Marxism: *silence* (in the hope that it will disappear) and *scare tactics* (playing on people's fears about the great bugaboo of Communism).

Not so very long ago, of course, red-baiting was all the fashion in America. The right wing was on the offensive; and Joseph McCarthy struck terror into the Hollywood film industry.

At present the shoe is on the other foot. Crippled by the obvious moral, political, and economic bankruptcy of its policies on Watergate, Vietnam, and inflation, the right wing in America is very much on the defensive. And in an era of expedient détente with the Soviet Union and a new "open door to China" policy, red-baiting is not on the immediate agenda.

In the cinema, of course, the McCarthyist repression of Hollywood "pinkos" was a red herring all along. Capitalism had nothing to fear from Hollywood; and that has not changed in the slightest. What has changed, however, are the critical attitudes and intellectual foundations that a growing number of people are applying to the analysis of films. Such a change, of course, can hardly be said to threaten capitalism at its very roots.

On the other hand, one should not minimize its potential importance. With the American economy so dependent on widespread consumption of the type of goods that are luxury or indulgence items, the cinema and television play an extremely important role in shaping the average citizen's fantasy-image of what the "good life" is like. Denouncing and demystifying the ideological distortions of the cinema and television can be important contributions to the growth of political consciousness.

In American intellectual circles, of course, there is still a solidly entrenched reluctance to deal with Marxist concepts and methods of analysis. But this ideologically conditioned attitude may be weakening somewhat. And the traditionally "liberal" circle of intellectual film buffs is a likely place for this bias to begin to crack. This is precisely what happened in France, for example, around the time of the May Events of 1968. Thus, by applying rigorous theoretical foundations to the analysis of cultural products (films) that achieve fairly wide distribtuion (compared to other cultural products like paintings, sculptures, stage dramas, or even books). Marxist film criticism can even function as an important vanguard both in breaking down intellectuals' reluctance to acknowledge the validity and usefulness of Marxist approaches and in helping the film-goer to understand how so many films are manipulating the public in ways that make them easy prey for continued capitalist exploitation.

Among film scholars now in America and England there is a growing tacit awareness of the important emergence of interest in Marxist approaches to the cinema. Increasingly, students of our film schools and universities are applying Marxist concepts and methods of analysis to the study of films. But ideological prejudices don't disappear overnight. And among the higher echelons of our educational institutions—and in our intellectual journals—there is only tacit acknowledgment, if that, of the fruitful new insights being achieved by Marxist film criticism.

Work that is explicitly Marxist is often simply ignored. Work that utilizes Marxist concepts and methods but not explicitly is praised for everything but its Marxism; and the insights produced by such work are attributed to anything but the Marxism from which the insights actually derive. (This is the case with Charles Eckert's analysis of the film *A Marked Woman*.) Sometimes even the explicitly Marxist orientation of a critical approach is ignored if the work in question can somehow be passed off as an offshoot of structuralism or semiology. (An example of this is found in English-speaking film scholars' treatment of the *Cahiers du Cinéma*'s collective text "John Ford's *Young Mr. Lincoln*.")

Let me state quite openly, however, that it is clear to me that what has wrought the profound changes in our current thinking about film is precisely Marxism. In particular *the Marxist concept of ideology,* which was given new impetus and refinement by the self-reflexive questioning of "culture" in the late 1960's, has provided the theoretical framework for, among other things, a rigorous reevaluation and deconstruction of the old Bazin aesthetics of ontological realism. And yet, in discussions about current film criticism, people will talk glibly about the shattered unity of discourse now that we have entered a post-Bazin era of film aesthetics, but they will have no clear notion of what shattered the old foundations and of what new foundations are being set forth. As usual, there is among bourgeois intellectuals a conspiracy of silence rather than an acknowledgment of the validity and effectiveness of Marxist thinking.

In this state of affairs confusion is not only tolerated, it is ideologically preferred over the clarity, the *threatening* clarity, of Marxist analysis. At present the confusion in film theory and criticism takes many forms. Largely it is centered around misconceptions regarding structuralism and semiology. In fact the confusion has even reached the point where structuralism, semiology, and Marxist criticism get lumped together in the most indiscriminate fashion.

Let us consider, as a case in point, the 1973–74 debate in *Film Quarterly* between John Hess and Graham Petrie.[55] Agreeing with Petrie that auteur criticism is dead and at the same time pointing out the abortive character of Petrie's own approach to "alternatives to *auteurs*," Hess has roundly criticized Petrie for a vaguely delineated, backward-looking approach that is characterized by glaring omissions. For example, "When Petrie calls for a reassessment of film criticism, he purposely ignores the three areas from which new discoveries about the cinema and our relation to it are emerging: structuralism, semiology, and Marxist criticism."[56]

For his part, however, Hess is very vague about just what constitutes each of these critical approaches. As Petrie somewhat bitterly points out in a rejoinder to Hess, "having chided me for not providing any acceptable alternatives to *auteurs* after all, Hess hastily wheels out the fashionable *troika* of structuralism, semiology, and Marxism, and urges us to take his word for it that it is a sound investment for the future. . . . Like most advocates of these techniques in the English-speaking world, Hess prefers to assert rather than to demonstrate their usefulness."[57]

One cannot help sympathizing with Petrie on this point about name-dropping, whatever failings there may be in his own "alternatives to *auteurs*." (And Hess has done a reasonably good job of pointing them out.) Moreover, Petrie's indignation at the superficiality of Hess's assertions is all the more likely to enlist our sympathies when we see the amazing way in which Hess goes on to lump together indiscriminately these three critical methods he is touting. For example, in Hess's opinion "structuralists, semiologists, and Marxist critics all deny the autonomy of art, considering film an ideological link between individuals, groups, classes and societies. . . . In all three cases the examination of a film's social context becomes more important than the film itself. Social ills, maladjustments, and manipulations come to be seen as more important than their manifestations on celluloid."[58]

In the first place it is simplistic, if not downright false, to say that "structuralists, semiologists, and Marxist critics all deny the autonomy of art, considering film an ideological link between individuals, groups, classes and societies." It is not at all clear from the texts of various structuralists and semiologists that this statement in any way characterizes their positions. In fact, quite the contrary. For example, where the semiology of Christian Metz is concerned, as we have seen in the preceding chapter, Metz sets forth a critical methodology which in its systematic *avoidance* of ideology might just as well openly reaffirm the old bourgeois notion of the autonomy of art—so severely and, to our mind falsely, delimited is its object of research.

Second, it is also simplistic, if not downright false, to say that "in all three cases the examination of a film's social context becomes more important than the film itself." Once again, one has to go no further than the work of Metz to find this assertion totally inapplicable. For Metz focuses neither on the social context of a film nor on individual films but rather on the notion of *cinematic language*. And where Metz does devote any attention to an individual film (the one film he has chosen to study in any detail is the rather pedestrian *Adieu Philippine* by Jacques Rozier), the peculiar methodological blinders of Metzian semiology force him to ignore not only the social or ideological context of the film but also nearly everything that is not simply an element of the denotation of the narrative.

The fact that Hess blithely attributes the above positions to all three—semiology, structuralism, and Marxist criticism—is bad enough; but worse yet is the fact that in Hess's hasty gloss, semiology and structuralism are made to sound almost indistinguishable from Marxist criticism; and the position—seemingly a Marxist one—ascribed to all three of them is so poorly formulated that in fact it does justice to *none* of them.

Where Marxist criticism is concerned, Hess seems to have in mind a "social issues" criticism that simply looks for political *themes* in films. This might have been characteristic of the old-style Marxist film criticism of John Howard Lawson, for example, but it is not at all true of contemporary Marxist film criticism. When Hess states that "social ills, maladjustments, and manipulations come to be seen as more important than their manifestations on celluloid," this remark makes it sound as if Marxist film critics (and structuralists and semiologists) don't really deal with films and how they work but only with their social and political *content*. Aside from making a naïve separation between form and content, Hess here seems to ignore the fact that Marxist film criticism today refuses to make an artificial distinction between form and content, and refuses to fall into the old habit and old theoretical impasse of treating film merely as a "window on the world's problems." Instead, with detailed analysis of the specifically cinematic relations between images and sounds, contemporary Marxist film criticism focuses precisely on the way the world's problems— or, better yet, its *contradictions*—are manifested in images and sounds on celluloid.

In short, Hess's pervasive confusion has unwittingly served those who would jump at the opportunity to discredit Marxist criticism and question its relevance to films. Thus, Petrie, in his rejoinder to Hess, is able to claim that "in effect, whatever titles he prefers to give them, Hess's alternatives come down to little more than an obsolete and dogmatic Marxism."[59] And Petrie is quick to imply that perhaps if purified of the contamination by this "obsolete and dogmatic Marxism," structuralism and semiology—either singly or in some new alloy—just might make a pot that, theoretically at least, might hold water.

This insidious attempt to boost structuralism and semiology at the expense of Marxist criticism not only reveals Petrie's prejudices, it flies in the face of what little clarity has emerged thus far from all the critiques and counter-critiques of structuralism and semiology. For example, whatever disagreements there may be between Charles Eckert and Brian Henderson,[60] it is at least clear that structuralism has not been capable of providing itself with valid theoretical foundations.

Moreover, in an extremely lucid piece of self-criticism, Eckert now recognizes that even the one structuralist approach that seemed useful—Lévi-Strauss's analysis of the dialectical systems that operate in mythic thought—remains locked in an idealist, transcendentalist metaphysics, at least if one sticks to Lévi-Strauss's eminently *ahistorical* conception of myth as a "found object," *authorless* and without a history. Criticizing (without repudiating, however) his own insightful analysis of the way class conflicts are diluted into ethical dilemmas in Hollywood films (he focuses on the 1937 Warner Brothers production *A Marked*

Woman, directed by Lloyd Bacon), Eckert rejects the Lévi-Straussian terminology of "transformational operations" for remaining at the level of "a pure mental activity—the activity of what Husserl calls a 'transcendental ego' exalted above, severed from, the contingencies of psychology, biology, and society." As Eckert acknowledges, the conceptual shifts that occur when class conflicts are diluted into ethical dilemmas have, after all, a *material* base; and they can "only be *comprehended* through the Freudian operation of displacement, and *accounted for* by a recourse to the Marxist notion of class conflict and its censorship in ideology."[61]

This acknowledgment of the primacy of the Marxist notion of ideology is most heartening, especially coming from a perceptive critic like Eckert. But even without Eckert's admirable insistence on setting matters straight, it ought to have been possible to see from his analysis of *A Marked Woman* that at a foundational level the basic theoretical framework of his insights was not structuralism but the Marxist theory of class struggle and its censorship/repression in ideology. In any case, now that Eckert has made this point explicitly, there will be no excuse for film scholars to persist in mistakenly treating his excellent materialist analysis of *A Marked Woman* as if it were somehow derived from structuralism or semiology.

Likewise, only bourgeois capitalism's ideologically inculcated reluctance to acknowledge Marxism can account for English-speaking film scholars' insistence on treating the *Cahiers du Cinéma*'s collective text "John Ford's *Young Mr. Lincoln*"[62] as if it were a product of structuralism or semiology rather than Marxist analysis. (The editorial board of *Cahiers du Cinéma* has openly declared its Marxist orientation since as far back as the winter of 1968–69.) Once again, as with Eckert's work on *A Marked Woman*, the *Cahiers* analysis of the various ways *Young Mr. Lincoln* dilutes "politics" into "moral questions" and transforms work and struggle into mythic destiny ultimately derives from the Marxist theory of ideology. The *Cahiers* text itself makes this point repeatedly; and yet English-speaking advocates of structuralism or semiology have persisted in trying to annex this text as a province of the vast empire of ambitious Lévi-Straussians. Certainly any analysis of the structure and function of myth will have to reckon with Lévi-Strauss; but without explicitly criticizing Lévi-Strauss the *Cahiers* text certainly goes against the grain of Lévi-Strauss's *ahistorical* conception of myth. In fact the whole thrust of the *Cahiers* analysis is to dismantle and expose the mythmaking function of Ford's *Young Mr. Lincoln*. And the *Cahiers* text very pointedly observes that the film's ability to make history and politics disappear in favor of myth and destiny is actually a very effective ideological maneuver. In fact, with detailed analysis of the political and economic background at the time *Young Mr. Lincoln* was produced, the *Cahiers* text shows how the seemingly innocuous terms in which the Lincoln myth is couched actually cover up (and thereby make more effective) the political biases (on behalf of Big Business and the Republican Party) which are cleverly set to work within the film's mythic structure.

Clearly the basic theoretical framework of the *Cahiers* analysis of *Young Mr. Lincoln* is the Marxist one. And even their treatment of myth in this film owes infinitely less to Lévi-Strauss's notion of myth than to the Marxist notion of the way *ideology* deforms our understanding of history. Granted, there are crossfertilizations from several strains of thought, especially from Lacan's psychoanalysis; but even the Lacanian insights are set to work within the fundamental matrix of Louis Althusser's Marxist concept of ideology.

Certainly the cornerstone to contemporary Marxist film criticism is to be found in the concept of ideology, whose specific relevance to the cinema I elaborated in the opening section of Chapter 6 on *British Sounds*. My arguments there (and elsewhere: see particularly the chapters on *Le Gai Savoir, Wind from the East*, and *Pravda, Struggle in Italy*, and *Vladimir and Rosa*) took as its starting point Louis Althusser's emphasis on the extremely important economic function of ideology in assuring the reproduction of the labor force and of the existing relations of production.

A given mode of production, like, for example, capitalism, will entail certain "relations of production," which must be *reproduced* constantly, day after day, by inculcating in individual consciousness values and a world view that reflect these dominant relations of production. (There can exist, of course, in any epoch several different, and antagonistic, relations of production. And, as Althusser aptly puts it, in class society the dominant relations of production (that is, the relations of production controlled by the ruling class) are also necessarily the *"relations of dominance"*— they are in fact the structural relations that ensure the dominance of the ruling class.[63]

The task of reproducing the relations of production is largely carried out at the level of *ideology*. In this, incidentally, it differs from the simple "reproduction of the labor force," which is carried out through the payment of wages sufficient for the worker to sustain himself more or less acceptably, to render himself each morning at the factory gate (or the office), and to produce offspring who will ensure the future labor force. Nonetheless, "reproduction of the labor force" and "reproduction of the relations of production" are critically interdependent: the wage that ensures the reproduction of the labor force simply ensures that workers will continue to be *physically* available, while the function of ideology is to ensure that *psychologically*, in their consciousness (and even in their unconscious), each individual acquiesces not only to the working conditions offered by a given mode of production but also to the patterns of consumption entailed by that mode of production, as well as to a whole host of related values and attitudes that serve to perpetuate the dominant relations of production on which that society is based.

What happens at the level of ideology, according to Althusser, is that through the various "ideological apparatuses of the state," such as the schools, churches, courts, political parties, labor unions, family, press, and even the arts, the individual's real relations to the relations of production get distorted because they are short-circuited by the process that establishes individuals as *subjects*.[64] (The implication here, which unfortunately Althusser does not spell out, is that in class society individuals are actually treated as *objects*—to be used for the personal or corporate accumulation of capital—while the whole panoply of the state's ideological apparatuses offers them the comforting illusion that they are being called upon—*interpellé*—as *subjects*.) Thus, conceiving of themselves as subjects, individuals do not make the conceptual connection that would enable them to see their real relations to the relations of production but instead get bogged down in imaginary relations in which ethical dilemmas conceived in terms of metaphysical Absolutes (in the schools, an idealist conception of Knowledge; in the churches, God; in the courts, Justice; in politics, the Party; in labor organizations, the Union; in the press, the Facts; in art, Truth and Beauty; and in the family, Proper Behavior) take the place of a materialist understanding of their real relations to the relations of production.

Ideology, then, in class society is above all a weapon used by the ruling class to inculcate in the masses the acceptance *as a given* of the existing relations of production which privilege one class at the expense of another. Ideology serves to suppress the asking of fundamental questions about society and its relations of production and to assure that what few questions do get asked are questions of *how* rather than *why*, of *reform* rather than *revolution*, of how to accommodate ourselves to "reality" rather than why this particular social system should exist at all, much less be elevated to the status of reality and accepted as a *given*.

Cinema and television, I have argued, have proved particularly useful ideological weapons in the past few decades, both because of the vast audiences they reach and because, as photographic media, they lend themselves so well to the ruling class's need to present the status quo as if it were reality itself. Photography, after all, is said to reflect reality. Moreover, there's an old adage that the camera doesn't lie; and whatever shows up on the photographic image, barring obvious tampering, is automatically raised to the status of reality.

It has even been argued by Jean-Louis Baudry that the technological development of the camera lens is wholly consistent with the ideological project of the capitalist bourgeoisie.[65] Thus, in this argument, the design of the camera lens has as its goal the achievement of "Renaissance perspective" (i.e., the illusion of depth on a two-dimensional surface, elicited by the geometric figure of the triangle, its apex functioning as the point on the "horizon" at which two diagonal lines are seen *not* to converge but to continue, as if parallel to each other, to infinity). And this Renaissance perspective—with its illusion of limitless space and its ability to *place* the spectator where it wishes, instead of leaving his eye free to wander and to create multiple relations among the elements of an icon, for example—thus offers the ascendant bourgeoisie, particularly the industrial bourgeoisie, an ideological tool expressly suited for passing off as reality the image it wants the world to have of itself and of the existing socioeconomic system.

In cinema of course, as I have pointed out, the aesthetics of André Bazin effectively codifies all the realist rationale of photography and sets forth a whole series of "thou shalt nots" in which such devices as superimposition, multiple exposures, slow motion, fast motion, expressionistic sets or décors, theatrically stylized action—and even most types of montage—are rendered suspect under any conditions and are downright *forbidden* under most if not all conditions. Their sin? Tampering with "reality," interfering with the "pure" reflection of reality.

For Bazin, who speaks of cinema's ontological realism, the cinematic practice of realism involves far more than the choice of one particular style among many possible styles: it amounts to a *religious* vocation. If in criticizing Bazin I have insisted on calling attention to the religious terminology in his writings, it is first to point out the peculiar notion of reality—a mystico-religious, transcendentalist "reality"—in whose service Bazin seeks to enlist the cinema. Second, I have wished to call attention to the *ideological* ramifications of Bazin's metaphysical, even *theological*, conception of reality and of the cinema's relation to reality.

However, a word of caution may be needed here to avoid misunderstanding. It is by no means necessary for Bazin's realist aesthetics to be built on such theological premises for them to be useful ideological tools in the hands of the ruling bourgeoisie. Today, in the mid-1970's, the religious cast of Bazin's thought may seem strangely anachronistic, for the ideological ramifications of his realist aesthetics continue to be exploited all too effectively by a capitalist ruling class which now finds alliance with the Church —any church—far less politically expedient, even in France or Italy, than it did immediately following World War II, when Bazin was writing.

Nonetheless, for an understanding of the concrete situation in which Bazin's work was produced—as well as for an exemplary lesson in the relation between ideology and the production of knowledge, even knowledge about the cinema—there are many useful insights still to be accomplished in analyzing Bazin's writings *in the historical context* of the postwar reconstruction of capitalist Europe. Although there has been some limited effort to sketch in at least certain intellectual currents of thought that influenced Bazin, there has been far too little recognition both of the *fact* that this intellectual context was part of an eminently political context (the postwar reconstruction of Europe was an extremely critical transitional moment for industrial capitalism) and, second, of the *consequences* of this fact, that is, of the specific repercussions by which the political pressures were felt in every sphere of social practice—including, of course, the cinema.

In Bazin's writings, for example, it is important to examine the relation between the privileged position in his work of the Italian Neo-Realist films and the presence in so many of these films of themes susceptible to a religious interpretation. And this latter fact needs to be put in relation to the Italian political situation which saw fragile coalitions dominated by the Christian Democrats (the very name of this political party should give us food for thought), who were—and still are—desperately striving to stave off the continuing growth and influence of the Italian Communist Party. Moreover, one can trace extremely direct ideological repercussions: like direct orders from the Christian-Democrat-controlled governments to Italian film production units that they must assign to each film project scriptwriters, including Catholics, representing each of the major political viewpoints. And this kind of direct intervention, too, needs to be put in relation to Bazin's appreciation of the "ambiguity" of the Italian Neo-Realist films.

And in France, the postwar situation needs to be understood as an eminently *political* situation in which the intellectual debates play their ideological part, however remote or specialized they may seem. Bazin's association with the progressive wing of the French Catholic Church (which included people like Gabriel Marcel, Jacques Maritain, Teilhard de Chardin and Emmanuel Mounier) needs to be put in relation to the fact that in France the Catholic Church, tainted by its association with the collaborationist regime of Pétain, sought to refurbish its image after the war by launching intellectual counteroffensives against those twin bugaboos the atheistic existentialism of Jean-Paul Sartre and "atheistic Communism."

At present, however, very little examination of these relations has been undertaken. The first effort along these lines—Gérard Gozlan's critical reading of Bazin[66]—is still the best that has appeared. (One hopes it will soon be made available in English.) Annette Michelson has attempted to outline some of the intellectual context of Bazin's writings and to draw up a general appraisal of his strengths and weaknesses; and her evaluation of Bazin[67] at least has the merit of taking the ideological ramifications of his theory into some, albeit sketchy, consideration.

Then, too, there is Bazin's English translator, Hugh Gray, who has also sketched in some of the influences on Bazin's thought in his introduction to the English edition of Volume Two of Bazin's *What Is Cinema?* But Gray's focus on Mounier as a direct influence on Bazin is too narrow to shed much light on the ideological context or ramifications of Bazin's work. Finally, Brian Henderson's recent evaluation of Bazin[68] neglects both the historical context of Bazin's work and the ideological ramifications (either then or now) of his aesthetics; concentrating instead on some rather hairsplitting logical inconsistencies Henderson purports to find (much to Gray's consternation) in Bazin's different uses of the

concept of *reality* and *relation to reality*. (Henderson has subsequently acknowledged the beside-the-point aspect of the rhetorical form he uses in ferreting out logical inconsistencies in
Bazin's writings; but, justifiably, I think, he steadfastly refuses to
recant, even at Gray's insistence, and pretend the inconsistencies
aren't there.)[69]

Today, of course, it is not so much the specifically religious
underpinnings of Bazin's aesthetics that are useful to the ideological needs of the ruling bourgeoisie, rather it is simply the
codification of the realist rationale of cinema as a reflection of
reality that fits in so well with the ruling class's ideological needs.
And the ruling class's *fundamental ideological task*, let us not
forget, is to pass off as reality—and thereby raise to the status of
a metaphysical *essence*—a system of social and economic relations that is not objective, as they would have us think, but subjective; not neutral, as they would have us believe, but partisan
(in *their* favor); not inevitable but *arbitrary* (and arbitrarily
imposed); and, above all, not immutable, as they would like to
have us think, but capable of being transformed in a revolutionary
way.

Where the cinema is concerned, our examination of the eminently ideological character of the cinema has led us to analyze
and to criticize Bazin's realist aesthetics not only for what it says
but also for what it does *not* say, for what it covers up and keeps
quiet—namely, the class struggle that has been the basis for all
social formations and transformations. And our continuing efforts
in the theory and practice of Marxist film criticism must implacably bring to light the class struggle that is going on all around
us but is so insidiously glossed over and hidden by the cinema
and the mass media in general. And this means that we have to
think not merely of the class struggle in the U.S.A. or in whatever country we happen to live, but of class struggle on a global
scale.

At the same time that we think globally we must also think
personally, for the division of society into classes and the struggle
between classes are not mere abstract concepts in some disem-

bodied and depersonalized thinking machine. We too are caught up in class struggle. And our revolution will not be liberating if it is aimed only at liberating *someone else* (the working class, the Third World, etc.). For each of us there needs to be a healthy, lucid coming together of the *political* and the *personal*. Revolution will only be genuinely liberating if it enables each of us to relate more freely in our own actual lives to men, women, and things.

Notes

Introduction

1. A collective text by the editors of *Cahiers du Cinéma,* "John Ford's *Young Mr. Lincoln,*" originally published in *Cahiers du Cinéma,* No. 223, (August 1970), 29–47; also translated into English by Helene Lackner and Diana Matias and published in *Screen,* Vol. XIII, No. 3 (Autumn 1972), 5–44.

2. Charles Eckert, "The Anatomy of a Proletarian Film: Warner's *A Marked Woman,*" *Film Quarterly,* Vol. XVII, No. 2 (Winter 1973-74), 10–24.

3. Louis Althusser, *Pour Marx* (Paris: Maspero, Collection: "Théorie," 1969).

Louis Althusser, *Lire le Capital* (in English), 2 vols. (Paris: Maspero, 1965 and rev. in 1969).

Louis Althusser, *For Marx,* trans. Ben Brewster (New York: Monthly Review Press, 1970).

Louis Althusser, *Reading Capital,* trans. Ben Brewster (New York: Monthly Review Press, 1970).

Louis Althusser, *"Lenin and Philosophy" and Other Essays,* trans. Ben Brewster (New York and London: Monthly Review Press, 1971).

4. Julia Kristeva, "Cinéma: Pratique analytique, pratique révolutionnaire," in *Cinéthique,* No. 9/10, p. 73, trans. James MacBean.

1. Politics and Poetry in *Two or Three Things I Know About Her* and *La Chinoise*

5. *Cahiers du Cinéma,* No. 194 (October 1967), 13–26, 66–70; also translated into English by D.C.D. and published in *Film Quarterly,* Vol. XXI, No. 2 (Winter 1968-69), 20-35.

2. Politics, Poetry, and the Language of Signs in *Made in USA*

6. Ibid., 32 (English translation).

7. Ibid.

3. *Weekend*, or The Self-Critical Cinema of Cruelty

8. Theodore H. Gaster, *Thespis* (New York: Harper Torchbook, 1966).

4. *Le Gai Savoir:* Critique Plus Auto-Critique du Critique

9. Quoted from Jonathan Cott's interview with Godard, published in *Rolling Stone*, No. 35 (June 14, 1969), 20–22.

10. Mao Tse-tung, "Talks at the Yenan Forum on Literature and Art," from *Mao Tse-tung on Literature and Art* (Peking: Foreign Language Press), p. 30.

5. *One Plus One*, or The Praxis of History

11. Quoted from Jonathan Cott's interview with Godard, published in *Rolling Stone*, No. 35 (June 14, 1969), 21.

6. "See You at Mao": Godard's Revolutionary *British Sounds*

12. Louis Althusser, "Idéologie et appareils idéologiques d'état," *La Pensée*, No. 151 (June 1970), 3–38; also translated into English by Ben Brewster and published in Althusser, "*Lenin and Philosophy.*"

13. Quoted from a text called "Premiers 'sons anglais' " (signed "on behalf of the Dziga Vertov Group: Jean-Luc Godard") published in *Cinéthique* (Paris), No. 5 (Sept.–Oct. 1969), 14. (English translations of this and other Godard texts are available by writing to *Kinopraxis*, 2533 Telegraph Avenue, Berkeley, California.)

14. Translated by Hugh Gray (Berkeley: University of California Press, 1967).

15. See Gérard Gozlan's critical reading of Bazin in *Positif*, nos. 46 and 47 (June and July, 1962).

16. The same conclusion is reached—specifically in regard to the way literature is studied (and taught) in America— by Frederick Crews. See his article "Do Literary Studies Have an Ideology?" in *PMLA*, Vol. 85, No. 3 (May 1970), 423–28.

7. Godard and Rocha at the Crossroads of *Wind from the East*

17. Glauber Rocha, "The Latest Godard Scandal," *Manchete* (Rio de Janeiro), No. 928 (January 31, 1970), 52–53.

18. Bazin, *What Is Cinema?*, pp. 41–52.

19. See "Summary of the Forum on the Work in Literature and Art in the Armed Forces with which Lin Piao Entrusted Comrade Kiang Tsing" (Peking: Foreign Language Press, 1968).

20. Quoted from "The Way to Make a Future: A Conversation with Glauber Rocha," by Gordon Hitchens, *Film Quarterly*, Vol. XXIV, No. 1 (Fall 1970), 28.

21. Lenin, *Que faire?* (*What Is to Be Done?*) (Paris: Éditions Sociales, p. 50). (All translations from the French edition are by James MacBean.)

22. Ibid., p. 52.

23. Ibid., p. 55.

24. Ibid., pp. 70–71.

8. Godard/Gorin/The Dziga Vertov Group: Film and Dialectics in *Pravda*, *Struggle in Italy*, and *Vladimir and Rosa*

25. Al Fatah was one of the first organizations to understand the Palestinian question as more than an Arab-Israeli confrontation and to concentrate on the urgent need for radical social and political change in the Arab countries, particularly in Jordan. Since the guerillas' military setback in Jordan in 1971, the Fatah movement has gradually emerged as the official spokesman for the Palestinian cause. Al Fatah's generally disapproving attitude toward airplane hijackings and other acts of publicity-oriented terrorism—such as the "Black September" group's murderous raid on the Israeli Olympic team at Munich—has earned the movement some international respect. (It is argued in some quarters, however, that Al Fatah has secretly supported such terrorism all along, and that the organization's public disclaimers are mere window-dressing to influence international opinion.)

26. For an intelligent but unnecessarily pedantic introduction to Vertov's own efforts to lay the foundations of such an epistemology, see Annette Michelson's "The Man with the Movie Camera: From Magician to Epistemologist," *Artforum* (March 1972), 63–72.

27. Althusser, "Ideology and the Ideological Apparatuses of the State," in "*Lenin and Philosophy*," pp. 127–86.

28. For excellent material on this subject, see Erving Goffman's *The Presentation of Self in Everyday Life* (New York: Doubleday, 1967).

29. I single out Brustein because he has been vociferous in denouncing both the growing "theatricalization of everyday life" and the avant-garde trends in drama (happenings, multimedia events, etc.) that encourage the breaking down of distinctions between theater and reality. For further discussion of these issues and of Brustein's position on them, see the sections entitled "Event as Theatre/Theatre as Event" and "The Film Revolution" in Albert J. LaValley's anthology, *The New Consciousness* (Cambridge, Mass.: Winthrop Publishers, 1972).

10. *La Hora de los Hornos:* "Let Them See Nothing but Flames!"

30. Quoted from Louis Marcorelles' "Interview with Fernando Solanas," *Cahiers du Cinéma*, No. 210 (March 1969), 64.

31. Althusser, "Ideology and the Ideological Apparatuses of the State," in *Lenin and Philosophy*.

11. The *Ice*-man Cometh No More: He Gave His Balls to the Revolution

32. Quoted from "Newsreel," *Film Quarterly*, Vol. XXI, No. 2 (Winter 1968–69), 46–47.

33. See "A Psychoanalyst Looks at Student Revolutionaries," *The New York Times Magazine* (January 17, 1971).

34. See Charles Derber, "Terrorism and the Movement," *Monthly Review* (February 1971).

12. Rossellini's Materialist *Mise-en-Scène* of *La Prise de Pouvoir par Louis XIV*

35. See interview with Rossellini in *Film Culture*, No. 52 (Spring 1971).

13. Sex and Politics: Wilhelm Reich, World Revolution, and Makavejev's *WR: The Mysteries of the Organism*

36. Wilhelm Reich, *The Mass-Psychology of Fascism* (originally written in 1933, revised and enlarged in 1935 and again in 1945), available now in a new authorized translation by Vincent Carfagno (New York: Noonday Edition, 1970).

Wilhelm Reich, *The Invasion of Compulsory Sex-Morality*, trans. Werner and Doreen Grossman (New York: Noonday Edition, 1971).

37. Joan Mellen, "Fascism in the Contemporary Film," *Film Quarterly*, Vol. XXIV, No. 4 (Summer 1971), 2–19.

38. For a penetrating analysis of Makavejev's earlier films—*Man Is Not a Bird, Love Affair: The Case of the Missing Switchboard Operator*, and *Innocence Unprotected*—see Robin Wood's chapter "Dusan Makavejev," *Second Wave* (New York: Praeger, 1970), pp. 7–33.

39. See interview with Makavejev in *Postif* (July-August 1971), 48–55.

15. The Working Class Goes Directly to Heaven, Without Passing Go: Or, The Name of the Game Is Still Monopoly

40. The call for a revolutionary, materialist psychoanalysis has recently been issued by Gilles Deleuze and Félix Guattari, whose book *Capitalisme et Scizophrénie: L'Anti-Oédipe* (Paris: Éditions de Minuit, 1972) denounces the idealist emphasis on the Oedipus complex (with its bias toward the bourgeois, paternalistic, and patriarchal family) that reigns in Freudian psychoanalysis. (Incidentally, it was Godard and Gorin who first called this book to my attention during a conversation in which they also expressed their admiration for Elio Petri's dramatization of the worker's underlying character in *The Working Class Goes to Heaven*.)

16. Contra Semiology: A Critical Reading of Metz

41. In this chapter references to Metz's *Essais sur la signification au cinéma* are to the original French editions (Paris: Éditions Klincksieck, Tome I, 1968, and Tome II, 1972). For convenience I have used the abbreviation *ESC, I* or *ESC, II* followed by the page number for the passage cited. For Metz's *Langage et Cinéma* (Paris: Librairie Larousse, 1971), I have used the abbreviation *LC* followed by the page number for the passage cited.

The English edition of *Essais sur la signification au cinéma*, translated by Michael Taylor and entitled *Film Language: A Semiotics of the Cinema* (New York and Oxford: Oxford University Press, 1974) was not available when most of this chapter was written; nor was the English edition of *Langage et Cinéma* (The Hague: Mouton, 1974). Thus, the English translations of Metz quoted in this chapter are, wherever possible, borrowed from material published in *Screen*, Vol. XIV, No. 1/2 (Spring/Summer 1973), and Vol. XIV, No. 3 (Autumn 1973). Where no English translation was available, I translated the passages myself from the original French editions.

42. Heath, "The Work of Christian Metz, *Screen*, Vol. XIV, No. 3 (Autumn 1973), 5–6.

43. Ibid., 8–9.

44. Eco, "Articulations of Cinematic Code," *Cinematics*, No. 1 (January 1970).

45. Heath, 9.

46. Cegarra, "Cinema and Semiology," *Cinéthique*, No. 7/8; translated and reprinted in *Screen*, Vol. XIV, No. 1/2 (Spring/Summer 1973).

47. Ibid., 146.

48. Ibid., 175.

49. Ibid., 170.

50. "*Cinéthique* on *Langage et Cinéma*," *Screen*, Vol. XIV, No. 1/2 (Spring/Summer 1973), 189–207.

51. Ibid., 192.

52. Heath, 13.

53. Ibid., 17.

54. *Cinéthique*, 198.

17. The Ideological Situation of Post-Bazin Film Criticism

55. John Hess, "Auteurism and After," *Film Quarterly*, Vol. XVII, No. 2 (Winter 1973–74), 28–37.

Graham Petrie, "Auteurism: More Aftermath," *Film Quarterly*, Vol. XXVII, No. 3 (Spring 1974), 61–63.

56. Hess, 35.

57. Petrie, 62.

58. Hess, 36.

59. Petrie, 62.

60. See Charles Eckert, "The English Cine-Structuralists," *Film Comment*, Vol. IX, No. 3 (May–June 1973), 46–51; and Brian Henderson's two-part "Critique of Cine-Structuralism," *Film Quarterly*, Vol. XXVI, No. 5 (Fall 1973), 25–34, and *Film Quarterly*, Vol. XVII, No. 2 (Winter 1973–74), 37–46.

61. Charles Eckert, "Shall We Deport Lévi-Strauss?," *Film Quarterly*, Vol. XXVII, No. 3 (Spring 1974), 63–65.

62. A collective text by the editors of *Cahiers du Cinéma*, "John Ford's *Young Mr. Lincoln*," originally published in *Cahiers du Cinéma*, No. 223 (August 1970), 29–47; also translated into English by Helene Lackner and Diana Matias and published in *Screen*, Vol. XIII, No. 2 (Autumn 1972), 5–44.

63. Marx and Engels, of course, had already pointed this out in the following passage: "The ideas of the ruling class are in every epoch the ruling ideas: i.e., the class which is the ruling *material* force of society is at the same time its ruling *intellectual* force. The class which has the means of material production at its disposal, has control at the same time over the means of mental production, so that thereby, generally speaking, the ideas of those who lack the means of mental production are subject to it. The ruling ideas are nothing more than the ideal expression of the dominant material relations, the dominant material relations grasped as ideas; hence of the relations which make one class the ruling one, hence the ideas of its dominance." Karl Marx and Friedrich Engels, *The German Ideology* (Moscow: Progress Publishers, 1968), p. 61.

64. Althusser, "Ideology and . . . the State," ibid., pp. 127–86.

65. Jean-Louis Baudry, "Cinéma: effets idéologiques produits par l'appareil de base," *Cinéthique*, No. 7/8, 1–8; also translated into English by Alan Williams and published in *Film Quarterly*, Vol. XXVIII, No. 2 (Winter 1974–75), 39–47, under the title "Ideological Effects of the Basic Cinematographic Apparatus."

66. In *Positif*, nos. 46 and 47 (June and July 1962).

67. In *Artforum* (Summer 1968), 67–71.

68. In *Film Quarterly*, Vol. XXV, No. 4 (Summer 1972).

69. For the Gray-Henderson exchange, see "Correspondence and Controversy," *Film Quarterly*, Vol. XXVI, No. 3 (Spring 1973).

Index